Z88

Portable Computing

Dave Oborne

SIGMA PRESS – Wilmslow, United Kingdom

First published in 1990 by

Sigma Press, 1 South Oak Lane, Wilmslow, Cheshire SK9 6AR, England.

British Library Cataloguing in Publication Data

A CIP catalogue record for this book is available from the British Library.

ISBN: 1-85058-204-1

Typesetting and design by

Sigma Hi-Tech Services Ltd

Distributed by

John Wiley & Sons Ltd., Baffins Lane, Chichester, West Sussex, England.

PREFACE

These days we cannot really get away from computers; they are all around us. Wherever we look it seems that someone, somewhere is tapping letters and numbers into these ubiquitous pieces of electronic wizardry.

But there is a reason for this: computers have so completely revolutionised our lives that we can no longer do without them. They help us organise our very existence; with them we can save time, maximise profits, optimise resources, and carry out a host of interesting and valuable activities.

A decade or so ago, however, such activities could only be done in large rooms via terminals that were linked (often physically) to powerful 'mainframe' computers. It is only in less than ten years that the modern (micro) computing revolution has come about, enabling us to do such things on increasingly powerful computers that sit on our desks at work and at home.

But it is just in the past year or so that equally powerful computing has managed to drag itself away from the fixtures dominated by a mains power supply, and into the era of truly portable computing. A variety of machines are now on the market that let you carry on your computing activity between home and the office – on trains, boats and planes.

Cambridge Computers' Z88 is not just a member of this new generation, it is a leader. As this book will illustrate, packed into its slim, A4-sized case is a variety of computing operations waiting to be used: word processing, spreadsheets, calculations, clock and alarm, and even the BASIC computer language. With this computer you can print material out onto a wide range of printers, communicate with other computers – even on the other side of the world – and use it to control other, even more complex, tasks.

The book will also illustrate, however, just how simple all of these operations are. The Z88 carries with it full help information and lets you switch from operation to operation with impunity. Within a couple of short hours most people should be able to master the main functions of this versatile computer so that the next train or bus journey will not represent wasted time. As they read through this book, newcomers to this computer, as well as the older hands, will realise that with their Z88 they are about to launch into a new computing experience.

No matter how excellent the product, however, no book of this nature would ever be written without the helpful co-operation of a number of people. I must record my grateful thanks to Peter King at Cambridge Computers who provided valuable information at critical times and who had the manuscript checked by those who know far more about the Z88 than I could hope to assimilate. At the other end of the Z88 knowledge scale, I am extremely indebted to Dr Brian Sweetman who was able to combine an enthusiasm for the Z88 with natural sense and wisdom. His pertinent comments on parts of the manuscript helped to create a book which, hopefully, will be of value to Z88 newcomers and experts alike.

And finally undying gratitude goes out to my wife, Susan, who endured months of disturbed sleep whilst I thoughtlessly got up early in the mornings to write the manuscript.

Dave Oborne

Contents

1

The most modern of modern technology

As we draw inexorably towards the end of a millenium, there are bound to be dozens of gurus who will come out of the woodwork and regale us with tales of our amazing technological development. They are likely to compare the state of our technology at the beginning of the age with that at its end. Some will point out that Harold was killed at the Battle of Hastings by a stray arrow in his eye; now it is more likely to be a bolt from a Star Wars satellite. Others will remind us of the unending toil of the medieval monks who took years to produce their beautifully illuminated manuscripts; now they are probably churning them out in their thousands on laser printers in their high-tech scriptoria.

In all walks of life, technology – particularly computer-based technology – has opened up exciting new horizons for us. We must be quick to capture and exploit the opportunities that these systems present. Otherwise, the pace of technological change being as it is, the new brave world will pass us by and our third millenium will begin with a sad and dejected whimper.

Enter the Z88

Cambridge Computers' compact little Z88 computer is just the kind of technological development that could point us in the right direction for the 21st century; while in the shorter term it has the potential to change the ways in which we think and work over the next decade. Indeed, future historians will probably recognise the Z88 as being such a major advance in computing facilities that it symbolises the end of one computing era and the beginning of another.

What is the evidence for such a sweeping statement?

Over the past year or so there have been significant changes in the great electronics revolution which began a couple of decades ago. The continual search for miniaturisation has abated slightly, to be replaced by an equally fervent desire for function. These days the important criterion is not so much how small the computer is, but what it can do with the power that it has got.

Many will see this as a natural progression. After all, the great valve-operated machines of the 1950s, which filled massive rooms and almost required the outpourings of a conventional power station to run them, were of little value to the average person.

With transistors and integrated circuits, however, miniaturisation soon followed. Computers became smaller and smaller until eventually you could harness their power in a small box on your desk. And then the ultimate: full-blown computers that were portable and could be used between desks as well as on them. These machines have had enormous benefits to the man in the street.

But there must be a limit to the growth of miniaturisation – if for no other reason than the fact that we are limited in our abilities to operate them. Keyboards may get smaller, but the sizes of our hands and fingers remain the same; display sizes may decrease, but our eyes are limited in the ways we can view small objects. Although small is beautiful there has to come a point when miniaturisation should stop – and many modern computers have just about reached that point.

Computing functions

Enter the need for increased functionality. Modern computers are multi-purpose pieces of electronic equipment, and the number and variety of functions that they can do have increased considerably over a relatively short period of time. With one program, for example, computers can be the most powerful word processor, helping people to generate textual perfection; another program can turn the same machine into a complex calculator, crunching numbers with incredible speeds. New computer-based applications are continually being generated with remarkable rapidity.

The only difficulty with this Utopian view is that although computers put on this show of apparent flexibility, their true versatility is rather limited. It extends only to the abilities of their programs – their software. Complete multi-functionality will only occur when you can take information from one application, say text in a word processor, and incorporate it directly into another, perhaps a desktop publishing program – *without having to power down one program and start up another.*

For example, maybe you want to take numbers from a spreadsheet and add them to a text-based document. Or perhaps you would wish to switch directly from word processing a document to sending it to another computer via the telephone line. Gradually, programs are emerging that can do some of these integrated activities – but they are in the minority at present.

The Z88 in Prospect

When he designed his Z88 computer, Sir Clive Sinclair took these two modern developments – size (portability) and multi-functionality – and wove them into as neat a package as one could hope for. As far as size is concerned, the Z88 takes up less space than a jumbo-sized pad of A4 paper, and its weight, at under 2lb., makes it easily transportable in most briefcases and other office carrying bags.

Added to this is the variety of functions that it performs. As well as being a sophisticated computer in its own right, providing you with the easy to use but powerful BASIC language, the Z88 comes equipped with built-in software that will allow it to act as a:

- word processor;
- spreadsheet;
- database;
- diary;
- interactive computer terminal;
- calendar;
- calculator; and
- alarm clock.

With gay abandon you can swap between these operations and back again, without losing any information. And you can transport information generated in one application directly into another. Indeed, as this book will show, with a little thought there are few operations that you *cannot* do on this mini-computer with maxi-power.

The Hardware

All of the hardware functions that you would expect to see on a powerful desktop computer are included in the Z88, and some more besides. It is sometimes difficult to realise that within its small, flat, shape there is a full-sized QWERTY keyboard, an eminently readable 8-line super-twist liquid crystal display, and a connector on the right hand edge via which you can transfer information to a printer or to another computer.

In addition, on the left hand edge of the A4 pad-sized machine is a small, recessed, button for resetting the machine if you ever get into difficulties (this is called a 'soft reset'). And a thumb wheel to vary the display contrast so that it can adapt to different lighting conditions.

The front edge contains a set of three cavities, covered by a protective flap, into which you can slot additional memory to expand the computer. Theoretically, the Z88 can contain up to three megabytes of memory.

This whole system is powered by just four AA-type (1.5v) batteries slotted into the under-side of the machine. These will supply up to 20 hours of continuous use (mainly because the machine provides sophisticated systems for conserving power when it is not being used). In addition, the Z88 can be run from a mains supply through a suitable power adapter – without having to remove the batteries.

Integrated Activity

Most modern computers can only operate one program at a time (although some programs have multiple functions). The Z88, however, can operate a number of different programs at the same time. How does it do this?

The answer lies in a jargonised term called 'context switching'. This lets you swap between applications instantly, without having to exit from them. And when you return, you go back to the original application in exactly the same place as when you left it. All the time you are away, the application is said to be 'suspended'.

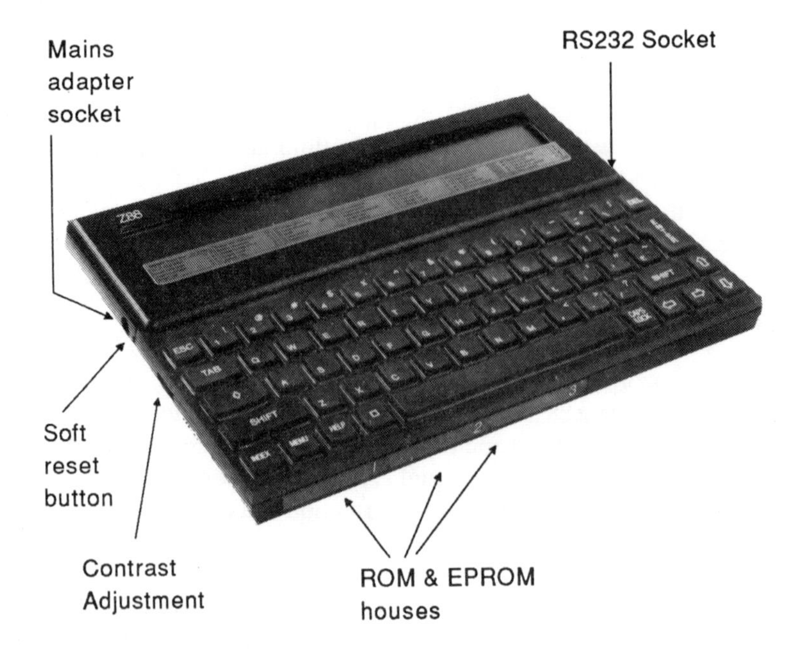

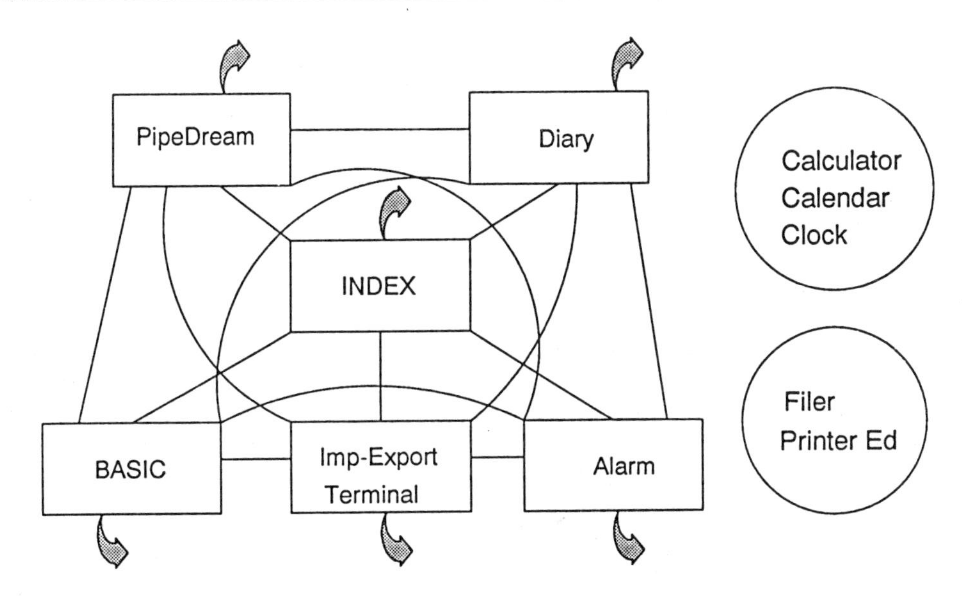

Integrated applications

Context switching

To get a feel for this new way of working, imagine yourself in the control room of a building, surrounded by different rooms. From the control room you can see what is happening in each other room, and you can also manipulate objects in these rooms. In each apartment, there is a telephone that connects with each other room, and which also connects through to the outside world.

Ensconced in your control room, context switching lets you switch your attention from room to room. You can deal with things in one room, switch to another and do something else. When you return your attention to the first room, as you would expect things will have remained the same as when you left.

And while in each room, via the telephone you can contact other rooms – and even request outside help, such as from a calculator to do some arithmetical operations, or the clock to see the time.

Once inside the Z88, therefore, you can switch between each application to each other, either going directly from application to application or via the control room. This control room is called the Index in Z88 parlance. In addition, for most of the Z88's applications, you can take information with you when you switch between them.

The Great Switch On

The next question is how do you access this power? New users will quickly discover that the Z88 lacks an on/off switch, so how does one switch it on? We shall consider the power behind the Z88 later in this chapter. For the moment, however, it is important to understand another innovation of this machine: the Z88 is always on – even when it is off.

Take your own body as an analogy: you never 'switch off', even when you are sleeping. Your eyes may be closed and your brain resting, but the slightest sound or even the faintest smell of smoke can bring you instantly awake, with your memory intact and ready for action.

So, too, does the Z88. In its resting, 'sleeping', state the Z88 is actually 'ticking over'. To conserve battery power the display is switched off and all software functions are eliminated, except for one which constantly checks to see whether the two SHIFT keys, one on each side of the keyboard, have been pressed. If you press these two keys together you will wake the Z88 from its slumber and bring the 8-line display alive and ready for action.

So, to switch 'on' the Z88 press both SHIFT keys together. To switch it 'off' (to return it to sleep) press both SHIFT keys together again. When you next turn it on the display will be exactly as you left it.

Timeout

While using the Z88, you may notice that the machine sometimes automatically goes to sleep without any action from you. This is one of its power-saving features. After a pre-determined number of minutes of inactivity (that is, of having no keys pressed) the Z88 switches itself off. You can determine how long this should be – indeed, whether it happens at all.

As you would expect by now, of course, when the machine goes to sleep like this you just need to press both SHIFT keys together to return it to the precise point you were at when it went comatose.

The Z88's keyboard

The layout of the Z88's keyboard is very similar to that seen on most common computers. It contains the standard QWERTY key set, with numbers along the top row. The keys that control the cursor are arranged in the bottom right hand corner, and there is a 'control' key at the far left hand end of the middle row. This is called the diamond key (◇); if you press this key along with certain others when you are working within an application you will make particular functions happen.

The four keys on the bottom row to the left of the space bar are peculiar to the Z88. First is the INDEX key, which we shall discuss in more detail below. Next is the key that generates pages of helpful information. Then there is the HELP key itself.

Finally, the key with a square design on it (□) is used like the diamond key, although this time you use it to begin an application. So, whatever you are doing in the Z88, if

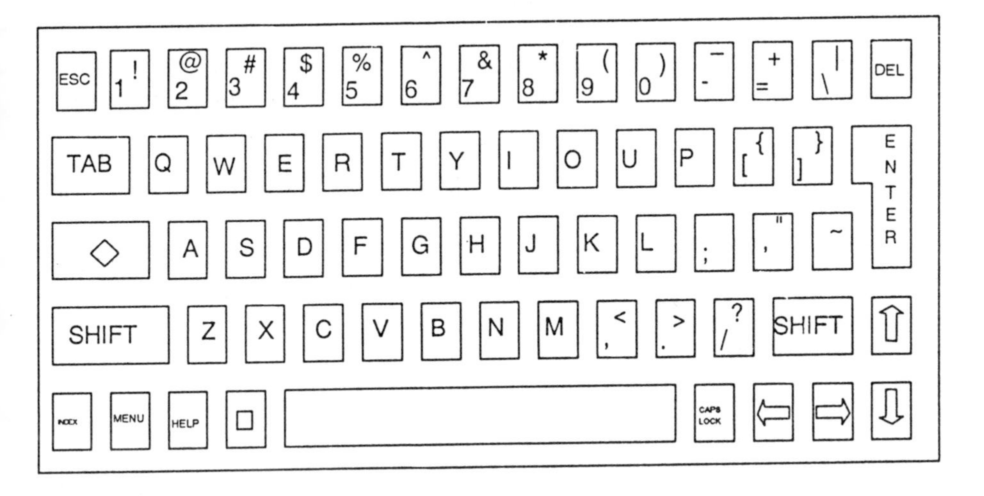

you press □P you will move directly into PipeDream. Pressing □B takes you into the Basic computer language, □R displays and activates the calculator, and so on.

The Helpful Menu

The MENU key provides access to the comprehensive help pages supplied within the Z88's software. This particularly concerns the control key (◇) functions that you can use within any specific application. To this extent, then, the Menu key is 'context sensitive'.

In whatever application you happen to be working, when you press the Menu key for the first time you will be presented with a list of functions which temporarily overlay whatever work you were doing. This work is not lost, of course, because when you press the ESC(ape) key at the top left hand corner of the keyboard the help information disappears and your work is returned to you. Indeed, you will find yourself at exactly the same point that you left to read the Menu material.

Listed down the left hand side of the Menu screen are all of the help menus which are available within that application, one of which will appear in bold print. The main portion of the Menu page comprises a list of all the functions available under that heading and the ◇ -key combinations which you have to press in order to access them.

Press the Menu key a second time and you will move on down the list of menus available. As you will see, the information page changes each time as appropriate.

In whichever help menu you find yourself, if you take the cursor to a particular function and press the ENTER key that function will be carried out. Of course, you can also perform the function at any time, without having to go through the rigmarole of displaying the menu, by pressing ◇ plus the appropriate letter sequence.

To illustrate using the Menu key, press both SHIFT keys together to switch on the Z88 and then press □P to enter PipeDream. For the moment we shall not worry about what PipeDream can do. The list of Menus available is displayed in the left hand column, with the first ('blocks') bolded. You can move the large cursor around the three columns of functions using the cursor arrow keys at the bottom right hand corner of the keyboard.

Now press the Menu key again to view the functions that deal with cursor movement, and so on.

Remember, pressing the ESC key at the top left hand corner of the keyboard always takes you out of the Menu system and back to your original application.

The Help Key

As its name suggests, the Help key provides basic help information about some of the activities you may wish to carry out within your application. It works in much the same way as the Menu key, except that the help information is simply displayed onscreen – you cannot activate a function by taking the cursor to it and pressing the ENTER key.

As well as telling you about the Z88's applications, the Help key also supplies information about the machine itself.

A little-known trick with this computer is to return to the Index page by pressing the Index key (or □I). Next press the Help key to read about the Index page and then press the *left* arrow key. Details about the version of the machine you have purchased, and the companies which were responsible for producing it, will appear on the screen.

The Index

Initially at least, you will perform all of the Z88's activities from the Index page. This appears immediately when you press the Index key which is located at the bottom left hand corner of the keyboard (you can also call up Index by pressing □I). Also, if you switch on the Z88 for the first time you will find that this page appears from the start.

You should remember that whatever you are doing with the Z88, in whichever application you happen to be, pressing the Index key returns you to this initial state. Any application you might have been performing will be 'suspended', ready to return to later.

The Index page is divided into two major sections, or windows, with the additional Menu list at the far left. In the left window you will see all the applications that you can carry out on the Z88, as well as their shorthand (□-key and letter) combinations. You can immediately switch into any of these applications simply by taking the cursor down the list to the appropriate place and pressing the ENTER key.

Or, you could just press □ and the relevant letter:

□D	Diary	a flexible diary for thousands of years
□P	PipeDream	word processor and spreadsheet
□B	BASIC	computer language
□R	Calculator	and metric/imperial converter
□C	Calendar	from 23rd November 4713 BC until 31st December 18253 AD
□T	Clock	onscreen time
□A	Alarm	alarm clock and time manager
□F	Filer	file storage and memory management
□E	Printer editor	for operating different kinds of printers
□S	Panel	setting various Z88 defaults
□V	Terminal	interactive computer-computer communications
□X	Imp-export	file transfer between computers

The right-hand window supplies a list of all of the suspended activities that are still in the Z88's memory, and the day and time when they were suspended. This is very useful information. As we shall see in Chapter 2 the Z88 can be very profligate with its memory, particularly when it suspends activities. Now and again, therefore, you

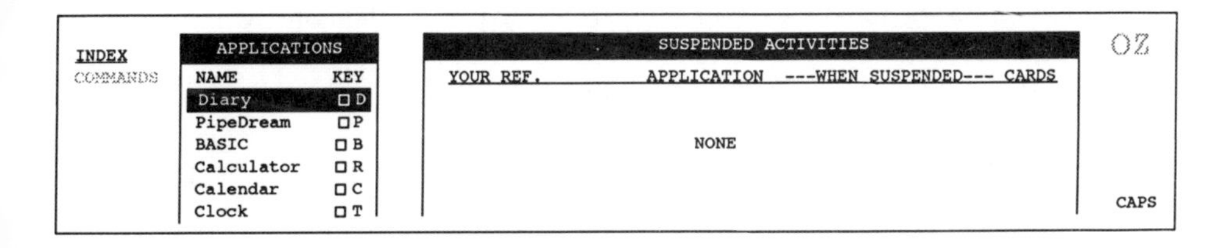

The Index page

will need to eliminate suspended activities to recover some memory. By letting you know when the activity was suspended, the Z88 will help you to decide which application to remove.

The suspension day is shown as 'today', 'yesterday' or the actual date. Both the date and time are taken from the Z88's own internal clock, which you can change by pressing □T.

As well as showing you which activities remain suspended in the Z88's memory, the right hand panel on the Index page has another very useful function: you can use it to switch immediately into a suspended activity without having to go through any of the rigmarole of setting up a file or whatever. Furthermore, you enter the activity in exactly the same position, and with the computer in precisely the same internal state, as when you left it. If the activity you suspended was associated with a particular file, then the file name will be shown in the 'Your Ref' column of the suspended activities panel.

To use this facility, simply take the cursor to the activity you wish to resume and press the ENTER key.

Multiple activities

Although you can switch into any of the Z88's activities in three ways: via the left hand window on the Index page, highlighting a suspended activity, or by pressing the square key (□) followed by an appropriate letter, the precise effects of these approaches can differ. We shall look at these effects in reverse order:

If you take the third route of pressing □ plus a letter (say □P) from wherever you are in the Z88 (even if you happen to be using a different application), then you will be taken to the *first* suspended activity that is associated with that application. And if you take the second route (highlighting a suspended activity) you will go directly to *that* activity.

However, if you take the first route and use the left panel on the Index page then the Z88 will *add* another activity for you. So you can have more than one word processed file suspended, for example, or more than one BASIC program on the go at the same time. We will see how to 'name' these activities later.

You can switch through these multiple suspensions by repeatedly pressing the relevant □ plus letter combination of keys. So, on the first press of □P you will be taken to the first suspended PipeDream activity; press the two keys again and you will move to the PipeDream file that was suspended next; and so on.

Kill and Purge

You can remove activities from the suspended list by 'killing' them. Rather more radically the system can be reset to its default state by 'purging' all the activities at once. Both of these tasks are carried out from the Index – if you press the Menu key you will see them shown in the third panel of the list of commands available.

To 'Kill' (remove) a single suspended activity, simply take the cursor to it in the right hand panel and press ◇, K, I, L, L. Notice that as you press each character in turn it appears on the far right hand side of the screen. Also, you do not have to keep the ◇ key depressed while you are entering the letters; you only have to press it once initially.

Killing an activity removes it from the list of suspended activities and makes more memory available for other Z88 computing applications. But once the activity has been killed you cannot switch back into it. However, it does *not* remove any material that you may have saved as files, as we shall see in Chapter 2.

Sometimes you may wish to 'purge' the system of all suspended activities and reset it to its default state. You do this by issuing the ◇PURGE command at the Index page. Since this also resets all the machine's internal settings, however, it is not an action that you should undertake lightly. Nevertheless, if you are happy with the standard settings, or you do not mind resetting the machine each time, then purging provides a simple way of removing a large number of suspended activities at a stroke.

Before issuing this command, however, you *must* make sure that there are no files stored in a special area of the machine called ':RAM.-'. If you are a newcomer to the Z88 and have not been doing any fancy operations with it then you do not need to worry about this problem. Nevertheless, Chapter 2 explains in more detail how you can check that this area of your Z88 is free from files before you purge the system.

Z88 Power

No computer can work without electrical power and, despite its revolutionary nature, in this respect the Z88 is no different from any other machine. To enable it to operate in as many environments as possible the Z88 comes equipped with two sources of power: batteries and mains.

For computing on the move, in trains, boats and planes, the Z88's power is supplied by the four AA-sized batteries that slot neatly into its under-side. These provide a 6-volts power supply, which should be enough for up to 20 hours of continuous use, or many months in its 'sleep' mode.

As will become apparent later, however, the length of time for which the batteries will continue to function depends considerably on the *kind* of computing activities that you do: just entering simple text or numbers, along with the associated computing, uses far less electrical energy than saving a file to memory, for example. And if you use some hardware attached to your Z88, a modem perhaps, or a printer, or even an EPROM pack, then the battery life will be considerably reduced.

In situations where an easily accessible power supply is available, it is much better to use the power adapter that can be obtained with the Z88. When plugged into the mains supply it takes over the batteries' functions and so conserves them.

Battery Power

As well as maintaining the Z88's computing abilities, the batteries also supply power to the memory and conserve the information that you have stored in it. So it is extremely important that a stable power supply is sustained, and considerable thought went into this aspect when the machine was designed.

Well before the battery power falls to the critical level at which data may be lost from memory, the 'Bat Low' indicator will appear on the far right hand side of the screen. Although this does not interrupt your computing activities, you should take its appearance as a warning that the batteries need replacing very quickly (and that any files you are working on should be saved if possible).

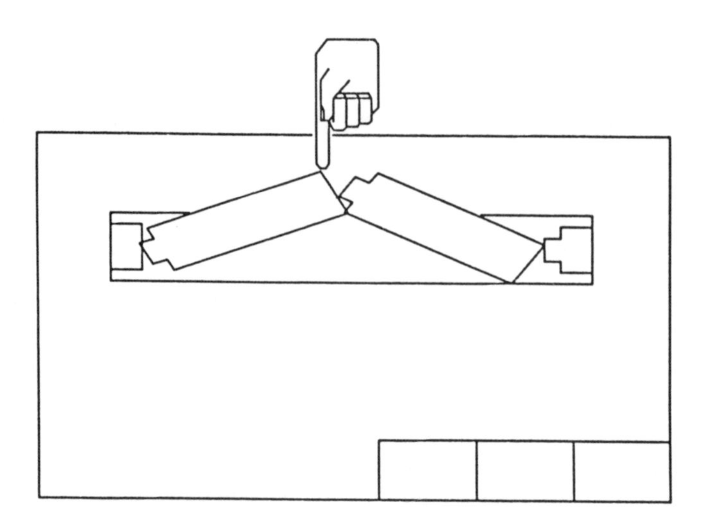

Inserting batteries

If you ignore this warning, as the power falls further the screen display begins to break up, and eventually the machine will preserve its integrity by entering its 'sleep' mode.

Changing the batteries

Changing the batteries is a very simple operation which can be done anywhere. Again, considerable thought has gone into the computer's design, since even after the batteries have been removed the machine has enough residual power to maintain its essential memory functions.

However, this residual energy only lasts for a limited time (minutes), so it is always best to change batteries while the Z88 is attached to a mains supply. But if you do have to change them while on the move ensure that your new batteries have already been taken from their wrappers before removing the old ones from the Z88.

When changing batteries it is essential that they are inserted the right way round inside the machine, with the negative (flat) part facing the right hand end of the Z88 when it is placed face down.

Inserting batteries

Having first switched off the machine, the easiest way of inserting new batteries is to extract the old ones and insert *two* new ones into the slot, pushing one to each end. Take the remaining two batteries and install them into the middle of the battery holder in an upside-down 'V' configuration. Then simply push gently at the apex of the V and replace the battery cover.

You are now ready for action again. Just press both SHIFT keys to continue where you left off.

The time of available to change the batteries depends on the kinds of memory cards that you have inserted into your machine. For example:

Cards	**Safe time**
No cards	6 minutes
One 128k	4 minutes
Two 128k	2 1/2 minutes

Obviously, you will have unlimited time available to change the batteries if your Z88 is connected to the mains supply.

Conserving batteries

If you are working on your Z88 without it being connected to a mains supply, the amount of power time that you will have available to do your work will depend on two features: the kinds of operations that you are carrying out and the kinds of memory that you have in your machine.

Some computing operations are more power hungry than others. This is particularly true of activities that involve data being transferred from one state to another, such as refreshing the screen by 'paging' through it, saving information in files, loading material from files, storing information in EPROMs, or communicating with other devices via an external cable.

Also, because the batteries have to conserve memory, the more RAM and EPROM memory which is added to your machine, the more power will be needed to maintain the information.

Timeout

Even displaying information onscreen can use battery power, which is why the screen is switched off when the Z88 enters its sleep mode. This is because during normal operation the computer actually prints the characters onto the screen many thousands of time each second, in much the same way as a television circuit scans the TV screen and continually refreshes the picture on it.

To conserve power, therefore, the most suitable state for the Z88 is when it is in its sleep mode. Unfortunately, this is the one state that is useless to the user because the display is invisible! However, the Z88 designers have produced an ideal compromise to the conundrum – by switching off the computer when it is not being used.

When entering data into a computer we rarely keep up a steady stream of key presses. For example, when composing a document using a word processor there will be periods when we need to sit and think, perhaps to look out of the window. Even copy typists have to stop work sometimes. During these periods of inactivity it would be wasteful of battery power for both the computer and its display to remain active.

For this reason the Z88 switches itself off after a certain period of time during which there have been no key presses, and the length of this timeout period can be varied by the user. If the machine does go to sleep in this way, you simply press the two SHIFT keys together to return to the same point at which you left the activity.

To alter the timeout period, wherever you are in the Z88 press □S and the cursor-down arrow five times to reach the 'timeout' option. The default value is 5 minutes, but you can change this to any length of time up to 99 minutes. If you enter zero here, the display will always remain active.

Pressing the ENTER key updates this value, which will remain in the machine until you either change it or you need to rest the Z88 for some reason (perhaps by issuing a ◇ PURGE command).

Battery types

Even when they are not supplying electricity batteries still lose their power, albeit very slowly. So it is sometimes possible to insert a 'new' set of batteries only to find that their life in the machine appears to be unexpectedly short. This may well happen because the batteries have remained on the shop shelf for too long and have lost much of their charge.

So it is always best to obtain batteries from stores that have a quick turnover of batteries. Also, it is unwise to maintain a supply of batteries for Z88 use, other than for 'emergencies'.

Because batteries can be costly, and 10-20 hours of continuous computing may not seem too long, many people use rechargeable, NiCad, batteries in their machines. These work almost as well as conventional ones, but they may not provide the added security that alkaline batteries supply when nearing the end of their working lives.

If you were to draw a graph of 'charge level' versus time for an alkaline battery, you would see a fairly constant level until the battery begins to fail. Then it decays fairly slowly. It is this slow decay that provides the safe time when changing batteries and also makes the 'battery low' indicator meaningful as a warning signal.

Rechargeable NiCad batteries, on the other hand, show a different kind of decay graph. Although they retain their power at a fairly constant level, at the end of their lives the power falls very quickly to the Z88's critical levels. This means that the battery low indicator may not give enough warning time, and the safe time for changing the batteries may be too short.

Nevertheless, rechargeable batteries can reduce costs considerably. If they are treated with caution and are changed at very regular intervals they can provide efficient service. However, they cannot be recharged inside the Z88; you will have to use a conventional battery charger for that.

Z88 power requirements

If you intend to use NiCad batteries you should realise that even under normal conditions, different machine activities require different amounts of power. For example, when it is active (when you are entering information into an application) the computer may extract up to 120 milliamps (mA) of power from its batteries; in 'snooze' mode (when the display is active but the keyboard is not), this drops to around 70mA with a 128K RAM pack inside the machine (see below). And when it is 'asleep' it takes about 1mA from the batteries.

Whereas a full complement of normal alkaline batteries inside the Z88 will supply about 2200mA (which means that it can sustain a current of 2200mA for one hour), rechargeable batteries supply only about a quarter of this amount. So, assuming that you use the Z88 to its fullest extent (in other words, you keep entering information into a PipeDream application, say, so that it is continually 'active'), then alkaline batteries will give you about 18 hours use (2200/120). NiCad batteries, on the other hand, will supply only about 4 hours (500/120) of continuous use.

Power leakage

Before leaving the tricky subject of power requirements, it is important to understand a little about the Z88's behaviour when it is off and asleep.

To be able to change instantly from sleep to snooze, ready to be 'active' when you enter information, the Z88 must actually be working even though it appears to be asleep. For example, the machine must 'know' that you have pressed both SHIFT keys together to wake it up. For that reason, even while asleep the Z88 constantly checks the keyboard to determine whether or not a key has been pressed and, if so, whether it is a SHIFT key. If a SHIFT key has been pressed then it moves into an intermediate 'doze' state to check whether the second SHIFT key is also being pressed. In this state the Z88 consumes more electrical power than when in its sleep mode.

The implications of this are quite far-reaching as far as storing the Z88 is concerned. If you keep the machine in a briefcase, say, or under a pile of books, and a key is continuously depressed on the keyboard because of the weight of material above it, then you will use your battery power much quicker than if you had allowed the computer to sleep uninterrupted. And if you use NiCad batteries in your machine, then this could have some disastrous consequences.

To reduce the likelihood of this kind of problem occurring, it is possible to buy hard covers for the Z88. Appendix 3 supplies some useful addresses.

Memory and Data Storage

Officially, the Z88 stores the information that you supply in one of two ways - either as random access memory (RAM) or on removable computer chips that provide more permanent storage facilities. These are called EPROMs (Erasable Program Read Only Memory). Each has its benefits and disadvantages.

The main advantage of RAM memory is that information can be stored in it, manipulated, extracted and erased at will. This is ideal for most computing operations such as those performed on the Z88 in which information in the machine is constantly being altered. For example, a word processor will accept text and let the user manipulate it to create other text; the same with a spreadsheet. In both cases the manipulated text 'overlays' the unwanted material and so makes maximum use of the memory space in the computer.

The process is fast and requires relatively little power from the batteries. However, RAM is critically dependent on an external power source; if the batteries are removed or the power supply fails for longer than the safe period, then all the information currently stored inside the machine will be irretrievably lost.

For this reason, most computers have some means of storing valuable information on a more permanent basis. These days that normally implies using computer disks and external drives so that the information can be stored and read. The drawback of these devices is that they are large, can be heavy and consume considerable amounts of power. Each of these three features contravenes the Z88's philosophy of minimum size, weight and power requirements.

To overcome the problem Cambridge Computers decided to use EPROMs for permanent data storage. These are solid state devices that look similar to the RAM 'packs', although they have a small 'window' on side through which you can see the chip. EPROMs operate almost as quickly as does RAM and require comparatively little power (although more than RAM does).

The disadvantage of EPROMs lies in the permanence of their storage mechanisms. Once a file has been written to an EPROM it cannot be removed other than by exposing the EPROM to considerable amounts of ultra-violet light using a device that can be obtained from Cambridge Computers. However, this process will also destroy every other file on the device. For this reason EPROMs should only be used to store important files in their finalised state, rather than working versions of a file.

RAM packs

When you buy a new Z88 it will arrive equipped with 32k of internal RAM, which will let you store about 32,000 characters. However, the size of your documents will have to be considerably smaller than this, because of the way in which the Z88 uses its internal memory. To overcome these limitations, it is possible to expand the Z88 by using specially designed 'RAM packs' supplied by Cambridge Computers. These are slotted into the transparent section at the front of the machine.

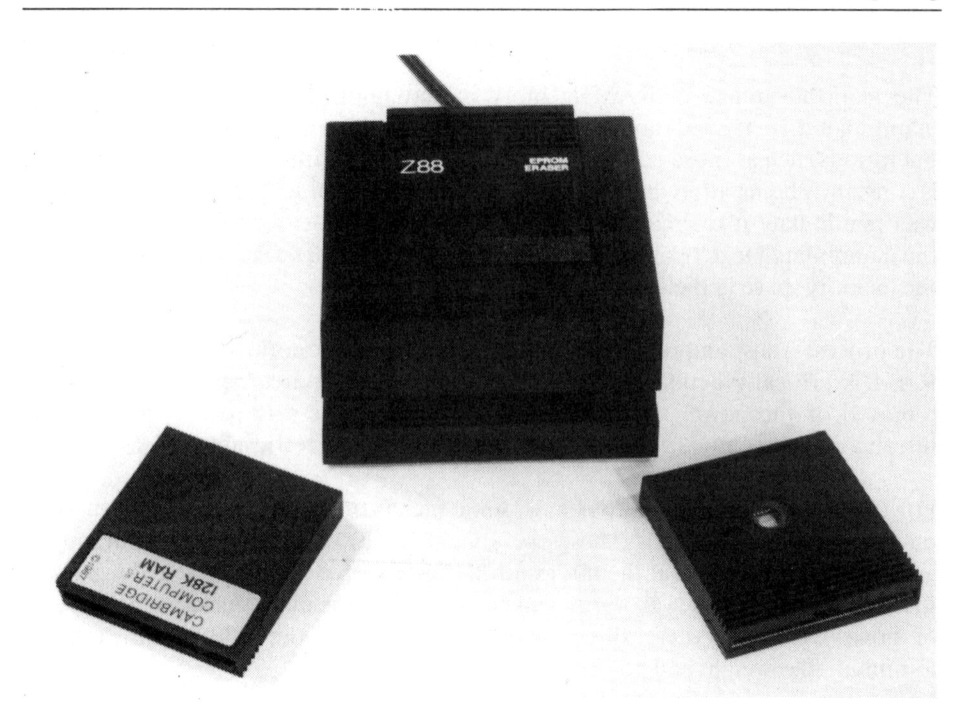

Adding RAM

Inserting a RAM pack is very easy. Switch into the Index page (by pressing the Index key or □I) and then switch off the machine by pressing both SHIFT keys together. Next open the transparent cover on the front edge of the computer; this hinges on the under-side of the machine. Now simply push the RAM pack into the first available slot so that the label on the front edge of the pack is upright and the red strip is underneath. Snap back the cover and switch on the Z88 by pressing both SHIFT keys together.

When you add a RAM pack to your machine the Z88 tries to retain as much information inside its memories as it can, so after the pack has been added your Index page will reappear as you left it. However, sometimes you may have to perform a 'soft reset' by pressing the small button on the right hand edge of the machine. Whenever you add a RAM pack, therefore, to be on the safe side it is always good practice to extract valuable files from the machine before you begin – perhaps by sending them to another computer (see Chapter 10) or saving them to an EPROM (see Chapter 2).

Of course, if you take a RAM pack out of the machine all the information in the RAM's memory will instantly be lost.

Inserting a RAM pack

When inserting a RAM pack it is important to decide which slot it should go in. Cambridge Computers have supplied additional power to the third slot for EPROMs (which do not have the red strip on their under-side), although you can also use it for RAM. If you insert a RAM pack into slot 1 then the machine is said to be 'expanded', which allows you to do some more advanced tricks with the Z88, as we shall see in later chapters. If the RAM pack is inserted into slot 2 while slot 1 remains free, however, the RAM is still available for use but the machine is not expanded.

As far as the Z88 is concerned, two consecutive RAM packs will operate in much the same way as a single pack. For example, a machine fitted with two 128k RAM packs (in slots 1 and 2) will act as if it contained 256k of continuous RAM.

Viewing the cards

Although the packs installed in your Z88 are perfectly visible through the transparent cover at the front of the machine, you can also find out about the state of such add-ons (and ensure that the Z88 also recognises them). Just issue the command ◇ CARD at the Index page and you will see a table of the various kinds of packs (cards) inside the machine, the slots they occupy and their values.

Summary

This chapter has introduced you to the Z88, its power, flexibility and ease of use. Whatever you are doing with the machine you can switch between applications with impunity simply by pressing the □ key and another key simultaneously. And, when you switch, everything will remain as it is, ready for your return.

Flexibility is not the only advanced feature of this machine, however. Its use of power is innovative. For example, you do not have annoying waits while the computer loads programs before you can begin work. Being in a permanently active state – albeit with varying degrees of activity – just press the two SHIFT keys together and the Z88 will be ready for work.

Finally, the chapter considered the memory facilities provided by this machine. Combinations of conventional RAM and less conventional EPROMs supply a range of opportunities for storing data on semi-permanent and permanent bases.

Chapter 2 will consider this last aspect in more detail, and will delve into the depths of file manipulation on the Z88.

2

Dealing with files

Before we look in more detail at the specific functions provided by the Z88, it is important to appreciate how information is stored in the machine and how we can organise, retrieve and manipulate different files. After all, the Z88 would have little value as a computer, word processor, spreadsheet, or whatever, if we could not store and retrieve material at will.

As was explained in Chapter 1, information that is currently in the major applications (like the word processor, Diary, BASIC language, and so on) remain accessible inside the Z88 without your having to store it in any permanent or semi-permanent way. When you switch from one application to another the applications that are no longer active become 'suspended', and full information about them always appears in the 'suspended activities' panel on the Index page.

Unfortunately, there are two major drawbacks against storing information like this. Firstly, the material is extremely vulnerable to attack, either from an inadvertent ◇ KILL or ◇ PURGE instruction or by being overwritten with other information that you subsequently enter. Secondly, you may decide to enter an application using the □ plus letter key combination route, in which case you will probably have to 'overwrite' the one that is currently in memory.

For these reasons the Z88 carries with it an extensive filing system, allowing you to file away various documents and other kinds of material for recall on subsequent occasions. These can be filed into a special part of the machine's memory (especially if you have increased the space available by adding additional RAM packs) or into EPROMs for more permanent storage.

As was discussed in Chapter 1, material that is stored somewhere in the Z88's RAM will be safe for as long as power is supplied to the machine, either from the batteries or from an external power supply. EPROM-based files, on the other hand, are stored on a permanent basis. Since they can only be erased by specifically applying ultra-violet light to the EPROM, important files should be kept in these devices.

File Names and Devices

To store information in either RAM or an EPROM, the file must be given a name with which you can address it. The choice of the name for any file is entirely up to you, although the Z88 follows the same convention for naming files as is used by many desk-based micro computers. Thus, the file name is composed of a set of alphabetic or numeric letters, optionally followed by a full stop and an 'extension' of up to three characters. Since the part of all Z88 file names before the full stop can be up to 12 characters long, you can create an almost infinite number of different file names.

Although you can choose any set of characters for each of your document's file names, to make things easier for yourself when interpreting the information in the file directory it is sensible to choose meaningful names such as LETTER, FRED, HOUSE and so on. Furthermore, since different extensions create different file names, you could use the same base and vary the extension.

For example, up to 1000 different letters could be stored (memory permitting) using the different file names LETTER.000 to LETTER.999; similarly, you could produce up to 1000 different documents each for various people: FRED.000, JIM.123, WILLIAM.543, and so on. Add to this the possibility of using extensions like LETTER.AAA, LETTER.AAB and so on, you can see how it is possible to create an almost infinite series of file names if you so desire.

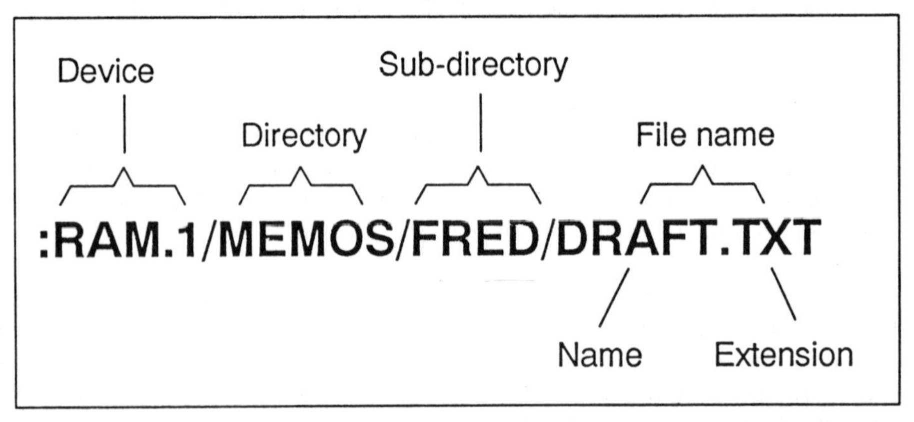

The structure of a file name

Traditionally, the file extension, the three-character part of the file name that follows the full stop, has been used to show the *kind* of file that has been stored, but this convention does not need to be followed blindly. In the past, for example, computer aficionados have used the extension '.BAS' to indicate a BASIC program, '.TXT' to express a piece of text, '.COM' to signal a 'command' program, and so on.

Although you may define your document with a file name having up to 12 + 3 characters, the Z88 needs a little more information before it can know *where* the document should be stored in the machine. This information must be added to the file name – although, as will be discussed later, it is possible to set up the machine to accept a 'default' storage position which removes the need to supply this additional information.

As far as the Z88 is concerned only the two devices of RAM and EPROM can be used to store data (other 'devices' can be used for other applications, but these will discussed in Chapter 9). Which device you use will be defined by the 'slot' in which it resides inside the machine – either the internal memory slot or one of the three slots at the front.

The internal memory slot is called device 0, while the three slots at the front are called devices 1, 2 and 3 respectively (from left to right).

So, the full storage information that needs to be provided when saving a file consists of the following: a colon, the letters RAM, a full stop, and the slot number. For example, the Z88's own internal memory is represented by:

```
:RAM.0
```

A RAM pack in slot 1 is represented by **:RAM.1**.

All of this information is put together to create a unique name for each file which is composed of the separate components:

```
the storage area or device / filename
```

So, to store a file in the Z88's internal memory (or at least in what is left of the 32k memory after suspended activities and other pieces of information have taken their toll), the full filename information would be:

```
:RAM.0/filename
```

For example, :RAM.0/LETTERS.001

To store the same file into an externally available plug-in RAM in slot 1, you would use the filename:

```
:RAM.1/LETTERS.001
```

:Ram.-

As well as the obvious RAM devices 0 (internal), 1, 2 and 3 (external), the Z88 also provides a very temporary storage area called :RAM.-. Although it uses this area for some of its own activities, as we shall see in later chapters you can also use :RAM.-. However, you should use the device with extreme caution since, under certain circumstances, unrestricted use can cause peculiar errors to occur in your Z88's functioning. More will be said about this problem, for certain Z88 users, in Chapter 8.

Default devices

Having to enter the device information, like :RAM.0, each time you want to save a file can be a little annoying and more than a little time-consuming. To overcome the problem the Z88's designers have incorporated into the system a way of changing the 'default' device. The Z88 will automatically store files there unless it is told otherwise by a different device name being added to the front of the file name.

You can change the default device from the screen options menu, by pressing □S at any time. The appropriate option lies at the bottom of the first column. Simply press the ↓ key three times to take the cursor to the bottom, the right cursor key six times to take the cursor to the right hand edge of the current default device (or press ◇ →), DELete the number shown, and insert your own (which will probably be 1 if you have installed an external RAM pack).

When you press the ENTER key you will update the default options. From now on, when you save a file, simply provide the file name (without giving the device number, that is); the file will automatically be saved into the default device.

Naturally, you can always override this action – either by changing the default device or by supplying the device plus file name information when saving a file.

Device Directories

To see a list of the files that are stored inside the Z88 (as opposed to suspended activities) you simply switch activities into the file directory (called the Filer) by issuing the command □F at any time and within any application. This provides a screen that looks like the Index page, with possible actions in the left hand window and a list of the files stored in the directory on the right.

FILER
COMMANDS

COMMANDS	DIRECTORY :RAM.1		
CATALOGUE FILES	draft.txt	draft	draft.doc
CATALOGUE EPROM	memo.d	memo.c	memo.b
SAVE TO EPROM	memo.a	letter.002	letter.001
FETCH FROM EPROM			
COPY			
RENAME			
ERASE			

OZ

The Z88's Filer

It is important to realise, however, that the list shows files that are in the *currently selected* directory, not the default one. So, although you may have defined :RAM.1 as your default device, if the currently selected directory deals with device 0 there may be no files shown.

Changing the device display is very easy with the Z88. From within the Filer simply press ◇ SV (Select deVice) and alter the device number in the same way that you did the default drive in the options screen. Now when you press the ENTER key, the name of the new device will be displayed at the top of the right hand panel and the files that are stored in it will appear in the panel.

Matching names

If you have a particularly crowded filing system, you may not wish to have all of the files displayed on your directory at the same time. Perhaps you only want to see those having the extension '.TXT', or all files that begin with the letters 'fred'. The Z88 supplies a simple way of 'filtering' out the unwanted files from the display (but not from the memory).

While still in the Filer press ◇ NM (Name Match) and you will be asked to supply a matching criterion. Already provided will be a single asterisk (*) character, which is universally accepted by the Z88 to mean 'any sequence of characters'. So, by default, all files are displayed in the directory.

To see all files with the extension .TXT, however, simply enter the matching name *.TXT, which means 'display files which have any character before the full stop and the letters TXT after it'. When the name matching filter is in operation, the file name panel shows the letters NM at the top to remind you. Similarly to display all files beginning with FRED, enter FRED*, and so on.

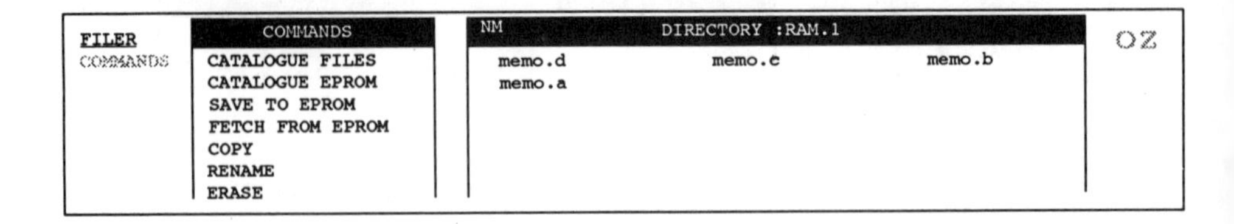

Using Name Match

If you use the matching name *.*, you will only see files that have an extension. So you would see a directory of files like FRED.TXT and LETTERS.001, but not FRED or LETTERS.

This generalised matching facility is extremely useful. As well as using the convention of using an asterisk to mean 'any sequence of characters' you can use a question mark to mean 'any character at that position'. So, matching for FRED*.T?? will find:

FRED.TXT
FRED.TOP
FRED.TIP
FREDS.TXT
FREDERICK.TAP

and so on.

Sub-directories

If you save a considerable number of files to your RAM pack, the situation can quickly arise when the file list becomes extremely cluttered and difficult to manage, even using the Z88's file matching features. Then is the time to consider developing sub-directories, and even sub-sub-directories.

A typical office filing cabinet with four drawers, say, is often used as an analogy for this kind of activity. As far as the Z88 is concerned, we can imagine each of the four drawers as being equivalent to a device. So a file is saved into device (drawer) 0, 1, 2 or 3. In each filing cabinet drawer, however, there will also be a set of file holders, perhaps grouped into subsets. So, maybe drawer 1 has a set of letter files, another set of report files, and so on. In our Z88 filing system analogy these sets of files are classed as a sub-directory: Drawer1/letters or Drawer1/reports.

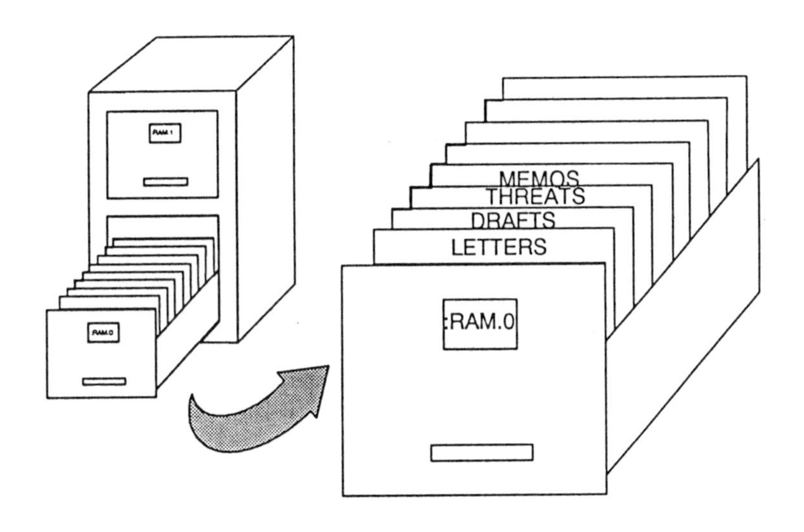

Sample file names:
:RAM.0/LETTERS/Jim
:RAM.0/LETTERS/Fred
:RAM.0/DRAFTS/Plan
:RAM.0/THREATS/Goods

Sub-directories on the Z88

It can also be the case, of course, that our letters sub-directory in drawer 1 could be divided into separate folders: Fred's letters, Jim's letters, and so on. So now we have a three-tier filing system: Drawer/letters/individual.

Exactly this kind of tree-based filing system is available on the Z88 to help you organise files sensibly within the machine, particularly for easy access. To see all of Jim's letters in RAM.1, for example, you would simply change the directory to :RAM.1/LETTERS/JIM – or whatever.

Dealing with directories

You can create as many sub-directories as you wish, simply by issuing the command ◇ CD (Create Directory) and supplying a directory name. So, to create a letters directory within :RAM.1, press ◇ CD and type 'letters' at the prompt. On pressing the ENTER key you will find that the letters sub-directory has been added to the file list for :RAM.1. Notice, however, that the word 'letters' is printed in small-sized capitals. Normal-sized lower and upper case characters indicate file names.

To switch into the letters sub-directory, press ◇ SI (Select dIrectory), supply the directory name (letters) and press the ENTER key. Now the file display will show all the files that are contained in this directory (note that the full directory path is shown at the top of the screen).

Again, to create a sub-directory off this sub-directory which will contain all of Jim's letters, simply issue the ◇ CD command and enter 'Jim' as the directory name. Once again, the new directory 'Jim' will be displayed in the :RAM.1/LETTERS file list in small capitals.

Selecting the :RAM.1/LETTERS/JIM directory from within the (current) :RAM.1/ LETTERS directory is not quite as straightforward as was selecting the :RAM.1/ LETTERS directory when we were at the root of the structure (:RAM.1).

As you will see if you press ◇ SI, the Z88 retains the last directory name supplied (/LETTERS) and tells us that we are in this directory. We now want to 'move into' the directory called :RAM.1/LETTERS/JIM and we can do this in one of two ways. First, we could take the cursor to the end of the name line (◇ →) and add the characters '/JIM', or we could delete the name supplied and simply enter JIM. Whichever way you do it, the complete directory display of :RAM.1/LETTERS/JIM will appear when you press the ENTER key.

To return to the basic (root) directory at any time, press ◇ SI and delete any directory name that has been supplied (a quick way of doing this is to press ◇ D). The Z88 interprets no name as the root directory.

Erasing directories

To erase a sub-directory select the directory from the Filer panel by taking the cursor to it, press the ENTER key to mark it, and then press ◇ ER to initiate the erasing option.

For example, to remove the sub-directory JIM from :RAM.1/LETTERS select the :RAM.1/LETTERS directory (◇ SI) and use the arrow keys to take the cursor to the JIM directory. Press ENTER to mark this directory (a triangular marker will appear next to it) and then ◇ ER. Press the ENTER key again, to confirm that you want to remove this directory.

Only directories that do not contain any files can be removed in this way, however. If a sub-directory contains files the Z88 will return an error message saying that the directory is 'in use'.

Manipulating Files

Storing files into a directory or sub-directory is all very well, but often you will want to manipulate them in some way – perhaps to make a back-up copy of one or other of them, maybe erase unwanted files, and so on. All of these activities, and more, can be done from within the Filer (□F).

Catalogue

Whereas the directory screen provides a simple list of the files contained in the directory, the information supplied is not all that comprehensive. Users often want to know more about a file than simply its name. For example, knowing when it was created might help to decide on its value; knowing its size (how many characters it contains) could guide you as to its importance, and so on.

This kind of information is provided by the directory catalogue. It is activated either by taking the cursor to the first option in the menu list in the left hand Filer window (and pressing the ENTER key) or by pressing ◇ CF (Catalogue Files) from within the Filer operations. This operation initiates a request for a name match, enabling you to catalogue all files beginning with 'C', for example (C*), or all files with a '.TXT' extension (*.TXT). If you simply press the ENTER key at this point you will see a catalogue of all files in the Z88 (*).

The catalogue supplies the following information displayed across the screen: file name, the date and time it was created, the date and time it was last updated, and its size in characters.

If you have more than seven files in the machine you should press the Space bar to scroll through the list.

As well as displaying the catalogue onscreen, you can also print it if you have a suitable printer attached to your Z88 (see Chapter 7).

At the Filer page (□F) press the three keys: □, +, P. This will send all the information that normally is displayed on the screen also to the printer. Now issue the catalogue command (◇ CF) and tell the Filer which kinds of files you want information on (press ENTER for all files).

As the catalogue information is displayed onscreen, it will also be printed. Press the three keys □, -, P to switch off this process of echoing all the screen information to the printer.

Copying files

To make a second copy of a file (known as a backup file) you first need to identify the file that is to be copied.

Take the cursor to the right hand Filer window (the directory), choose the file to be copied (using the arrow keys to direct the cursor), and press the ENTER key. This adds a small marker at the left hand edge of the file name. Now either return the cursor to the left hand window and take it to the Copy command (and press ENTER), or press ◇ CO (COpy)to begin the operation.

The Z88 will request a new file name, which can reside in another directory of course, and then asks for confirmation that the process should proceed. So, to copy your file 'FRED' from :RAM.1 to :RAM.0 you need to supply the new name :RAM.0/FRED.

You can also use the Copy command to join files together. In this case you need to select all the files to be joined before issuing the Copy command. The process of selecting multiple files is the same as you went through to select the first file, but you mark subsequent files by pressing the SHIFT and ENTER keys together, instead of just ENTER.

So, to join the files LETTER.001 and LETTER.002 to produce a new file called LETTER, take the cursor to the right hand window and find the LETTER.001 file name. Mark it by pressing the ENTER key. Now find LETTER.002 and add this to the active list by pressing SHIFT and ENTER together. When the Z88 asks for the new file name, simply indicate that you want the two files to go together into a file called LETTER.

Tree copy

As well as copying single files from one place to another, and even into the same directory with a different name, you can also copy whole directories and sub-directories using the 'tree copy' command (◇ TC).

Say, for example, you have a sub-directory called LETTERS in :RAM.0, which contains two further sub-sub-directories: JIM and FRED. Each of these sub-sub-directories contains files relating to Jim's and to Fred's work.

You can copy the complete tree structure, including all the files, across to :RAM.1, say, using the tree copy command.

From the Filer, press ◇ TC and supply the device :RAM.0 as the source and :RAM.1 as the destination. When you press the ENTER key all the files will be copied automatically, including :RAM.0's sub-directory structure.

Partial tree copying

If you wanted to copy just the sub-directories JIM and FRED to :RAM.1, along with the files they contain, then enter :RAM.0/LETTERS as the source. Any files saved in the directory :RAM.0/LETTERS itself will also be transferred across, but files in :RAM.0 will not.

It is important to note that the tree copy operation will fail, and the Z88 will display the message 'in use', if the destination device already contains file names which are the same as either files or directories in the source device.

Rename

It is often useful to be able to rename a file, and the process for doing so is similar to copying a file. However, it is not possible to rename a file and send it to a different directory at the same time.

Again, it is easiest to highlight the file to be renamed using the ENTER key (as with copying a single file this is not absolutely necessary – you can enter the file name yourself at the appropriate point). Then it is simply a case of using the 'rename' option in the left hand window, or pressing ◇ RE.

You can also use Rename to change the name of a directory.

Erase

You can erase single files or a complete batch of them at the same time. In either case, you just indicate the file(s) to be erased (using ENTER for the first file to erase and SHIFT/ENTER for subsequent files), and then either take the cursor to the erase option in the left hand window or press ◇ ER.

Because erasing a file can be a drastic step to take, the Z88 asks each time whether you want to erase the file selected. If you have only selected one file the Z88 will ask for permission to go ahead (pressing ENTER completes the operation; 'N' stops it). If you have selected more than one file, however, it will first ask whether you wish to confirm each erasure. The default response is 'yes', in which case you simply press the ENTER key to proceed; subsequent presses of the ENTER key confirm each erasure.

If you do not wish to confirm each erasure, however, press 'N' and the ENTER key. The process will be executed automatically.

EPROMs

Saving and manipulating files in Eproms is very similar to dealing with RAM, although it can be slightly slower and will certainly use more power from your batteries.

Files can only be transferred to an EPROM after having first saved them to a directory within the Z88's RAM. It is then a simple matter of saving (copying) them to an EPROM that has been fixed into slot 3 at the front of the Z88. The process is very similar to the Copy command, except that multiple files are saved separately rather than being joined as one.

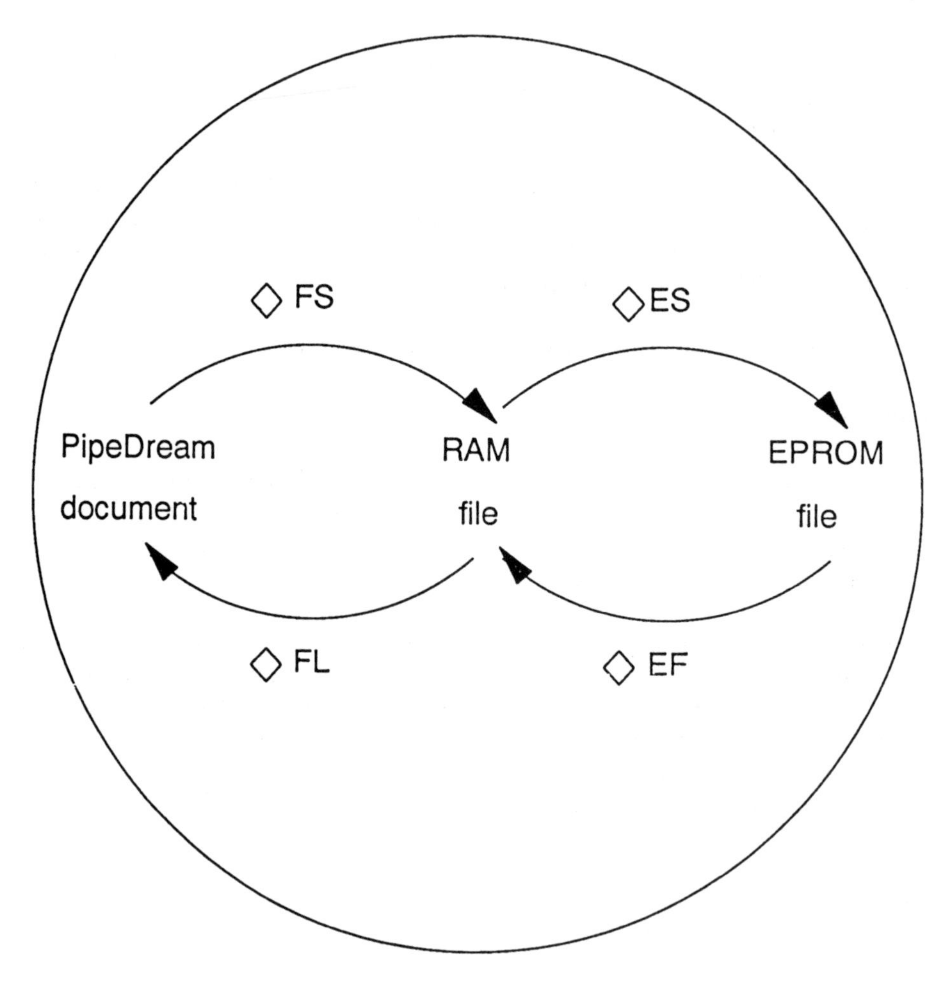

Saving files

Files are saved with the same names as they have in the RAM. As with the Copy command, mark the files you wish to save to the EPROM and then either take the cursor to the 'save to EPROM' option in the left hand window, or issue the command ◇ ES (Eprom Save).

When you save files to an EPROM the Z88 temporarily enters a semi-sleep mode in which the display goes blank, but flashes now and again. This is a power-saving feature of the Z88, which is necessary because of the additional power that is required for the process.

Multiple copies in an EPROM

If you save a file to an EPROM with a name that is already there, the Z88 does some fancy tricks to 'overwrite' the existing one. The effect of this is that the latest version of your file will always be ready for you, despite the fact that in reality old files cannot be erased from EPROMs without recourse to ultra-violet light.

Unfortunately, however, when it saves a subsequent version of the same file, all the Z88 really does is to direct its directory's attention to the new version – the old one is still present. So saving the same file name too often can mean that the EPROM may quickly become filled with unusable information.

Dealing with the EPROM files

Since the EPROM system is used solely for storage, it is not possible to manipulate files in EPROM in the same way as you can files in RAM. The only options open to you are to catalogue the EPROM-based files (◇ CE – Catalogue Eprom), in the same way as you do RAM-based files, and to fetch the files back from EPROM to RAM (◇ EF – Eprom Fetch).

Fetching files from the EPROM to RAM does not remove or destroy them in the EPROM; it simply copies them into RAM.

The only way in which you can remove files from an EPROM to erase the whole EPROM by exposing it to ultra-violet light. You do this with a specially designed eraser and it can take about 20 minutes (depending on the size of the EPROM). If you do wish to save some files from obliteration, therefore, it is imperative that before erasure you copy the relevant files into RAM, and then copy them back again to the erased EPROM later.

Summary

This chapter has taken a detailed look at the Z88's filing system (□F). With it you can store information that you have generated within an application, ready for use subsequently. Indeed, you have considerable flexibility when doing this – files can be moved, copied, catalogued and erased at will.

Despite the flexibility, however, most people will want to use the Z88 for creating documents of various kinds rather than storing them. So Chapter 3 will take an in-depth look at probably the most popular office-based computing application: word processing on the Z88.

3

Words, words, words

Although the Z88 is a powerful computer with the capability of performing a wide range of integrated activities, it is likely that most people will use it, initially at least, for one application only – word processing. But this A4-sized laptop computer gives all kinds of people, from travellers to executives to students, more than just the ability to process words. As we shall discover in other chapters, within the same plastic case they can develop their literary masterpieces, build complex mathematical models, manage their time and resources, and even print out all this information or send it, electronically, to other computers – maybe even on the other side of the world – for further treatment.

In this era of electronic sophistication, most people already know about the basic features of word processing and the benefits that can accrue from using them. In essence, they are computer programs that let you manipulate characters and words, so that text-based information has to be entered into the computer only once, say in 'draft' form. Then, using the word processor, you can manipulate the words *ad infinitum* until you are happy with the result.

Text (characters, words and blocks of text of varying sizes) can be moved, deleted, copied and so on. Specific text can be searched for, and changed automatically. Many word processors will also do quick and accurate word counts, check your spelling, create indexes, do mathematical calculations, and maybe even let you include electronically generated pictures, such as graphs, in your text.

PipeDream

Interestingly, the Z88's built-in word processing package (called PipeDream) was designed mainly as a spreadsheet – a program which is used to manipulate numbers rather than characters. While developing the program, however, Cambridge Computers sensibly 'twisted' a simple feature of standard spreadsheet applications to enable the same program also to perform powerful word processing procedures.

Spreadsheet word processing

Although more will be said about the Z88's spreadsheet facilities in the next chapter, it is appropriate here to delve a little into the ideas behind spreadsheets in order to understand how PipeDream's word processing functions work.

A spreadsheet is simply an electronic table which is composed of 'cells' that are created by combining a set of rows (labelled with letters) and columns (numbers) – rather like graph paper. Data, which generally take the form of numbers, words and even formulae, can be entered into any cell – and the formulae can relate cells to other cells.

For example, to calculate current VAT rates a formula might be entered into one cell which would multiply the value of another cell by 0.15. Standard spreadsheet technology generally lets you alter the width of any column of cells, from zero to

Row	Column A	Column B
1	This is an example of using the spreadsheet as	
2	a word processor. Note that the words wrap at	
3	the right margin of the column in which we are	
4	working. The width of the 'page' is set to be the	
5	column width. The length of the page is	
6	determined by the number of rows you want	
7	printed on a piece of paper.	
8		
9	For most word processing purposes we take no	
10	notice of other spreadsheet columns.	

A word processor from a spreadsheet

upwards of 250 characters, in order to accommodate large numbers or descriptions (of the contents of rows or columns, say).

It is the dual ability to alter the width of a column of cells and to enter alphabetic characters as descriptors that lets us use the Z88's in-built spreadsheet program, PipeDream, as a word processor. For example, if we deal only with the first column of cells (column A) and set its width to 80 characters, say, then the standard spreadsheet provides us with the beginnings of a normal page outline. As with a sheet of lined paper, the page will be composed of a series of rows down it, in this case each row being 80 characters wide. The number of rows down the page, then, defines the page length.

Entering PipeDream

The PipeDream word processor is conjured up simply by taking the cursor to the PipeDream option on the Index page and pressing the ENTER key, or by pressing □P at any stage in your Z88 use.

In whichever way you enter the program, assuming there are no PipeDream documents currently suspended you will be presented with the standard spreadsheet screen: an electronic table composed of six columns (A – F) and a flashing cursor on row 1. You should note that the row of dots at the top of column A are closer together than on the other rows. This is PipeDream's way of letting you know that the text cursor (the small flashing square) is currently situated in column A. That the cursor is in row 1, in cell A1, is shown in the top left hand corner of the screen.

You can give your PipeDream document a name right at the beginning of your activity by issuing the command ◇ FC (Filename Change). When you save the file PipeDream will use this name – and will display it on the Index page if you suspend the activity.

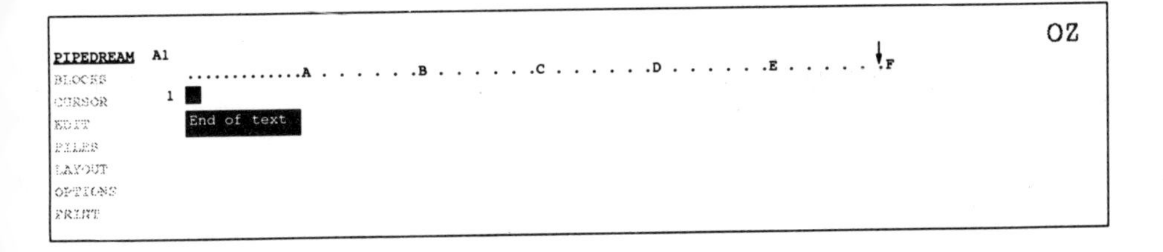

A clean PipeDream page (□P)

PipeDream cursors

The empty spreadsheet that confronts you when you first enter PipeDream contains two kinds of cursor: the column cursor, which is the row of closely spaced dots at the top of the active column, and the text cursor – the flashing square which shows where the next character will appear.

You can move the column cursor horizontally, left to right, by pressing the TAB key. Pressing the SHIFT and TAB keys together move it back again, column by column, from the right to the left hand sides of the screen. You can move immediately to column A from any column by pressing ◇ and TAB.

There are also other ways of moving the text cursor within a column, but there will be described in more detail later.

TAB

A word of warning at the beginning of your excursion into word processing on the Z88: the TAB key on the left hand side of the keyboard is not a 'tab' key in the conventional sense. It switches between columns for you. The effects of this can be quite dramatic; all of your text may suddenly disappear because you have switched from column A, say, to column B. To jump back a column, press the SHIFT and TAB keys together (◇ TAB always takes you back immediately to column A).

Experienced typists often use the TAB key to indent each new paragraph by a certain number of spaces. Because PipeDream operates in this specific way, you cannot use the key for this function.

Helpful information

When you begin a new PipeDream document the program highlights the words 'End of text' in the next available row. As these words imply, they indicate the end of the

PIPEDREAM	Mark Block	◇Z	Search	◇ BSE	Word Count	◇ BWC	MENU	OZ
BLOCKS	Clear Mark	◇Q	Replace	◇ BRP	New	◇ BNEW	ADVANCE	
CURSOR	Copy	◇BC	Next Match	◇ BNM	Recalculate	◇ A	← → ↓ ↑	
EDIT	Move	◇BM					SELECT	
FILES	Delete	◇BD					ENTER	
LAYOUT	Sort	◇BSO					ACTION	
OPTIONS	Replicate	◇BRE					ESC	
PRINT							RESUME	

A PipeDream menu

document as it is stored in memory. Since a new document will have no text stored in it, the end of text indicator appears under row 1. As you enter text and fill up rows, these highlighted words drop down the screen accordingly.

As with most of the Z88's in-built applications, the PipeDream screen can also display a helpful list of functions for you to scroll through with sequential presses of the 'Menu' key at the bottom left hand of the keyboard. Remember, pressing the ESC key from within a MENU page will return you to the PipeDream document where you left it.

The PipeDream Page

Although you could start to enter text as soon as your PipeDream screen appears, without making any changes to the underlying page dimensions and in much the same way as you would use a sophisticated electronic typewriter, most users will probably want to define the page that they are about to work on. This is particularly so when it comes to considering the page width (in this case the position of the right hand margin) and its length.

In addition, the continued presence of the row and column labels can be annoying to clean-paper purists, and this information takes up a valuable text display line. It is often easier to work on a page if these labels are removed first.

The width of a PipeDream cell (which Cambridge Computers calls a 'slot') can be changed with the command ◇ W. In many respects you can conceive of this as being the same as the width of a piece of paper in a typewriter. Simply enter the new width in terms of the maximum number of characters you want to see across a page. Since there are ten 10-pitch characters to an inch, and twelve 12-pitch characters, you can easily calculate the width of your page in terms of character positions.

When you press ◇ W, as well as enquiring about the column width PipeDream will also ask you to define the column whose width you want to change. At this stage do not worry about this request. Unless it is told otherwise the Z88 assumes that you intend to alter the column that contains the cursor which, when you are dealing with a 'clean' page, means column A.

When you change the column width you will see that the column labels move across the screen to accommodate the alteration. Indeed, if you request a width which is greater than 73 character positions the column labels disappear entirely.

Whatever width you request (and even if you do not change the width at all) you will see a downward facing arrow on the top line towards the right hand side of the display. This shows where the right hand margin of the page will occur (it is initially set to 72 characters). At this point the words will 'wrap' around to the next line when you are entering text, and they will do this irrespective of the column width.

For future reference, it is important to realise that different columns can have different column widths.

Margins and page lengths

To alter the right hand margin position simply press ◇H and supply the relevant information. Again, do not worry about specifying the column, as long as the cursor is currently in the relevant column.

It is also possible to set the right hand margin dynamically. Each time you press □← the right margin at the top will move one step to the left; □→ sends it scurrying to the right.

Having set the page width and right hand margin you can change the page length from the PipeDream Options page (◇O), along with many other features. For example, you can use the options in the first column of this menu to turn off the

```
PIPEDREAM                                                                          OZ
   Text/Numbers T   Insert on wrap R   Margins: Top 0      File No file
        Borders Y   Calc: Auto/Man A         Header 2      Page 1        Insert
        Justify N     Columns/Rows C         Footer 2      Free 137216
           Wrap Y   Decimal places 2         Bottom 8
 Page length 66    Minus/Brackets M            Left 0     Title
 Line spacing 1          Lead chs. £         Header
     Start page         Trail chs. %         Footer
```

The Options page

borders (enter ‘n’), set right justification and word wrap (these will be discussed later), and the line spacing. The page length option is the fifth one down in the first column.

The third column on this page of options lets you determine how the page should be laid out if you intend to print directly from the Z88. These options will be discussed in more detail later.

It is important to note that the settings you make in the Options menu page remain with a file, even when you save it. So, once set there will no need to alter them again for any specific document – unless you wish to do so, of course.

Mapping the words

No matter how powerful a word processor may be, and as we shall see the Z88's PipeDream is a very powerful word processor indeed, for many people its value will be limited by the amount of text that they can see on the screen at a time. When writing on a normal page of paper, for example, an author can see a whole page of material at a time, so that paragraph structure and even text layout is immediately apparent, as will be the flow of ideas between paragraphs and through the text. This all helps to create readable and meaningful material.

When working with a normal computer-based word processor, however, generally you can only see a part of the page at a time because of size limitations of the computer's screen. For most IBM-based programs, for example, this limitation is generally in the region of about 20 lines of text at a time, each with about 80 columns.

To overcome this restriction, and to let you 'see' all of the text, modern word processors allow you to 'scroll' through the material, often either a line at a time or a screenful at a time.

Naturally, as the number of lines of material you can see on the screen at a time decreases it becomes increasingly difficult to see whole blocks of text. This question becomes particularly important with the Z88's eight line display (only seven of which can contain user-entered information).

To overcome some of these problems, Cambridge Computers have given PipeDream users the option of displaying an interesting 'map' display which illustrates the whole page as it is created. Although you cannot distinguish individual characters on this map (each character is represented by a small dot), it is certainly possible to distinguish paragraphs and word groupings. In addition, the position on the page of the seven lines being displayed is indicated by a moving

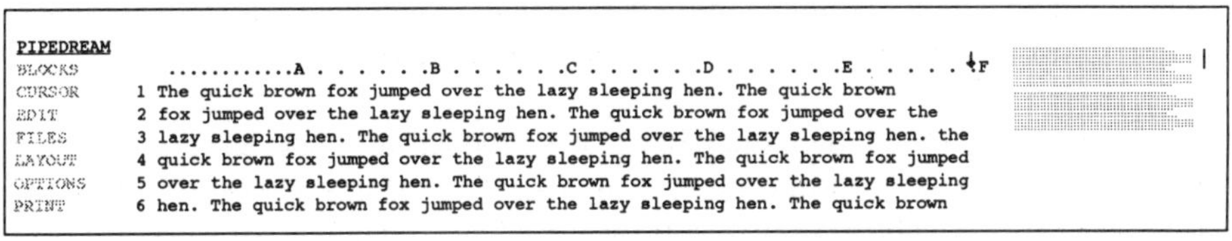

```
PIPEDREAM
BLOCKS     ............A . . . . . .B . . . . . .C . . . . . .D . . . . . .E . . . . . .F
CURSOR   1 The quick brown fox jumped over the lazy sleeping hen. The quick brown
EDIT     2 fox jumped over the lazy sleeping hen. The quick brown fox jumped over the
FILES    3 lazy sleeping hen. The quick brown fox jumped over the lazy sleeping hen. the
LAYOUT   4 quick brown fox jumped over the lazy sleeping hen. The quick brown fox jumped
OPTIONS  5 over the lazy sleeping hen. The quick brown fox jumped over the lazy sleeping
PRINT    6 hen. The quick brown fox jumped over the lazy sleeping hen. The quick brown
```

The page map

vertical bar. This makes it much easier to understand how the screen is acting as a 'window' on the underlying page structure.

To obtain the map display you simply enter the screen-based options menu (□S), take the cursor to the middle column and move three options down to 'Map'. Pressing the 'Y' indicates 'yes' (a map is required) and 'N' indicates 'no'.
The next option in the column lets you alter the map's size (width). Obviously it is sensible to set this in relation to the width of the PipeDream slots, although the screen's finite width means that the larger the map width the smaller can be the word processor's page width. Indeed, if you set the page and map widths to inappropriate values, the Z88 shows its displeasure by not displaying the map properly.

A sensible compromise is to set the right margin to column 75 and to leave the map width at 80 characters.

Having set the map width to an appropriate value, the display shows exactly how the page will appear when printed. For example, if you enter header and footer information (see below) this will show up on the map display, as will changes to the left and right margins, text justification, and so on.

Keyboard Click

As well as providing a range of word processing features, PipeDream also has the ability to provide click-type sounds every time you press a key.

The advantages of the silent, rubber-based, keyboard should be obvious in many different situations such as a lecture theatre, board room or even travelling by train. However, many experienced typists make considerable use of the sound from keys hitting the platen of a normal typewriter. This is called 'auditory feedback' and helps skilled users to maintain a rhythm, detect when they've pressed a wrong key, and so on.

You can make the Z88 give you a key-click sound by changing the relevant option on the screen display menu (□S). This is the second option in column one. It should not be confused with the 'sound' option that appears in column two, which concerns the Z88's use of a bleeper to let you know when you've made a mistake.

If you 'turn off' the sound, then the Z88 will not produce key clicks either. Changing these options can be appropriate if you wish to perform almost silent word processing, say in a lecture theatre or anywhere where you might not wish others to know that you are computing in private.

Inserting text

Another of the control panel options (□S) concerns whether you want text to be *inserted* into the document, or merely to overwrite characters as you enter new information.

To understand the difference, imagine a standard typewriter. Say that you have entered a line of text only to find that you have missed out a word. If you take the type head back to the position of the missing word in the line and begin entering it you will overwrite the existing text. Clearly, this is not much use. Word processors, on the other hand, can *insert* the new text so that all material to the right of each inserted character shifts rightwards by one character at a time.

Sometimes, however, it is useful to overwrite text rather than insert it – perhaps you want to insert a word into a gap, or complete a screen-based form.

This option, therefore, allows you to decide in which mode you wish to conduct your text entry. The default situation is for PipeDream to operate within insert mode, so if this is how you want to behave you do not need to worry about changing the option. If you change it to overtype, however, the Z88 will remain in that mode until it is reset.

Repelling Borders

Finally, it is useful to know that you can add an extra row of text to the PipeDream screen. For people who like to compose their documents 'at the keyboard', this additional row of displayed information can be very useful.

Simply enter the document options (◇ O) and change the 'border' choice to 'n'. Now the screen will display the maximum amount of text, since the cell labels at the top and the right hand margin indicator will have disappeared.

Text Entry

Perhaps the easiest of all PipeDream's operations involves entering text into your document. Whether you are composing your masterpiece 'at the keyboard' or are typing material into the document from a previously written hand copy, once you have organised your document's page dimensions all you have to do is type in the words as they appear. When the cursor reaches the right hand margin it will automatically move to the beginning of the next line – there is no need to press the ENTER key.

Indeed, with this kind of word processor you only need to press the ENTER key when you want to force the cursor to return to the first column on the next line, probably at the end of a paragraph. For reasons that will become apparent later, it is probably best to leave a clear row between paragraphs – so press the ENTER key a second time between paragraphs.

Word wrap

While entering text, as the cursor moves to the beginning of the next line you will notice that it probably takes the last whole word with it. This is known as word wrap. It means that you do not end up with a document that has split words at the right hand margin.

Although the default position is to wrap words, you can turn this facility off in the document options menu (◇ O). If you change the 'wrap' option in the first column to 'n' you will find that the text you enter takes no notice of the right hand margin and continues forever onwards along the same row.

Justification

Also in the document options (◇ O) you will notice that the third option in the first column asks whether you want the text to be 'justified'. This refers to process by which spaces are added between words in order to ensure that all the text aligns perfectly down its right hand, as well as its left hand, edge. This is a useful facility for 'blocking' pieces of text, say when you want to highlight paragraphs or indicate quotations. (In both cases you would probably want to reduce the right hand margin by using ◇ H or □← and □→.)

Page breaks

As you enter increasing amounts of text you will begin to fill up the document's page, as opposed to just the screen. The length of the page (in terms of the number of rows), remember, is set by the page length option in the first column of document options (◇ O). Eventually you will see a row of carat signs across the screen, and if the page map is operational the dots representing the characters will disappear.

This row of caret signs indicates the end of the document page and can be extremely useful in helping you to lay out pages properly. For example, if you are typing a letter it can alert you to the fact that the salutations will end up hanging at the top of the last page.

You will also notice that if you move the cursor up a row or two to rest at the bottom of the previous page, the page map display reappears – and it disappears again when you return across the page boundary. This merely emphasises that the display map represents the page as it will appear in printed form. It is not a scrollable window as is the case with the Z88's screen itself.

Finally, you might notice that the page shown on the page map contains fewer lines of text than you had set in the document's options menu. This is because of the lines reserved for header and footer margins at the top and bottom of each page. We shall consider this feature in more detail later.

Forced page breaks

You can force a new page by issuing the command ◇ EIP (Edit Insert Page) at the appropriate point in the document. PipeDream will ask you whether you want the page to break immediately, or only if fewer than a certain number of lines are left before it would break naturally. For example, say your natural page length is 66 lines, and you have already used 60 of them. If you request a conditional page break if only three lines are left, then PipeDream will not make the break for you. If you add another three or four lines of text to the page, however, then the page break will appear.

If it decides not to make the page break, on the other hand, PipeDream adds a special, non-printing, marker into column A to remind you that the conditional page break is operational. This marker is the tilde sign (~) followed by the number of lines on which the page break is conditional.

This conditional page breaking feature is very useful for stopping 'hanging headings' occurring in your document. There is little worse, for example, than seeing a heading left hanging at the bottom of a page while its associated text starts at the top of the next page. By inserting a ◇ EIP command immediately before the heading, with the condition that the page breaks if only six text lines are left, say, you can rest assured that the heading will never hang.

Moving Around

Before we start entering text, it is sensible to understand how you can move quickly through material, both within the memory and onscreen. This is all done by judicious combinations of the ◇, SHIFT, and four cursor arrow keys.

You move the cursor to the right and left by one character at a time, and up and down by a row at a time, by just pressing the appropriate arrow key in the cluster of four at the bottom right hand corner of the keyboard. If you have to move through large portions of text, however, this can be time consuming.

Things can be speeded up by using the cursor keys in combination with either the SHIFT or the ◇ keys.

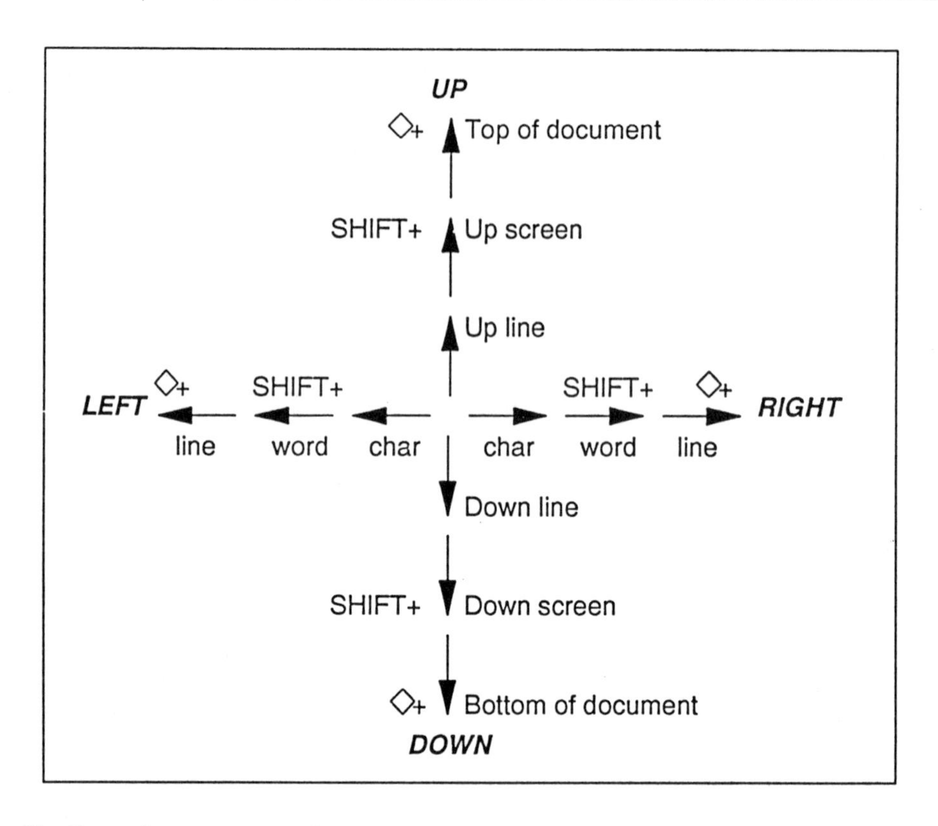

PipeDream's cursor control

The arrow keys in combination with the SHIFT key move the cursor in small, manageable, steps through your document. For example, if you press the SHIFT and right arrow keys together, then the cursor moves to the right by a word at a time, stopping each time at the first letter of the next word. (A word is generally defined by PipeDream as being a cluster of characters separated on each side by a space.) The SHIFT and left arrow keys together make the cursor travel leftwards a word at a time.

The SHIFT and ↑ keys move the cursor up the text one screenful at a time. One anomaly of the fact that the screen represents a 'window' on your document, however, is that when you press SHIFT and ↑ together the text actually moves downwards while the cursor remains stationary. This happens because the cursor is moving up the text in memory. Similarly, SHIFT and the ↓ key moves down through the text by a screenful at a time (so the text scrolls upwards).

The ◇ key moves the cursor in similar directions, but in much larger steps. When the ◇ and → or ← are used together the cursor speeds to either the left or the right end of the current line. If you press the ◇ key together with either the up or ↓ keys you will immediately reach the top or bottom ends of the file in memory.

Finally, PipeDream also provides a useful function for marking a place in the text and returning to it later. If you enter the characters ◇ CSP (Cursor Save Position) at the place where you wish to return, issuing the command ◇ CRP (Cursor Return to Position) from anywhere within the text will return the cursor to the beginning of the 'marked' row.

Editing the Text

Deletion

The simplest level of text editing occurs as you are entering the material at the keyboard. You can easily change simple mistakes, either immediately by pressing the DEL key at the top right hand side of the keyboard or by moving the cursor to the appropriate part of the line and either inserting characters or deleting them.

You should notice that the DEL key only operates on the character that is immediately to the left of the cursor. So, to remove (delete) the character at the end of the line, say, you should move the cursor to one character further on before pressing the DEL key. The easiest way of doing this, of course, is to press ◇ → to get to the end of the line quickly, move back a character by pressing ← once (because the last character will actually be a space), and then DELeting the last alphanumeric character on the line.

To delete the character *under* the cursor you should press ◇ G (although pressing SHIFT and DEL together also performs the same operation).

Once we pass beyond simply changing the characters on the line being typed, however, we enter a slightly more complicated phase of PipeDream editing. This is because of the nature of PipeDream itself: remember that it is basically a spreadsheet, and with a spreadsheet we deal with a sheet of cells rather than the conventional page composed of lines and columns.

◇ Y	Line
◇ D	Rest of line
◇ T	Word
◇ G	Character under cursor

Deletion commands

Imagine a series of slots, each one row deep and 80 columns wide, say. This is how PipeDream conceptualises its own arrangement as a word processor. Entering characters into a particular slot is easy enough, as is editing them while the cursor is still in the slot. PipeDream is even intelligent enough to realise that when you enter more characters than the slot can accommodate the additional text needs to 'flow' over into the next one down. This is the word wrap facility we considered earlier.

Unfortunately, the program is not intelligent enough to realise that when *deleting* characters, backwards along a slot as it were, when the cursor gets to the left hand edge it should continue upwards from the right hand end of the slot above. This simple idea seems to be beyond its capacities for logical 'thinking'. So, although we can have word wrap when entering text, we cannot perform the equivalent backwards process when deleting characters.

To accomplish this simple act we have to move the cursor up the screen by one slot and then to the right hand end of the slot (by pressing ◇ →). Then we can continue with the deletion process.

As well as simply deleting text character by character, PipeDream also incorporates faster routines that let you delete more than one character at a time.

You can delete whole words at a stroke by pressing ◇ T. The action actually deletes all characters up to and including the next space. So, to be totally effective the cursor should be on the first character of the word before deleting it. However, you can also use this facility to remove end parts of words that need to be changed. For example, if you place the cursor on the 'L' of CATALOGUE and press ◇ T, you will be left with just the letters CATA. It is now a simple job to add the letters COMBE to change the word completely.

Wherever the cursor is on the line, the whole line can be deleted by pressing ◇ Y. You should use this option with caution, though, since PipeDream does not have a facility for reinstating deleted blocks of text. And if you leave your finger on the 'Y' for too long you may find that more than one line disappears.

Finally, the command ◇ D is very useful for deleting the rest of the text on the line *after* the cursor.

Insertion

Inserting characters into the text is generally simply a matter of taking the cursor to the correct place and typing in the text that you want to appear. This assumes, of course, that the insert/overtype option is set to 'insert' in the screen-based options (□S) – although you can temporarily set the insert/overtype toggle in the document by pressing ◇ V.

This method of inserting characters can have disadvantages, however, in situations when you do not want the cursor to move along with the text being inserted. Sometimes you may want the cursor to stay where it is, but to move the the text to the right of it by a specific number of spaces. On this special occasion you can insert spaces into the text simply by pressing ◇ U. You could think of this as the insertion equivalent of ◇ G for deleting the character under the cursor.

As far as inserting a row (slot) is concerned, pressing ◇ N does this for you. The cursor remains where it was on the original line while the text below moves down by a row. The interesting aspect of this command is that you can issue the ◇ N command from anywhere within a line; a whole line opens up to drop the text down. Since the cursor remains in the same place on the now empty line, this can be a very useful feature for adding rows to a document.

Splitting, joining and cleaning up the lines

Although ◇ N works very well when you want to insert a line of text into a document, often you will want to split a line – perhaps to create a new paragraph from the middle of an existing piece of text. Because it inserts a *whole* line, ◇ N is no use for this purpose.

At this point you need to invoke another of PipeDream's commands: ◇ ESL (Edit Split Line). With this instruction the line splits *at the cursor position*.

The equivalent instruction for joining two lines together is ◇ EJL. In this case the line below the one containing the cursor moves up and joins up with the cursor's line.

Obviously, when you join lines together like this there may be too much text on the newly combined line to show on the screen at once, in which case it will extend beyond the right hand margin. To reset all the text in the new paragraph so that it lies within the margin positions you will need to issue an additional command: ◇ R (Reformat).

A word of caution though: slap-dash use of ◇ R can lead to unfortunate side effects, for two reasons.

Firstly, the reformatting occurs for the remainder of the paragraph *from* the line that includes the cursor – not the whole paragraph. So you may end up with a part of the paragraph that has a different line length from the other.

More importantly is the question of where PipeDream decides that a paragraph (and thus the reformatting) ends. It takes this to be the next *blank* line in the text. So it is imperative that you get into the habit of leaving at least one blank line between paragraphs. If you do not, then you will inevitably end up with the *whole* of your text reformatted – which may not be what you wanted!

This problem can be alleviated with a little foresight by defining a specific paragraph as being 'left aligned' (◇ LAL). As will be described later, the effects of this are to ensure that each row is treated as a separate 'paragraph' which cannot be reformatted without reversing the left alignment.

Block Operations

So far we have dealt with relatively simple pieces of text, characters, lines of text, and so on, and we have looked at how to enter and edit them within PipeDream. But, like many word processors, PipeDream also lets you carry out all these operations, and more, on pre-defined blocks of text. So, you could move paragraphs around your document, for example, delete sentences quickly, or copy tables to another part of the document. With these block operations you can do all manner of interesting things.

PipeDream places just one slight restriction on its block operations, though. Whereas most modern word processors let you define a block of text with a resolution down to a single character – so that you could 'block' a part of a word, for example – with its slot-like mentality PipeDream does not allow such refinements. Only whole lines of text (slots) can be blocked, so you might need to do some line splitting (◇ ESL) in order to create the right blocking environment.

For example, say in the paragraph above you wanted to move the first sentence to the end of the second. You would first need to split the line which contains the second sentence at the word 'Whereas'. Then you could treat the first sentence as a unique set of text lines and manipulate it at will.

Defining the block

A block of lines is defined simply by placing the cursor on the first line of the block and issuing the command ◇ Z. Then you move to the last line of the block (using all the cursor movement facilities available) and issue ◇ Z again. PipeDream highlights the block that you have defined in this way.

If you find that you have defined the wrong block, simply issue the command ◇ Q (Quit) and the highlighting disappears.

Copy, move and delete

Once a block has been defined in this way you are ready to manipulate it in a variety of ways.

```
PIPEDREAM
BLOCKS       ...........A . . . . . .B . . . . . .C . . . . . .D . . . . . .E . . . . . . .F
CURSOR     1 This is an example of how a block of text is highlighted. You may first
EDIT       2 have to split the lines using <>ESL.
FILES      3 Then take the cursor to the first line in the block to be highlighted
LAYOUT     4 and press <>Z; next take it to the last line in the block and press <>Z
OPTIONS    5 again.
PRINT      6 The whole block will appear onscren in inverse video.
```

Highlighting a block of text

To *delete* the block simply issue the command ◇BD (Block Delete). Be careful, though – there is no way of retrieving a deleted block of text. Of course, the block is only deleted from the current document – not from any copy that has been filed away.

Once a block of text has been defined it can be *copied* to another part of the document by taking the cursor to the place it is to go to and issuing the command ◇BC (Block Copy). Similarly, the block can be *moved* to another part of the document by issuing the command ◇BM (Block Move). The difference between the two is that the first creates a second copy of the text. Moving, on the other hand, deletes the block from the first position after moving it to the second.

Naturally, when you copy or move blocks of text like this you will probably have to reformat the new paragraph to align the text within the relevant margins (◇R).

Saving and reading blocks

As well as moving them about within your document, you can also save previously defined blocks of text to a file of their own. Having defined a block, simply go through the normal procedure of saving a text file (◇FS) and supply a new file name (this is important, otherwise you may overwrite the original file in memory). Before pressing the ENTER key, however, take the cursor down three lines to the option that asks whether you wish to 'save (the) marked block'. Reply Y(es) to this option and press the ENTER key. Your block will now be saved as a separate file – although it is also still in the original file.

The reverse of this option, reading a file into the current document, is just as easy. Put the cursor where you want the new file to be entered in the document (this can be anywhere in the document – not just at the end). Then enter the usual command to load a file (◇FL), supply the name of the file to be loaded and answer Y(es) to the option 'Insert at slot' (if you do not change this option in the menu the new file will overwrite the that you are currently working on). When you press the ENTER key the file will be inserted at the correct place.

You can use these two very useful features to create new documents from amalgamations of old ones. Simply create small files of appropriate blocks of text and build up a new document by loading the relevant file each time.

Stylistic Enhancements

If you want to produce professional looking documents, these days you will have to revert to some of the tricks of the secretarial trade and enhance parts of the document, using techniques like bolding, underlining and so on. In addition you ought to ensure that the textual layout is suitable, with blocked text, centred headings, and the rest.

PipeDream provides facilities for all these kinds of enhancements – and more.

Blocking the text

Sometimes you will want to make a piece of text, such as an important paragraph or perhaps a quotation, stand out from the rest. The trick of the trade of doing this is to block the text, in which the left and right margins are reduced by a certain amount – say 10 column spaces, and ensure that the text is right justified. This has the effect of taking the reader's eye directly to that piece of text since it is so obviously different from the rest.

Most word processors let you do this by temporarily altering the left and right margin positions and by setting the paragraph layout to be justified. Unfortunately, PipeDream does not have the ability to create this kind of temporary indent – the page layout options available for setting the left and right margins and so on alter the whole document, not just the paragraph you want to change. So you will have to use some of the program's other facilities to achieve your aim.

Perhaps the easiest way of producing a blocked text effect is to use PipeDream's columnar structure and vary both the width and the right margins of the relevant columns.

Let us say that you want to block a piece of text by reducing its left and right margins by 10 character positions, within a document whose normal right margin is set at 60 characters. You can create this blocking effect by putting PipeDream's column B 'inside' column A:

Ensure that the right margin for column A is 60 characters (◇ H), but that its width is set to 10 characters only (◇ W). Now TAB the cursor to column B and make *it* 40 characters wide (60-10-10); you will see that the right margin indicator for column B (the downwards facing arrow on the top line) jumps 10 spaces leftwards from where column A's right margin resides.

```
PIPEDREAM
BLOCKS        .........A . . . . . .B . . . . . .C . . . . . .D . . . . ! .E . . . . . .F
CURSOR      1 To  indent  a  block of text in PipeDream simply enter your
EDIT        2 text using the standard right margin for column A - say 60.
FILES       3           When  you want to indent, TAB to column
LAYOUT      4           B and set the  right  margin  (<>H)  to
OPTIONS     5           column A's margin minus twice the width
PRINT       6           of  column  A  -  in  this  case,   40.
```

Indenting a block of text

Now return to column A (by pressing SHIFT and TAB) and enter your text; it will wrap as normal at column 60. When you want to enter the blocked text, however, TAB to column B and type it into PipeDream. This will wrap at column 50. Having entered the blocked text, return to column A and continue as normal.

To give the text its fully blocked effect, though, it is always a good idea to right justify the piece. You can do this either before you enter it or afterwards. Beforehand, simply enter the document's options page (◇ O) and change the 'justified' option to Y(es). If you decide to block it after entering the text you will have to reformat the paragraph (◇ R) after having changed the justifying option.

Right justifying the text in this way, of course, is only 'temporary'. If you reformat the block again with the justifying option turned off, the right justified effect will disappear. You can stop this occurring by using the right align function (◇ LAR) as described below.

Centring

Centring text, perhaps for a heading, is an easier operation than blocking it. Either a single line on which the cursor is positioned, or whole pieces of text that have previously been blocked using ◇ Z, can be centred simply by issuing the command ◇ LAC (Layout Align Centre).

If you centre a line at a time, it will only appear centred on the display when the cursor moves off it.

Right align

When writing a letter, say, it is generally accepted that one's address should be written at the top right hand corner of the first page, aligned so that the text is justified on the right hand margin only. The left hand margin is left to be ragged.

As with centring, this effect can easily be obtained by issuing the command ◇ LAR (Layout Align Right), either on a row-by-row basis or for a marked block of text.

Left align

When you normally enter text into PipeDream you begin typing from the left hand edge of the screen. So the text is naturally left aligned. However, you can insist that a line or a block of text should *always* be left aligned (that is, it will never by changed by a centre or a right align command) by issuing the command ◇ LAL (Layout Align Left).

Left, centre and right

You can immediately see the effect of each of the three above alignment commands, particularly if you are using your Z88's map facility. The 'left, centre, right' command, however, only makes its effects known when you print the document. Nevertheless, it is a very clever and interesting command to use.

Quite simply ◇ LLCR (Layout on the Left, Centre and Right) lets you divide a line of text into three parts and print them left, centre and right aligned. This can be very useful for different kinds of headings.

The program's cleverness lies in the way in which you define which text should be printed in each of the three positions: it is up to you. All you have to do is think of a unique character (like $ or } perhaps) and use it to divide the text. PipeDream assumes that the first character in a line that's to be printed 'LLCR' is the text separator.

For example, take the three words 'left', 'middle' and 'right'. If you enter them into your PipeDream document as:

```
%left%middle%right%
```

and issue the command ◇ LLCR while the cursor is on this line, they will be printed in their respective positions.

When using this command you must ensure that you have *four* occurrences of your unique character. For example,

```
%left%%right%
```

will miss out the centre.

Bolding, underlining, and so on

As long as you have access to a printer that can print textual enhancements like underlining or bolding you can indicate in your Z88 document which pieces of printer output should be highlighted like this. Much more about this aspect of the printed output will be discussed in Chapter 8. At this stage it is useful to know that you can incorporate up to eight print enhancements in your document. The beginning and end of each is indicated by a different command:

1	Underline	◇ PU
2	Bold	◇ PB
3	Extended character sequence	◇ PX
4	Italic	◇ PI
5	Subscript	◇ PL
6	Superscript	◇ PR
7	Alternative font	◇ PA
8	User defined enhancement	◇ PE

So to underline a word, for example, simply place the cursor on the first character and enter the command ◇ PU. Then put the cursor on the last character of the word and enter ◇ PU again. Each time you enter the command a highlighted number is displayed that corresponds to the enhancement type (1 for underlining, for example).

Having highlighted something in this way, as soon as you move the cursor off the row the actual enhancement appears on the display (at least for enhancements 1 to 4). So underlined characters are shown as being underlined and bolded characters are displayed in a bold typeface. Italicised characters are indicated by a small font size, while extended characters appear feint.

```
PIPEDREAM
BLOCKS          .........A . . . . . .B . . . . . .C . . . . . .D . . . . . .E . . . . . . .F
CURSOR        1 To enter highlights into your PipeDream document simply begin and end
EDIT          2 the words to be highlighted with the appropriate highlight commands.
FILES         3 For example <>PU underlines and the command <>PI italicises.
LAYOUT        4 While the command <>PB bolds.
OPTIONS       5 Note the onscreen appearance ■only■ changes when the cursor leaves the ■
PRINT         6 line.
```

Highlights in PipeDream text

The use of the extended character sequence, alternative font and user defined enhancements will be discussed in Chapter 8.

As well as entering highlights by issuing the command ◇ P plus a letter, you can also enter them directly as a number. When you press ◇ PHI (Print HIghlight) the Z88 asks which highlight number you wish to use. Your answer will be entered into the text in just as if you had issued the ◇ P command.

When they are embodied in the text you can think of the highlight commands as just being additional characters. So they can be deleted, moved and copied in the same way as you can any other text-based characters.

Finally, each of these enhancements only operate within a single line of text; a normal carriage return turns them off – unless you have specifically turned off this facility within the Printer Editor, as we shall see in Chapter 8. This is a very useful 'safety' feature: there are few things more irritating than finding that the whole of a chapter is printed out underlined because you have forgotten to turn off that particular enhancement!

Specified blocks of text can also be enhanced in one operation using the command ◇ PHB (Print Highlight Block). Similarly, specific highlight numbers can be *removed* from specified blocks by issuing the command ◇ PHR (Print Highlight Remove).

Headers, Footers and Page Layout

Glance at any page of text in a book and you will probably also see various kinds of information printed at the top and/or the bottom of each page, outside of the standard text area. This will probably include page numbers, and might also contain a description of what is on the page, chapter identification, and so on.

Information that is printed at the top of a page is called a 'header'; that at the bottom of the page is a 'footer'. Within PipeDream you can add either or both to your documents. You simply enter the header or footer text into the list of options associated with the document (◇ O). In this case the relevant options appear at the bottom of the third column. Whatever text you enter here will be printed on each page.

Often, of course, your page will demand that certain kinds of information should appear in specific positions within the header or footer – say in the centre of the page, or aligned with the right hand margin. To accommodate such requirements PipeDream lets you enter text in up to three separate fields within the header or footer line: left, centre and right.

```
PIPEDREAM                                                                                   OZ
BLOCKS     Text/Numbers T   Insert on wrap R   Margins: Top 0        File No file
CURSOR          Borders Y   Calc: Auto/Man A         Header 2        Page 1        Insert
EDIT            Justify N     Columns/Rows C         Footer 2        Free 137216
FILES              Wrap Y   Decimal places 2         Bottom 8
LAYOUT    Page length 66    Minus/Brackets M           Left 0      Title
OPTIONS   Line spacing 1         Lead chs. £         Header /Chapter 1/Page @P@//
PRINT       Start page          Trail chs. %         Footer //Date @D@/DRAFT/
```

Headers and footers

As with the ◇ LLCR command, the text which is to appear in each area should be bounded by an arbitrary character that does not appear within the text itself. So, the following header information will ensure that the three words 'test' will be printed at the top of each page at the left hand edge, in the centre, and at the right hand edge:

`/test/test/test/`

To print the same word, but just in the centre of the header or footer, you would enter:

`//test//`

And the following would print it right aligned only:

`///test/`

Page numbers

PipeDream prints page numbers sequentially wherever you include the characters `@P@` in the header or footer text. For example, if you put `//Page @P@//` into the footer field the program will print 'Page 1' at the bottom of the first page, centred; 'Page 2' at the bottom of the second page, and so on.

You can even change the page number from which you wish to start printing, again within the options menu (◇ O). This option appears at the bottom of the first column of options; the number you enter here will be the first page number that PipeDream prints when it recognises the `@P@` counter.

Dates and other information

As well as updating page numbers PipeDream can also cope with other variable information in its documents, again using the @letter@ convention.

`@D@` Inserts the current day and date – taken from the clock (□T)

`@T@` Inserts the document title – defined in the options page (◇ O)

`Oref@` the value that appears in the cell 'ref'. For example, `@B1@` inserts into the document the value in cell B1. We shall use this facility more in later chapters.

These functions could be very useful when writing a letter on one day to be printed and sent on some other day, say. In this case, instead of entering the date into the letter, simply enter `@D@` at the appropriate point. PipeDream will insert the correct date when it is time to print the letter.

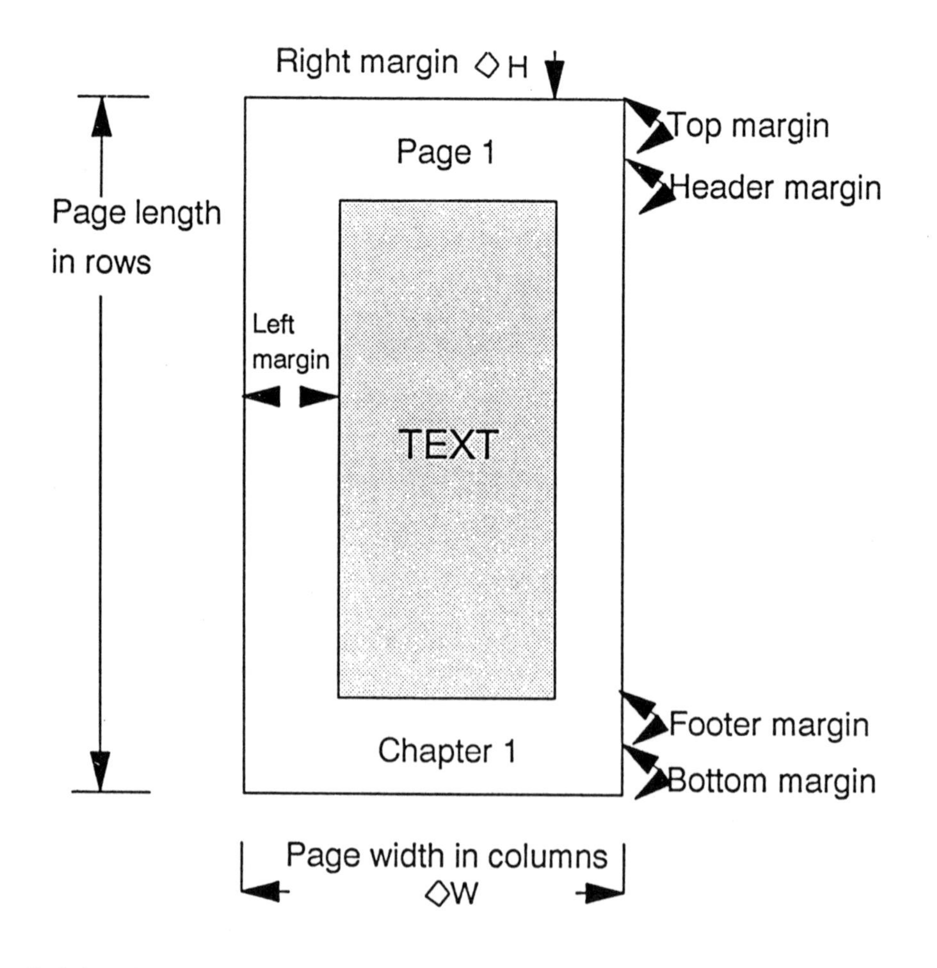

Defining the margins

Margins

Finally, it is important to consider where on the page all this information is to be printed. The layout will be determined by the margin positions you choose and the amount of space that you decide to leave between the text and its associated headers and footers.

Again, of course, the options menu (◇ O) provides a comprehensive group of margin settings. Within a particular page length, the top margin represents the number of lines to be left between the top of the page and the header information; the bottom margin creates the same effect for the footer. The header and footer margins, on the other hand, indicate the number of rows left blank between the header and footer text and the main text. Judicious use of these four settings, with the left margin setting, enables you to lay out your text on the page to suit all manner of requirements.

Columns

When discussing layout, we should remember that not all page layouts demand that the text is printed across the page in just one column. Newspapers and magazines, for example, have multiple columns across the page. Again, PipeDream can help you achieve this effect very easily.

At this point we have to use more of the spreadsheet features than we have encountered so far, although this should not come as much of a surprise. After all, a spreadsheet makes considerable use of columns – albeit for manipulating columns of figures. So there is no reason why this feature should not be used to create columns of text.

Working with newspaper-style columns of text is as easy as working with single columns. All you need to do is to divide the page into as many columns you wish, and to set the right hand margin of each column separately in order to ensure that a

```
PIPEDREAM                                   ↓
BLOCKS     ..................................A . . . . . . . . . . . . . . . . B . . . . . . C . .
CURSOR     1 Entering   information  in  a     order  to  create  a 'gutter'
EDIT       2 columnar format is very easy.     effect between columns.  Then
FILES      3 Simply  set the width of each     simply  enter  your  text  as
LAYOUT     4 column (<>W)  as  appropriate     normal, switching to the next
OPTIONS    5 and  the right margin (<>H) a     column at the page break.
PRINT      6 few   characters   shorter in
```

Columns in PipeDream

'gutter' of space remains between the right hand edge of one column and the left hand edge of the next.

To work in columns in this way, we first need to set the document's 'insert on wrap' option to 'columns' (the default setting is for rows). This option can be found at the top of the second column of options in the ◇ O menu. Change the 'R' to 'C'.

It is now time to decide on the page and column layout. Say you want a two-column page, with a total width of 70 characters. So each column needs to be 35 characters wide, although the right hand margin of each may only be 30 characters, for example. This would provide a 5-character gutter between the two columns.

First, then, we must set the column widths. With the cursor in column A, alter the width and right margin using the ◇ W (=35) and ◇ H (=30) commands. Now press the TAB key to take the cursor to column B, and do the same again.

Remember that you can swap between columns by pressing the TAB key to go from column A to B, and the SHIFT and TAB keys together to go back from B to A. Also, you could have altered column B's width and margin while the cursor was still in column A by simply specifying the column.

Now you can progress with your text entry. With the cursor in column A, simply enter text in the normal way; it will happily wrap at the right hand margin and continue downwards across the relevant page break. When you see the page break switch to the next column (TAB), go to the top of it (◇ ↑), and continue entering text.

If you want to delete a row of text within a column, you should not use the normal ◇Y command. That will delete the row across all columns. Use the command ◇ EDRC (Edit Delete Row in Column) instead.

Similarly, to expand the column by inserting another row, do not use ◇ N. Use ◇ EIRC instead.

Searching for text

PipeDream contains fairly sophisticated search and replace features which enable you to seek out any combination of characters and, if necessary, change them for others.

Following the command ◇ BSE (Block SEarch) PipeDream displays a comprehensive menu of options, although many are unnecessary at this point. Most important are the first, which defines the string of characters you want to find, the third (which searches by the letter case) and the fourth (search within a marked block).

```
PIPEDREAM
BLOCKS          ....  String to search for                  ■    B . . . . . C . .
CURSOR        1 Ente  Search only range of columns          No
EDIT          2 colu  Equate upper and lower case           Yes
FILES         3 Simp  Search only marked block              No
LAYOUT        4 colu  Search from current file              No
OPTIONS       5 and   Search all files in list              No
PRINT         6 few
```

Search options

PipeDream will search for, and find, any legitimate string of characters in your document. For example, you could find all occurrences of the word 'PipeDream' or every time the phrase 'PipeDream is excellent' is mentioned in the document.

Having entered the string you wish to search for, pressing the Enter key begins the search and takes the cursor to the first occurrence of the string in your document. The next occurrence of the string can be found by issuing the command ◇BNM (Block Next Match), and so on. When PipeDream cannot find any more matches of the string the Z88 gives a polite bleep and displays the number of times your string was found in the document.

Wildcards

You do not have to be too precise when you define your character string. It is possible, for example, to use 'wildcard characters' to find all words that begin with 'b', say, or to seek out all three-lettered words in the document, and so on.

There are two wildcard conventions:

^# finds any combination of characters (including none); and
^? matches any single character.

So, if you enter the five characters 'hat^#' into your search string, PipeDream will find the words 'hat', 'hats' or 'hatter' in your document. On the other hand, 'hat^?' will only find 'hats' and the 'hatt' part of 'hatter'.

Case

Sometimes it is important to take into account the case of the characters for which you are searching. For example, the name 'PipeDream' contains two upper case letters in very specific positions in the name. If you alter the third option in the search menu, however, the program will not find occurrences of the word 'pipedream', 'Pipedream' or 'pipeDream'. If you want to make sure a that the letter cases are ignored, keep the third option as Y(es).

Blocks

Finally, you can search for your string in the whole document (by default) or only within a block that you have previously defined using the ◇ Z command. You must change the fourth option in the search menu to Y(es) to use this facility.

Exchanging Characters

As well as simply finding text in your document, PipeDream also lets you replace all or some of the discovered text with other material. To use this function you should issue the ◇BRP (Block RePlace) command instead of ◇ BSE. It operates in a very similar way to ◇ BSE, except that a couple of additional options are supplied.

Obviously, the first addition is to supply the characters which will replace the text when it is found. So, say you want to change all (or some) occurrences of the word 'cat' with 'dog' you should enter 'cat' in the 'string to search for' option and 'dog' in the 'replace with' option.

As with the searching facility, you can include wildcards in the search string. In this case, though, as well as the ^# and ^? wild cards PipeDream lets you search for and replace several special characters within your document:

Highlight characters	`^1 .. ^8`
^	`^^`
Space	`^S`
One or more spaces	`(space)`
Beginning of a line	`^B`

All the facilities for searching on a case-wide basis, and within a specified block, are provided with ◇ BRP, and they work in the same way as they do with ◇ BSE.

The other additional option concerns the request for confirmation. If you leave this option as 'yes' (the default condition), each time it finds the specified string PipeDream will ask whether you want to replace it with the new string. You should press 'y' to make the change, or 'n' to move to the next match without changing the string.

Changing the option to 'no', on the other hand, will cause PipeDream to change each occurrence of the string *automatically*, without asking first. This may be a much faster way of proceeding through a document – especially if the string to be changed is a unique one – but it can be 'dangerous'. For example, automatically changing the word 'and' to 'but' will cause 'hand' to end up as 'hbut'.

Sorting alphabetically

Sometimes you will want to sort rows of text within a document – for example, you might have a list of topics that you want sorted into an index. PipeDream contains a very simple, though quite sophisticated, sorting system.

The sort function, which is initiated with the ◇ BSO (Block SOrt) command, only operates on a block of text that has been marked using ◇ Z. You should define the column you wish to have sorted (which will be column A for most word processing operations) and then decide whether you want the rows of text to be sorted in increasing or decreasing order.

When they are sorted in increasing order, rows that begin with a number will appear above those starting with an alphabetic character. Lower case letters appear above upper case ones, though the program is intelligent enough not to block all the lower case rows first and then the upper case ones. The sorting is done in a proper alphanumeric order. Decreasing order, of course, is the reverse of this.

It is not necessary to worry about the third option in the sorting menu ('Don't update references'). We might use this when sorting cells in a spreadsheet.

Printing out

It is very easy to print your document. Simply issue the command ◇ PO (Print Out) while the document is onscreen and active. At this point the only option in the print menu that you need to consider is the last one: wait between pages. Changing this to Y(es) will mean that the Z88 suspends printing at the end of each page, to let you insert a new page into your printer if necessary.

If you do change this option, PipeDream tells you the page that it is about to print and waits for you to tell it to continue. If you press 'M' then it misses this page and goes on to the next one. Pressing C will turn off the page waiting option so that pages will be printed continuously. Any other key (other than ESC) will tell PipeDream to print that page, and then wait again for the next instruction. ESC abandons the print run altogether.

Counting words

A simple word counting program is included within PipeDream. Simply issue the command ◇ BWC (Block Word Count) and the number of words in your document (defined, as always, as strings of characters having a space at each end) will be displayed in the top line of the screen.

If you have highlighted a specific block of text (using ◇ Z) then the word count will show the number of words present in the block only.

Case conversion

It is possible to change the case of single characters easily using the command ◇ S (Swap case). This changes the case of the letter currently under the cursor and then advances the cursor one character to the right. So, you can change the case of whole words, or even lines, simply by keeping your finger on the ◇ key and pressing 'S' each time.

Files

Saving files

Having created your text, edited it and turned it into a masterpiece, now comes the time to save the document to a file for safe-keeping.

You should use the command ◇ FS (File Save) to save the file for future use. If you've worked on a file that was loaded using the ◇ FL command, or if you have change the file name using ◇ FC, the relevant file will be supplied for you. Simply press the ENTER key and your document will be saved with the name supplied. If the document was started from scratch or you want to change the file name, however, you will need to supply a relevant file name; but remember the importance of directories, as discussed in Chapter 2.

The option to save only a marked block of the file has already been discussed; the choice of saving the file as 'plain text' will be discussed below. For the most part, therefore, all you need to do to save a file will be to supply the filename and press the ENTER key.

Plain text files

By now PipeDream's power and flexibility should be apparent. With it you can vary layouts, change highlights and develop a variety of different kinds of document. To do all this, however, PipeDream must contain a number of control codes that will have to be saved with the file. Unfortunately, these codes are meaningless as far as the text itself is concerned.

So that you can create a document that is composed of just the 'plain' text, therefore (perhaps you want to send it to a friend via the telephone line – see Chapter 10), when it saves a document PipeDream asks whether it should first strip out the control codes. If you reply Y(es), then it is still possible to load the document back into PipeDream (◇ FL) but the default options will operate.

Appendix 4 provides details of the internal file structure of PipeDream documents. For the most part it will be the column width, right margin, and document options which will be lost if you save a file as plain text.

Multiple files

As well as dealing with one file at a time, PipeDream supplies a very powerful facility to let you work on a complete list of files, without having to save or recall them when you want to do any editing. For example, your chapter may be composed of several sections, or your book built from a number of chapters. If you work with each of these sections or chapters as separate files, you can work on them in sequence.

To do so you must create a separate file, using PipeDream, called a 'file list'. As its name suggests, this simply lists the file names in their correct order. For example:

Chapter.1
Chapter.2
Chapter.3

and so on. Each individual file *must* appear on a separate line in the list, and there should be no blank lines in the file list document.

Now simply save this file list as *a plain text file*. You can give it any file name you want, although the name *must* have the extension '.L'. For example:

```
Book.L
```

Working with the list is very easy. You simply load the list file as if you were going to work on it like any PipeDream document – though you do not need to supply the .L extension. So, in our example, you would issue the command ◇ FL to load a PipeDream document, and supply the file name 'book'.

Whenever it is commanded to load a file, PipeDream searches through the current directory for files that have the .L extension. If it finds one with the same name that it is searching for then, rather than loading the file as a document in the normal way, it uses it as a command file, loading the files in the list in sequence.

In this case, then, asking PipeDream to load 'book' will first make it load the document called 'Chapter 1'. You can work on this document in the normal way.

As soon as you are ready to move on to Chapter 2, issue the command ◇ FN (File Next). This loads the next file in the list – *but saves the current one first*. Indeed, whenever you move from one file to another PipeDream always saves the current file before moving on.

When you are using file lists like this, three other commands are available to you:

◇ FP Returns to the previous file in the list;
◇ FT Goes to the top file in the list; and
◇ FB Goes to the bottom file in the list.

Printing lists

To print all the files in the list, in one long sequence, simply go to the top file in the list (◇ FT) and issue the print command in the usual way (◇ PO). PipeDream will print each file in sequence, without a page break in between. So, if you want files to begin on a new page – as you may when printing a sequence of chapters, for example – you should ensure that a new page instruction (◇ EIP) is added to the end of each file.

Starting Again

There are two ways of beginning work on a new document. Either you can load a new file from the directory by issuing the ◇ FL (File Load) command or you can erase the document currently in memory by issuing the ◇ BNEW (Block New) command.

If you try to load a file from the directory without having first saved the previous file, PipeDream sensibly asks you whether you want the file to overwrite the current document. At this point you need to make a positive 'y' or 'n' response (although any response other than 'y' is taken as indicating 'no').

Similarly, when you issue a ◇ BNEW command, PipeDream asks whether you want to overwrite the current text.

Summary

This chapter has delved into the depths of the word processing aspects of PipeDream. We have considered ways of entering and deleting text, moving around a document, and manipulating blocks of various sizes. The chapter also introduced various ways of laying out your document, both onscreen and ready for the printer. Finally, we considered PipeDream's valuable feature of letting us deal with lists of files so that very large documents can be accommodated within small stages.

In the next chapter we shall look at PipeDream's number-crunching facilities: its spreadsheet. And, because we are actually dealing with the same program and the same document structure, we will see how it is possible to join text and spreadsheets together for the best effect.

4

Crunching the numbers

Often the simplest ideas are the most effective, and this truism certainly holds for spreadsheets – programs that do for numbers what word processors achieve for words. For years people having been using the backs of envelopes to do their complex calculations, profit forecasts, cash flows and whatever. But few considered how easy it would be to formalise the principles they were adopting, of creating simple tables in which any part of the apocryphal envelope comprised either some information (a number or a description) or a formula, to develop one of the most powerful and valuable pieces of computer software available.

And few would have realised that this simple concept could help a major computer manufacturer, Apple, break into the highly competitive world of computer sales *and* rise rapidly to be one of the leaders.

In 1978 two programmers, Daniel Bricklin and Robert Franckston, developed Visicalc, a program that would quickly and accurately perform the kind of 'back of the envelope' calculations that people had been doing for ages. Visicalc was simply a two-dimensional table of rows and columns, which formed 'cells' at each row and column intersection.

In the standard spreadsheet parlance, each cell is identified by a combination of the column label (expressed as a letter starting from A) and the row number. So, cell A1 appears in the top left hand corner of the table; A2 is the second cell down in the first column; B1 is the first cell in the second column; and so on. Any cell can contain either data or a formula.

The important feature of this cellular structure is that the formulae themselves are normally 'invisible' to the user. A cell that contains a formula either appears blank or it will display information that is associated with the formula in some way. And the formula will often make use of information in other cells, so that some very complex calculations can take place.

To take a simple example, say you want to calculate the gross cost of an item (including VAT at 15%), given its net cost. Into cell A2 you might enter the formula:

`A1 * 1.15` (which means 'multiply the contents of cell A1 by 1.15')

Whatever value you enter into A1 (the top left hand cell of the table), the gross value of the item will appear in cell A2. Indeed, every time you make a new entry into the spreadsheet the program recalculates the values in all active cells.

Once that simple leap in the notion of numerical planning had been made, people quickly appreciated the potential value of spreadsheet programs. And since Apple freely distributed Visicalc with their new computers, sales of Apple computers soon rose.

The spreadsheet story does not end there, however. Software manufacturers soon realised that cell formulae do not have to remain simply at the arithmetical level. With a little sensible programming it is possible to include mathematical and statistical functions such as summation (adding) of a row or column of values, obtaining the square root of the value in a cell, and so on.

It is also possible to include more complex facilities such as the computer's own branching and decision making capacities. For example, these days you can instruct a spreadsheet program along the lines of: 'if the value in cell A1 is greater than 10, then do something, otherwise do something else'.

Spreadsheets on the Z88

As was explained in the last chapter the spreadsheet program supplied inside the Z88, PipeDream, is fundamental to many of the facilities provided by this computer. For example, by altering PipeDream's margins it is possible to make it behave as a word processor. And, as Chapter 5 will illustrate, by entering specific kinds of information into the program's columns we can turn it into a useful database.

Indeed, because PipeDream *is* the fundamental program within the Z88's integrated suite, you can incorporate spreadsheet data into your word processed files, and vice versa – as we will see later in this chapter.

Since all these functions are represented by the same program the spreadsheet is accessed in exactly the same way as for the word processor: you press the two keys □P from within any of the Z88's activities, or highlight 'PipeDream' on the Index page. In whatever way you reach the program a simple six-column table appears, with just the first row highlighted.

Spreadsheet expressions

As it stands in this pristine state, PipeDream is expecting you to enter alphanumeric characters into the spreadsheet – in other words to treat it as a word processor. You can switch into its spreadsheet operation in one of two ways. Either:

- precede any data or formula entry with the command ◇ X (eXpression); or
- change the function of the program slightly using the options page (◇ O).

When you take the second route (◇ O) the first option you see lets you switch between text and numeric operations. If you change this to N(umbers) PipeDream will operate fully as a spreadsheet. But, if you make the change PipeDream will *always* operate as a spreadsheet for *this* document – you cannot change the document back into a text-based one. To add some text around the spreadsheet you will need to save it and then load it into a word processed document, as will be explained later.

Once a row contains a spreadsheet formula or a piece of data, the left and right cursor arrow keys move the cursor by cells, rather than by characters as they do when the program is in its word processor mode. There are special methods of moving around the spreadsheet, and of editing cells, that will be discussed later.

A Simple Example

Having set up the Z88 to operate as a spreadsheet we shall try out a simple example. Before doing so, however, it is important to understand the difference between a spreadsheet's model and its data.

Models and data

The spreadsheet's model refers to its underlying theme; the formulae that it contains and how these are arranged to produce the desired results. The data are the values which we enter into the spreadsheet. For example, the model for the VAT calculations described above is a very simple one – it just says 'take the value in cell A1, multiply it by 1.15, and display the result in A2'. In this case the data are the values that will be entered into cell A1.

We could have designed a slightly more complex model to make it more adaptable, of course. Say, for example, the Chancellor of the Exchequer decided that VAT rate should vary from week to week. And say you have a range of three items for sale, each of which needs to have its gross value calculated. Finally, to complicate matters a little further, say you need to display not just the gross amount but the VAT fraction that is due – maybe for tax purposes. Now we shall have to build a slightly more complex model which takes account of variable VAT rates, VAT fractions, and a number of items.

First, switch PipeDream into its spreadsheet mode by changing the first option in the option page (◇ O) from T(ext) to N(umbers). Press ESC to return to the PipeDream document.

Cell labels

With the cursor in cell A1 (PipeDream always displays the cell reference at the top left hand part of the screen, above the column labels), enter the following:

```
"VAT rate"
```

There are three important points to note. First, because you have told PipeDream to act as a spreadsheet, immediately you press a key the whole cell is highlighted and the information is entered on the top row of the screen above the column headings. This is the editing row, and we shall look at this in more detail later.

Second, because PipeDream is now expecting to receive numeric data you must enclose text in double quotes. If you fail to do this the message 'Typing error' will appear in the slot. Again, we will shall consider later how to edit the information in slots, including erasing errors. For the moment, though, if you have received the dreaded error message press ◇ X and edit the text that appears on the top line – and add the double quotes this time!

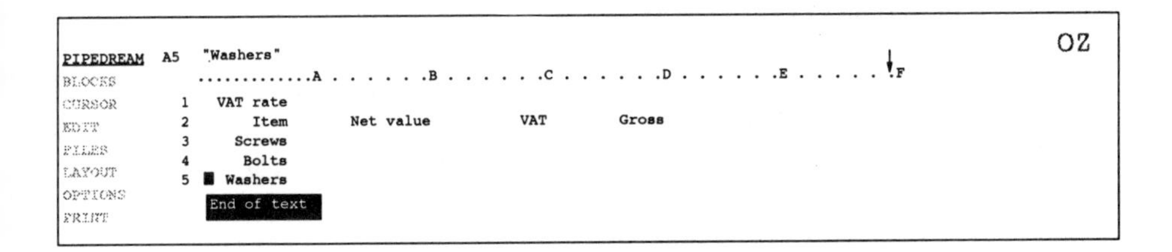

Defining the labels

The third point to note is that when you press the ENTER key the information that you have entered into the top line of the screen appears in cell A1, aligned with the right hand edge.

We shall put more accurate information about the VAT rate into cell B1 later. For the moment TAB to cell B1 and enter any number into it – say 15 – followed by the ENTER key. Note again that the cell is highlighted as you enter the data, and that numerical information is shown with two decimal places. Again, we shall see how to change this layout later.

Now return the cursor to the beginning of cell A1 by pressing SHIFT and TAB together (which moves the cursor leftwards by one cell at a time), and move down a row to A2 by pressing the ENTER key. To move immediately to column A, wherever you happen to be in the spreadsheet, you could also press ◇ TAB.

On the second row we shall insert some headings (remember the double quotes each time):

Cell	**Heading**
A2	"Item"
B2	"Net value"
C2	"VAT"
D2	"Gross"

Return the cursor to the left hand edge of the spreadsheet (cell A2) by pressing ◇ TAB and press the ENTER key to take it down to cell A3. Now is the time to describe our three items: "Screws" in cell A3, "Bolts" in A4, and "Washers" in A5.

Cell formulae

Having described the information in the various cells, we now have to conclude the model by entering the relevant formulae.

Later we shall enter the net prices of the goods into column B. Based on this information, relevant cells in column C will show the VAT fraction and the gross values in column D. So we need to enter the appropriate formulae into these cells in the table.

First the VAT fraction: TAB the cursor to cell C3 and enter the following:

`b3*b1/100` (you can use either upper or lower case letters)

```
PIPEDREAM  C3   B3*B1/100                                                          OZ
BLOCKS        . . . . . . A . . . . . . B. . . . . . . . . .C . . . . . .D . . . . . .E . . . . . .↓.F
CURSOR     1     VAT rate        15.00
EDIT       2         Item    Net value          VAT       Gross
FILES      3       Screws         4.50 ■       0.68        5.18
LAYOUT     4        Bolts         6.70         1.01       26.08
OPTIONS    5      Washers         1.25         0.19        3.75
PRINT         End of text
```

Entering the formulae

This means 'take the value contained in cell B3 (currently zero), multiply it by the value in B1 (currently 15) and divide by 100'. When you press the ENTER key the result (0.00) appears in C3. At the moment it is zero because cell B3 contains no information.

Now enter the same basic formula into cell C4, although this time it will be B4*B1/100. And in cell C5 you should enter the formula B5*B1/100. Notice that the same principles (model) apply to the formula each time; only the cell reference changes.

Next the formulae for the gross figures: the net value plus the VAT fraction. So put the following formulae into these cells:

Cell	**Formula**
D3	b3+c3
D4	b4+c4
D5	b5+c5

With this set-up we have created the spreadsheet model for calculating the VAT and gross amount on our three items for sale. It is now time to enter the data.

Take the cursor to cell B3 and enter a sensible figure for the cost of screws – say 4.50. Then enter information for bolts (6.70 in B4) and washers (1.25 in B5). As you enter each value, note that the values in the 'VAT' and 'Gross' columns change accordingly.

Now we can accommodate our fickle Chancellor. Whatever VAT rate he sets we simply have to change the value shown in cell B1. Say he decides to bring VAT down to 10%; you just need to alter this figure and PipeDream will make the appropriate changes for you within the table.

Cell functions

Finally, we could improve on this model to make it even more useful. Maybe we wish to add the information in each column to determine, automatically, how much VAT needs to be paid to the Customs and Excise.

Take the cursor to cell B6 (at the bottom of the Net value column) and enter:

```
sum(b3 b5)
```

As soon as you press the ENTER key the value 12.45 will appear in this cell. The function has asked PipeDream to add (summate) all the values shown in the range of cells B3 to B5 inclusive.

At the bottom of column C (in cell C6) enter sum(c3 c5), and in cell D6 enter `sum(d3 d5)`. Finally, if you label cell A6 with `"Total"` you will have produced a meaningful, and quite useful, VAT spreadsheet model – ready for whatever data you wish to enter.

Spreadsheet Basics

Having seen how easy it is to produce a spreadsheet, and how useful the tool can be for analysing data and for future planning, now comes the time to discover a little more about the spreadsheet facilities that PipeDream offers. Understanding these will enable you to produce sophisticated spreadsheet models for most purposes.

Cell width

Before entering any data into the spreadsheet, either to produce the model or to create the data, it is important to ensure that the widths of the columns are set to sensible dimensions. Obviously, if they are too small large numbers will not be displayed properly. But if they are too wide you are unlikely to see much of the spreadsheet at a time.

As with PipeDream's word processing functions, the cell width is set simply by issuing the command ◇ W and entering an appropriate value. As soon as you press the ENTER key the width of the column currently containing the cursor will be altered accordingly.

So that you do not have to move from column to column before you can change its width, PipeDream also offers the facility for defining which column you wish to alter. While within the width-changing menu (◇ W) take the cursor to the second column and change 'No' to Y(es). Then enter the letter of the column that you wish to change.

Zero width

Sometimes it is useful to 'hide' columns from public view – either when they are printed or when they are displayed on the screen. Maybe they will contain intermediate information that could be 'secret', or they could contain calculations that are not important to the final display.

Setting a column width to zero hides the column. To make it visible again you will have to alter its width to some positive value but, because you can't take the cursor to a hidden column, you will have to declare the column letter from within the ◇ W menu.

Editing the Spreadsheet

As with a word processed document, you can edit the information in the spreadsheet at two levels. Firstly, when you are entering material into a cell but *before* you press the ENTER key; and secondly after having pressed the ENTER key and the information has been transferred into the spreadsheet itself.

Simple editing of the first kind, when the information still appears on the top line of the display, is done using all the editing commands mentioned in the last chapter. So, ◇ G deletes the character under the cursor while DEL deletes the one to the left of the cursor. The command ◇ Y deletes the line, ◇ D deletes the rest of the line after the cursor, and ◇ T deletes up to the next space.

If you want to edit information that is already in the spreadsheet, however, you first need to get PipeDream to display it on the top line. You do this using the ◇ X command. Once in this mode, you can edit to your heart's content.

Finally, to erase the content of a cell, take the cursor to the cell and issue the ◇ D command.

ENT and K

As well as these editing facilities, PipeDream supplies a couple of others for use in special circumstances.

The command ◇ ENT swaps the content of a cell between 'text' and 'number' mode. This is useful in two circumstances: first, if you are working in 'normal' word processing mode (that is, you have not modified the text/numbers option in the options page) and you forget to issue the ◇ X command before entering data. Pressing ◇ ENT will change the word processed text into spreadsheet text.

Second, if you issue the ◇ENT command when the cell contains a formula the cell will display the formula itself rather than the value of the calculation. This can be useful for 'debugging' the spreadsheet and ridding it of various kinds of errors.

The command ◇K can be useful when entering formulae; it puts the cell reference of the cell that contains the cursor onto the top editing line. This is extremely valuable if you have to enter lists of cells, since it means that you do not need to remember them all.

For example, say you want to add the contents of a group of cells, as we did earlier. Take the cursor to the cell that will contain the summation function (B6) and press ◇X to show that you want to enter a formula into this cell. Begin the function by entering:

```
sum(
```

Now move the cursor to the first cell in the list (B3). You can use the up and down arrows with impunity, but to move right and left you will have to press TAB and SHIFT/TAB respectively. When you reach the correct cell press ◇K and the cell reference will appear in the top line. Now move the cursor to the cell that defines the end of the list (B5) and press ◇K again. Complete the function by adding the final right bracket and press the ENTER key. The cell cursor will leap back to its original cell and display the result of the summation.

Columns and Rows

When you start a new spreadsheet PipeDream displays only six columns (A-F), each of which is 12 characters wide. For many purposes this will be enough, although it could clearly be restrictive for some applications. To add more columns you issue the ◇EAC (Edit Add Column) command. In total, you can have up to 69 columns (labelled A to BL).

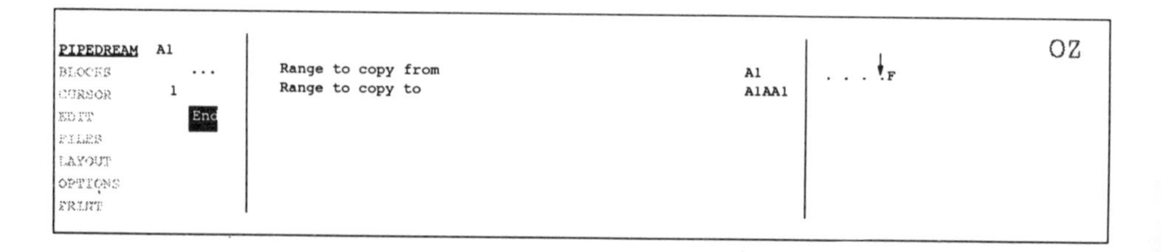

Extending the columns using ◇ BRE

Using ◇ EAC can be a little tedious if you have to add a large number of columns. However, it is possible to automate the process by using PipeDream's 'replicate' command, which will be discussed in detail later.

For the moment, say you wish to create a spreadsheet with 27 columns (A to Z and then AA). To replicate slots issue the command ◇ BRE (Block REplicate) and give as 'range to copy from' the label of an empty cell (say A1). For the 'range to copy to' provide a list of cells that covers the full width of your new spreadsheet – in this case A1AA1. When you press the ENTER key you will find that PipeDream has created a range of empty cells for you.

If you vary the row number in the 'range to copy to' – for example, copy from A1 to A1AA10, you will find that PipeDream creates a block of cells in other rows as well.

Whereas you are limited to 69 columns, there is a theoretical maximum of 32,768 rows. However, a spreadsheet that contained over two million (69 x 32768) cells would soon run out of memory.

To insert a column into the middle of a spreadsheet, rather than at the end of it, take the cursor to where you want the column inserted and issue the command ◇ EIC (Edit Insert Column). A new column will appear to the left of the one containing the cursor, and everything to the right – including formula references – will be shifted one column rightwards.

If you do add a column in this way, it is important to note that the cell references will also change accordingly. For example, say cell A1 contains a function that adds the contents of cells B1 and C1. Inserting a new column B, say, that is shifting what was column B into column C, C to D, and so on, will change the references so that cell A1's formula becomes 'C1+D1'.

This also happens for cell lists in functions. So 'sum(b1c1)' in cell A1 would become 'sum(C1D1)' if you insert a new column B.

Deleting a column is done in the same way, but by issuing the command ◇ EDC (Edit Delete Column). In this case, however, the column *containing* the cursor is deleted. Again, cell references are changed accordingly.

Adding rows to the end of your spreadsheet is simply a matter of pressing the ENTER key, as you do with a word processed document. Inserting and deleting rows is done in the same way as you would to insert and delete rows in a word processed document (◇ N and ◇ Y) – and the cell references change too.

Rows in columns

As well as adding, deleting, and inserting complete rows and columns, you can also add and delete blank cells into your spreadsheet. This is useful for shifting a group of cells upwards or downwards within a column, say, without changing the rest of the spreadsheet structure.

To do this, take the cursor to the cell you want to insert and issue the command ◇EIRC (Edit Insert a Row in the Column). To delete the cell and move all cells below it in the column upwards by one cell, issue the command ◇EDRC.

Moving Around the Cells

The facilities supplied for moving around a spreadsheet quickly are not quite as extensive as the ones for moving around a word processed document. In essence, you

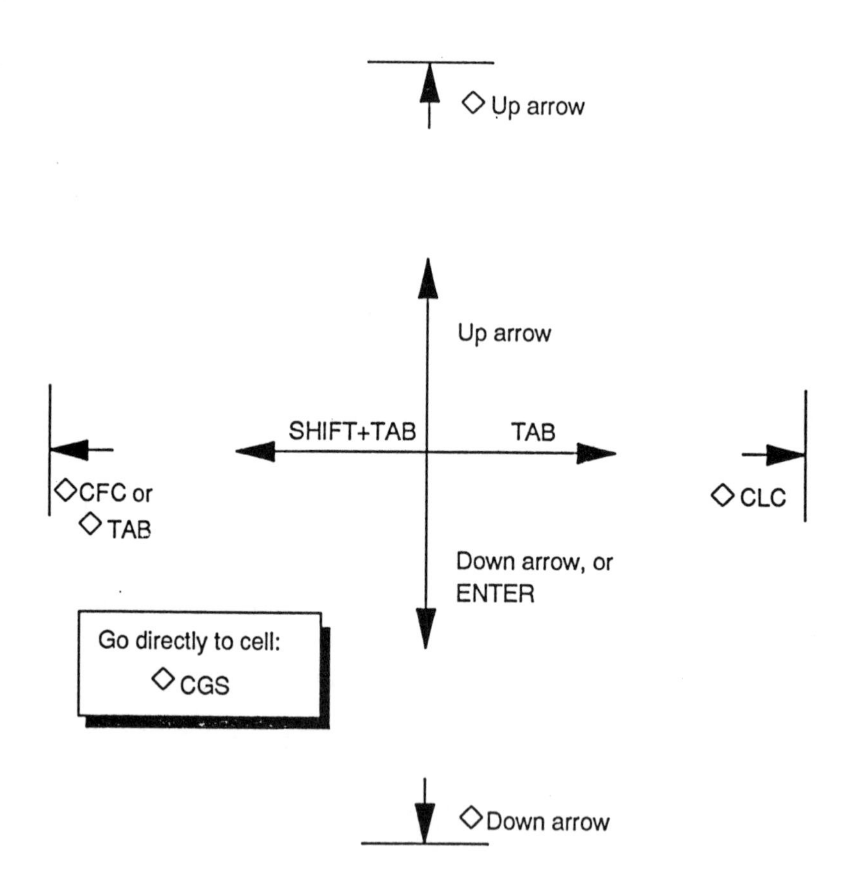

Moving around the cells

can use the cursor keys to move from one cell to an adjacent cell, and to move immediately to the top or bottom of the spreadsheet, or to the beginning or end of a row. There is also the facility to jump to a named cell.

Movement between adjacent cells is carried out simply by using either the cursor arrow keys or the TAB and SHIFT/TAB combinations for right and left movement respectively.

As with a PipeDream document, pressing the ◇ key along with the up or down arrow takes you to the top or bottom row of your spreadsheet – within a column. Fast movement to the first or last column in a row is performed by the commands ◇ CFC (Cursor First Column) and ◇ CLC respectively. But pressing ◇ and TAB together presents an even faster way of moving to the beginning of a row. This takes the cursor back to the first character of the line (that is, to the beginning of column A).

Finally, you can jump to any named cell by issuing the command ◇ CGS (Cursor Go to Slot). Used with the 'cursor save position' and 'cursor return to position' (◇ CSP and ◇ CRP) commands described in Chapter 3, this can be quite a useful facility.

Layout

Setting the cell width is not the only display feature available within PipeDream; you can lay out your spreadsheet with a fair degree of sophistication to make it look as you wish.

Aligning the labels

Perhaps the first feature to consider is aligning labels and figures within a column. When you enter a text-based column heading (between double quote marks) PipeDream automatically displays it in the cell with a right alignment. That is, it is entered over to the right hand side of the cell, with the final character touching the right hand margin. Numbers are also automatically displayed in the same format.

Sometimes, however, you may not wish to have right aligned numbers and headings. So, just as with a word processed document, it is possible to centre them or to set them to be left aligned. This is done with the commands ◇ LAC (Layout At Centre) and ◇ LAL commands respectively. To reset a slot to right alignment use ◇ LAR.

These commands do not only work on single slots. They will also operate on a block of slots that has been highlighted using the ◇ Z command.

Number formats

Spreadsheets are probably used most frequently for financial forecasting, so most numbers will need to have two decimal places for pence, cents and so on. But not all will require two decimal places, so PipeDream offers a chance to change the number of decimal places shown. To do this you should alter the fourth option in the second column of the document's options page (◇ O).

Unfortunately, if you use this option the number of decimal places that you define affects the whole spreadsheet. Nevertheless, PipeDream also offers the facility to have variable decimal place displays – either for single cells or for marked blocks – by using the command ◇ LDP (Layout Decimal Place). With this command you can also set the display to 'free format'; that is, to display only the significant values in the expression.

For example:

Number of decimal places	Display	
0	3	
1	3.0	
2	3.00	
Free	3	if 3.00 is entered
	3.2	if 3.2 is entered
	3.267	if 3.2670 is entered

Leading and trailing characters

The options page also makes provision for displaying leading and trailing characters for a cell or a marked block. For example, you could change numerical spreadsheets to financial ones by adding a pound or dollar sign before the numbers. Similarly, a column of numbers could be changed to indicate percentages by putting the % sign after each number.

The characters to be displayed in this way can be changed at the bottom of the second column of options within the Options menu. Then, when you issue the command ◇ LCL (Layout Character Leading) or ◇ LCT (Layout Character Trailing), the values in cells that contain the cursor – or in a marked block – will have the appropriate characters added to the beginning or end.

Negative values

PipeDream supplies one further display option for financial forecasters – the ability to show negative values with either a leading minus sign or, as used frequently in balance statements, enclosed within brackets. Again, this format can be imposed on either single cells or a marked block; this time using the ◇LSM (Layout Sign Minus) or ◇LSB (Layout Sign Bracket) commands.

Finally, it is important to note that once a slot's format has been specifically defined using the decimal places, leading/trailing characters, or signs commands, it will not be affected by changes to the default options in the options menu. This is extremely useful, and can lead to some very sophisticated spreadsheet displays, with a variety of leading characters, for example, as well as number formats.

To reset a cell or a marked block to the default values indicated in the options menu, issue the command ◇LDF (Layout DeFault).

Titles and Windows

```
PIPEDREAM  C3      B3*B1/100                                                              OZ
BLOCKS             ________ A ________ B...........C . . . . . .D . . .. . .E . . . . . .↓.F
CURSOR       ___ 1     VAT rate       15.00
EDIT         ___ 2         Item   Net value         VAT        Gross
FILES            3       Screws        4.50 ■      0.68         5.18
LAYOUT           4        Bolts        6.70        1.01        26.08
OPTIONS          5      Washers        1.25        0.19         3.75
PRINT              End of text
```

Scrolling titles and windows

When you are entering numbers into a spreadsheet, or interpret the results, you will often need to know what various cells represent. Unfortunately, as you scroll down or across a spreadsheet the headings and labels quickly disappear, particularly on the Z88's display which is only eight rows deep.

You can stop this happening by freezing the scrolling movement above and or to the left of the cursor. To do this you should issue the commands ◇LFR (Layout Fix Row) or ◇LFC (Layout Fix Column) respectively.

So, say you have a set of column headings across row 1. Take the cursor to anywhere on this row and issue the command ◇LFR. A short bar will appear to the left of the row number, and the display will now only scroll beneath this row. To remove this windowing effect, issue the same command again.

To set both column and row titles, take the cursor to the top left hand cell of the scrolling area that you wish to keep free. Now issue the commands ◇LFR and ◇LFC. All the rows that are frozen will be indicated by the short bar to the left of the row number, while the frozen columns are shown by a continuous line under the column label.

Search and Replace

Before concluding the discussion of PipeDream's features, we should not forget the facilities offered by many of its word processing options. In particular, the ability to search, replace and sort. These features can be useful for altering headings, say, or other text-based information within a spreadsheet. Unfortunately, it is not possible to use the commands to search for, or to replace, cell references within formulae.

The ◇BSE and ◇BRP commands we encountered in the last chapter work in much the same way for spreadsheets as they do for word processed documents. The only addition to note is that from within the search/replace menu you can define a set of columns over which these activities are to be carried out. The second and third questions in the respective menus ask whether you want to perform the operation over a range of columns. If you change the response to Y(es), PipeDream expects you to indicate the first and last column letter in the range (they must be separated by a space).

Sorting

When showing the results of a spreadsheet calculation it is sometimes useful to be able to display the rows in some kind of order. For example, you may wish to arrange the items in a list in alphabetical order or the values of goods in numeric order. You can do all this using PipeDream's ◇BSO (Block SOrt) command.

As the command's name suggests, it only operates on a block that has been marked and highlighted using the ◇Z convention. In this respect it is important that *all* the columns in each row are highlighted – otherwise you will end up with some peculiar results.

As an example, we will use the VAT model that we developed earlier. This comprised four columns of data: items in column A, net prices in column B, VAT fractions in C, and the gross price in column D. The three items we included in the spreadsheet were entered into rows 3, 4 and 5.

This means that the block that must be highlighted extends from cell A3 in the top left hand corner to cell D5 in the bottom right hand corner. So, take the cursor to A3 and press ◇Z; now take it to D5 and press ◇Z again.

When you issue the ◇ BSO command you will be asked which column you wish to sort on; we need column A (the item names). Ascending and descending sorts are obvious.

The third option ('Don't update references') refers to PipeDream's ability to look at every active cell in the spreadsheet and check whether it is associated with a cell that is being sorted. If so, then the 'reference' will be updated accordingly. Obviously, this can take some time, so it is best not to use this option if other cells are not affected.

As soon as you press the ENTER key, your sorting will be done for you.

To change the sort criterion simply vary the column to sort on. So, to sort items according to their gross price, ask for the process to be done on column D.

Replication

When we developed the VAT example earlier you probably found that entering the same formula into a range of different cells became rather tedious. Take column D, for example: the gross value of the goods (net + VAT). Into cell D3 we entered B3+C3, into D4 went B4+C4, and cell D5 ended up with the formula B5+C5. In each case the formula stayed the same, only the cell references changed.

Most spreadsheet programs, including PipeDream, allow you to 'copy' a cell formula into a range of other cells, updating the cell reference each time. This is called 'replicating' the cells.

If you issue the command ◇ BRE (Block REplicate), PipeDream asks you first to indicate the cell, or range of cells, that you wish to use as your base. Then you are asked for the range of cells to replicate this base into.

So, in the above example, you would wish to use cell D3 as the base and to replicate it into the range of cells extending from D4 to D5. When indicating a range of cells in this kind of option, PipeDream expects you to show the first and the last cell in the range separated by a space. So, the replication menu would look like:

```
Range to copy from   D3
Range to copy to     D4 D5
```

If you now take the cursor over the three cells D3, D4 and D5, you will see that the simple summation formula has been copied into all three cells, with the cell references altered appropriately.

Replicating ranges

Whereas replicating a single cell should be quite straightforward, replicating ranges of cells may be a little confusing. This is because the final outcome of cell references depends on how you make the move – from a column to an area, from an area to an area, or from a row to an area. The important point to remember is that however you

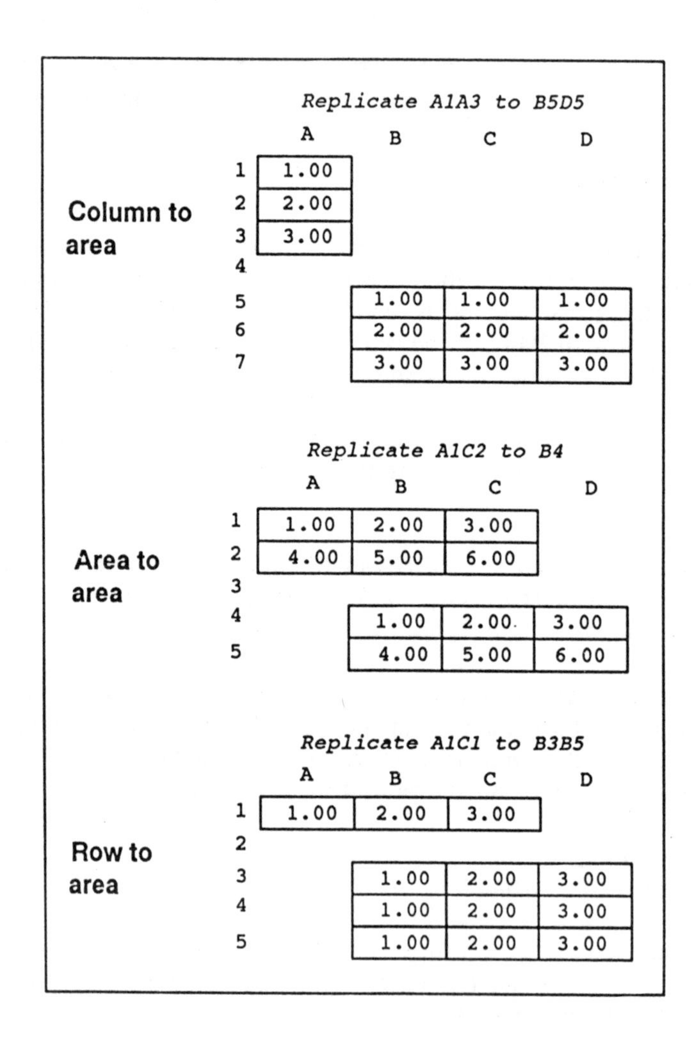

Replicating to cells and areas

define the range of cells initially, PipeDream will always end up by replicating it into an area of the spreadsheet that is the same size as defined by the initial column, row or area.

Probably the best way to illustrate these effects is to replicate ranges of cells which have specific numbers in them, rather than formulae. So, turning first to the *column to area* replication, into cell A1 enter 1, into A2 enter 2 and into A3 enter 3.

Now issue the replication command (◇BRE) and define the starting range as A1A3.

The range to copy into should be B5D5, say, (which means that we are going to use B5 as the upper left hand, and D5 as the lower right hand, corners of our area). When you press the ENTER key you will see how PipeDream has coped with the replication. Each of the three cells in row 5 (B, C and D) contains 1s, those in row 6 contain 2s and there are 3s across row 7.

Had you defined only cell B5 as the range to copy to, PipeDream would have simply produced the same column of figures as the original, starting at cell B5 and ending at B7. This is the basis of the *copy area to area* feature of the function.

Copying a *row to an area* produces the same effect as a column to an area, although the final cell values will be slightly different. By replicating the range A1 to C1 to the range B3 to B5, for example, cell A1's value will end up in cells B3, B4 and B5. B1's value will be replicated to cells C3 to C5, and C1 will copy to D3 to D5.

Although these examples used specific numbers to illustrate the replication effects, you should realise that cell formulae operate in much the same way, with the cell references updated appropriately.

For example, say cell A1 contains the formula A2+B2 – that is 'add the values contained in the cell immediately below A1 to the one immediately below and to the right of it'. If this is replicated to cell B5, the formula in this cell will become B6+C6. And so on.

Block Copy, Move and Delete

Although replicating a cell or a range of cells to another area of the spreadsheet is both simple and an effective way of quickly building up a complex model, the replication function suffers from a major drawback: the contents of any cells into which the original range of cells are replicated will be overwritten by the new values or formulae. So, you must ensure that replication is only performed into an area of the spreadsheet that is devoid of existing cells.

Using the standard block copy and move functions that we encountered while word processing, however, removes this problem. Block copy (◇ BC), for example, will copy the cell or range of cells that have been defined as a block using the ◇ Z command to the new area *and* will move the existing cells downwards by an appropriate number of rows. Not only this, but the cell references are updated as appropriate.

The Block Move (◇ BM) command performs the same function, but removes the expression from the original slot after the copying process has been carried out.

Block Delete (◇ BD), of course, simply deletes the contents of the defined block.

Fixing the Cell Reference

Let us return to our original VAT example. You will recall that cell B1 contains the current VAT rate, updated according to the Chancellor's decisions. Column C was designated to contain the VAT fractions, calculated by multiplying the net value of the goods (column B) by the VAT amount (B1) and dividing by 100.

For example, the formula in cell C3, the VAT fraction for screws, was:

```
b3*b1/100
```

If you now replicate this formula for all entries in column C, that is into cells C4 and C5, you will notice an unwelcome effect of PipeDream's cell reference updating facility. Although the reference to the net value cell changes appropriately each time (to B4 and B5), so does the reference to the VAT amount in B1.

So:

Cell C3 contains the formula `B3*B1/100`

C4	`B4*B2/100`
C5	`B5*B3/100`

This is clearly of no value at all. We need to 'fix' the reference to cell B1 so that it remains constant while the other cell references change.

PipeDream allows us to do this by prefacing the part of the cell reference that needs to remain constant with a dollar sign ($). In our case we want both the column label and the row number to remain constant (that is, the cell reference must remain as B1) so we should refer to it as:

```
$B$1
```

So, if you enter the formula

```
B3*$B$1/100
```

into cell C3, and then replicate this cell to the new area you will find that the net values of the different kinds of goods are always multiplied by the value in cell B1.

Being able to fix parts of the cell reference independently means that in more complex models you could allow one part of the reference to vary (say the column label) while fixing the other (the row number). Say, for example, cell A1 contains reference to cell B$1. Replicating this to the range of cells C5D5 will mean that cell C5 contains reference to D$1 and cell D5 contains reference to E$1.

Similarly, fixing the reference to $B1 will replicate to $B5 in both cells C5 and D5.

Spreadsheet Functions

As well as simple, and not so simple formulae, cells can also contain a variety of logical, mathematical, statistical and trigonometric functions that let you do some very detailed analyses. With appropriate combinations of functions, for example, it is possible to vary the displayed information in response to the *kind* of data being entered, to make comprehensive predictions on the basis of the spreadsheet's own calculations, and to do detailed calculations of various kinds.

The standard format of all PipeDream's functions include the function name (for example 'sum') and reference to either a cell or to a range of cells, both of which are contained between brackets. It is at this point that the 'insert cell reference' command (◊ K) we met earlier becomes useful.

So, instead of having to remember the cell range over which you wish to summate, for example, you simply need to take the cursor to the first cell in the range and enter ◊ K, and then to the last cell in the range – followed by ◊ K again. PipeDream inserts the appropriate references into the expression for you.

Arithmetical and Statistical Functions

SUM(range)

This will probably be the first function that the novice spreadsheet designer uses. It adds the values in the range of cells defined within the function. For example, the function SUM(A1A5) will display the sum of all the cells A1, A2, A3, A4 and A5.

COUNT(range)

It is often necessary to display the number of entries that have been made in a column or row. COUNT returns the number of non-blank cells in the range.

INT(cell or number) and SGN(cell or number)

An integer is the part of the number that appears before any decimal point. So, the integer of 4.5, for example, is 4. This function is very useful if you wish to round off numbers to whole values. So, if cell A1 contains the value 4.5, INT(A1) will return the value 4.

The sign (SGN) of the number is displayed as -1 if the number has a negative value, and 1 if it is positive. This can be very useful when combined with some of the logic functions that will be described later. For example, a bank manager might develop a spreadsheet that will write an unpleasant letter if the sign of the account's balance is negative – otherwise he will not write the letter.

ABS(cell or number)

The absolute value of a number is, simply, its positive value. So the absolute value of 4.5 is 4.5; the absolute value of -4.5 is also 4.5.

MAX(range) and MIN(range)

Sometimes it is useful just to know the maximum or minimum values of a list of numbers. On other occasions this information can be incorporated into more complex, logical, statements. For example, our friendly bank manager may develop a spreadsheet that decides:

'If the maximum value in column A (the overdraft column) is greater than 100 then write an unpleasant letter, otherwise do nothing.'

SQR(cell or number)

The square root of a value is frequently used in statistical calculations.

EXP(cell or number)

Mathematicians and statisticians often use the exponential value (2.71828184). The function raises this value to the power expressed in the referenced cell. So, if B1 contains 1, EXP(B1) will show 2.72; if it contains 2 the same function will display 7.39; and so on.

LN(cell or number) and LOG(cell or number)

These two functions return the natural logarithm, or the base 10 logarithm, of the value in the cell reference.

Trigonometric Functions

All of the trigonometric functions relate to either a cell or a number that is contained in the brackets:

`ACS()`	Arc cosine in radians
`ASN()`	Arc sine in radians
`ATN()`	Arc tangent in radians
`COS(radians)`	Cosine
`DEG(radians)`	Radians to degrees
`RAD(degrees)`	Degrees to radians
`SIN(radians)`	Sine
`TAN(radians)`	Tangent

PI

This function has no cell reference or range associated with it. It is the value 3.141592653 and is used to calculate aspects of curves.

Spreadsheet Display Functions

These functions relate to the spreadsheet design itself and can help the spreadsheet designer make use of the spreadsheet during calculations.

COL and ROW

Both functions return a number that indicates the cursor's column or row position in the spreadsheet. For example, if the cursor is in cell B5, then COL will return a value of 2 (B is the second column across) and ROW will return 5 (the fifth row down the page).

ROW can be very useful when designing a spreadsheet. Often, for example, you will wish to number the rows – maybe to remind the person entering the data which row he or she is dealing with (especially if you have turned off the borders). Or you may want the row numbers printed with the spreadsheet. Entering the function ROW into cell A1, for example, and then replicating it for the entire column (◊ BRE) will produce the desired effect for you. COL can be used in the same way.

The two functions might also come in handy when performing some calculations or logical functions. For example, say you have designed a spreadsheet which uses the first twelve columns to enter monthly returns. Since column A will return a value of 1 when you issue the COL function, you could use this to indicate January, or maybe incorporate it into a monthly return calculation.

INDEX(col,row)

This function returns the value contained in the indexed cell – where 'col' is the numeric value of the column (A=1, B=2, and so on) and 'row' is the row number. So, INDEX(3,4) will return the value contained in cell C4.

Used in this simple way, INDEX has no more value than simply referencing cell C4. Its importance, however, lies in the fact that the 'col' and 'row' values are variables. So, you could reference a different cell each time by combining INDEX with COL and ROW, for example.

So, INDEX(COL+1,ROW) will display the value contained in one cell to the right of the function. INDEX(A1+A2,5) will display the value contained in the cell whose column is represented by the sum of the values in A1 and A2, five rows down.

We shall use this function to good effect in Chapter 9 when developing a mail-merging facility for PipeDream.

DAY(cell or date), MONTH(cell or date), YEAR(cell or date)

These three functions split a specified date into its component parts. For example, if cell A1 contains the date 15.12.1947, then DAY() will return 15, MONTH returns 12 and YEAR returns 47.

Logical Functions

With the logical functions, spreadsheets enter into the decision making field and provide considerable forecasting powers.

IF(expression, then, else)

The IF function is probably the most frequently used of the logical functions. It evaluates the expression given and then performs one of two actions: the first if the expression is 'true' and the second if it is 'false'.

For example, say you enter the expression IF(A1>0,"surplus","overdrawn") into cell A2, then the display in A2 will change as the value in A1 changes. As long as A1 remains above zero, A2 will declare a surplus; if it falls below zero, however, then A2 turns into 'overdrawn'.

The expression that is evaluated can be extremely complex and can contain a range of relational and logical operators.

Relational Operators

<	less than
>	greater than
<=	less than or equal to
>=	greater than or equal to
=	equal to
<>	not equal to

Logical Operators

&	and
|	or
!	not

Also, when strings are being evaluated (for example, IF(A2="good",...)) the standard wildcard operations are available:

^?	matches any single character
^#	matches any number of characters
^^	matches ^

With these facilities, some very powerful expressions can be built up. For example:

`IF(A1>10 & A1<20...` will return a 'true' value if A1 contains values between 11 and 19.

`IF(A1="bo^#"...` will return a true value if A1 contains 'box', 'boy', 'bother' and so on.

`IF(A1>0,A1,"")` will display the value of A1 if it is greater than 0, otherwise the cell is left empty.

CHOOSE(key, list)

CHOOSE can be considered to be an extension of IF, insofar as it supplies a longer list of alternative actions than just the two of 'true' and 'false'.

There are two main elements to the CHOOSE function: the first is the key value or expression, and the second is the list of actions from which the choice is made. If the key expression is 1, then the first action in the list is performed; if it is 2 then the second in the list is done, and so on.

The list of actions can contain alphabetic strings of characters (between quotes) or cell references. So, say you want to display a label that describes the value in cell A1. Into A2 enter:

```
CHOOSE(A1,"good","bad","ugly").
```

Now, as long as the value in A1 is either 1, 2 or 3, its description will appear in A2:

A1	A2
1	good
2	bad
3	ugly

You could have produced the same effect by putting the expression "good" into C1, say, "bad" into C2 and "ugly" into C3. Then use the expression CHOOSE(A1,C1,C2,C3).

If the value in A1 is larger than the list of actions that you have put into your CHOOSE expression, you will get the message 'Too few arguments'; if it is less than 1 then the message 'Bad index' appears. Both can be trapped by judicious use of the IF function, of course:

```
IF(A1>0 & A1<4,CHOOSE(A1,"good","bad","ugly"),"")
```

This says "if the value in A1 is greater than zero and less than 4 (in other words it is between 1 and 3) then operate the CHOOSE function, otherwise leave the cell blank".

LOOKUP(key, range1, range2)

The LOOKUP function is used in much the same way as CHOOSE, insofar as it produces a particular 'value' to be displayed that depends on the value of an initial key. However, its use is rather more specific than CHOOSE. Whereas with CHOOSE you could index an action anywhere within the spreadsheet by referring to the relevant cells, with LOOKUP you reference one range of cells with another.

The function takes the key value and looks down the first range of cells to find a match. It will then display the value in the corresponding cell in range 2. In this way, the key can represent a number, a string or a date.

For example, say you have a spreadsheet containing two columns of data in columns A and B, with column A containing the names of friends and column B their house number.

	A	B
1	Name	Number
2	Fred	23
3	Jim	2
4	Freda	36
5	Sarah	12
6	Mike	1

Lookup could be used to answer simple questions such as 'who lives at number 36?'.

Into cell D1, say, enter the expression LOOKUP(36,B1B6,A1A6) and PipeDream will supply you with the answer. Becoming more adventurous you could enter a cell reference as the key: LOOKUP(C1,B1B6,A1A6). Now, whatever number you enter into cell C1, Lookup will supply the corresponding name. If it cannot make a match, then the program returns the error message 'Lookup'.

You could also ask the same question in a different form: "What number is Jim's house?" In this case the expression LOOKUP("Jim",A1A6,B1B6) entered into cell D1, say, will provide the answer. Similarly LOOKUP(C1,A1A6,B1B6) will do the same if cell C1 contains a string that PipeDream recognises within the range A1A6.

By incorporating strings in this way, the LOOKUP function becomes very powerful, even more so with the facility to include the standard 'wildcards' in the key string. So LOOKUP("Fre^#",A1A6,B1B6) will find either Fred or Freda's house number (although, actually, it will only find Fred's since despite the function's name it looks *down* the range of cells and reports the first match it finds).

One important point to note about this function is that the ranges specified in the LOOKUP function do not have to be next to each other. Indeed, they do not even have to be columns. So you could look up a key within a range of 10 cells in column A, for example, and report the corresponding values in cells C6L6.

Combining Functions

Many of the functions supplied with PipeDream can be combined to create some very powerful controlling and reporting features. For example, we have already seen how IF can be combined with CHOOSE to ensure that we do not get error messages appearing as a result of the keys being out of range.

You can also manipulate the results of functions mathematically. For example, instead of entering 'row' into a cell to display the row number, you could enter 'row-1'. In the same way, CHOOSE(key+1,list) will reference the list starting with values in the key cell that are as low as zero.

The restrictions of the combinations will be restricted only by the limitations of your imagination. It is these combinations that increase the power and value of spreadsheet models.

Recalculation

Each time you insert a new expression into one of the cells the spreadsheet program quickly recalculates all the cells in the spreadsheet, beginning at A1 and updating the display where appropriate. With only a small spreadsheet, this process is obviously very fast. As the spreadsheet grows, however, things begin to slow down.

Whereas it is nice to be able to see your calculations revised before your eyes as you enter new data, for most cases it is not imperative to the efficient running of the spreadsheet. So, when your spreadsheet is large enough to cause significant slowing down each time you enter information into a cell, this can obviously become rather annoying.

To overcome this problem the Z88 lets you turn off the automatic recalculation, using one of the options in the options page (◇ O). Changing 'Calc: Auto/Man' to M(an) means that the recalculation will only be done when you tell PipeDream to do so. And you do this by issuing the command ◇ A.

Word Processing the Spreadsheets

Because the Z88's spreadsheet and word processing functions use the same program, it is perfectly feasible to insert a spreadsheet (or a part of it) into a word processed document. The process involved is very similar to inserting one word processed file into another.

To do this, obviously the spreadsheet must first be saved to a file (see below) – or at least that part of the spreadsheet that you want to include. Then load or create the word processed document (using ◇ FL if you want to use a previously saved file and ◇ BNEW if you want to begin a document from scratch – but *do* remember to save the spreadsheet first.

It is then a simple matter of taking the cursor down to the point at which you wish to insert the spreadsheet file and issuing the ◇ FL command. As with inserting one word processed document into another, answer 'yes' to the question whether you want to insert the file 'at the slot' – otherwise the new file will overwrite the current document.

Whereas this process is very simple, it is prone to one important possible error: column widths. The newly inserted spreadsheet takes on the column widths of the document into which it is being inserted, irrespective of the widths that you might have set. On most occasions, of course, this will not cause you too much bother – you probably will not have altered the column widths for the word processed document, and it is a relatively simply task now to set them to fit in with the column widths needed for a neat and tidy spreadsheet.

However, if you have used the column widths to control the left margin of an indented block of text, for example, or you have created a document with multiple columns, then problems might arise.

Unfortunately, there is no solution to the confusion between the two documents' competing requirements.

Selecting cells

PipeDream provides a useful function that lets you incorporate information from a selected cell of a spreadsheet into your word processed document. If you add the expression '@cell ref@' (for example, @A1@) to your document, the value contained in the cell reference will be printed at that point. Again, we shall use this function to good effect in Chapter 9 when designing a mail-merging facility for PipeDream.

Spreadsheet Files

The process of saving and recalling a spreadsheet is exactly the same as for a word processed document – with one exception: you are more likely to want to save and recall particular ranges of rows and columns than you are with a word processed document.

As with saving a text-based document, if you simply supply a file name and press the ENTER key the whole spreadsheet will be saved. However, it is possible to be a little more selective by changing some of the options in the save menu before pressing the ENTER key.

Partial saves

To save only part of a spreadsheet, you can either define a specific range of columns (like A D) or a previously marked block with ◇ Z.

As well as these standard operations, it is also possible to save specific rows of the spreadsheet – for example, all rows that contain the word "good" in column D, say, or for which values in column A lie between 10 and 20. Because PipeDream actually evaluates each row against these criteria before saving them, it is possible to use all the conditional combinations we discussed earlier to create some very powerful sorting processes. For example, you could save all rows which:

have values in column A that lie between 10 and 20 ;*and*
have names beginning with D in column B; *but not*
those which have some value in column C.

To perform this complex manoeuvre issue the file save command (◇ FS) and provide an appropriate file name for the new file. Be careful, though. If you have recalled this file from one in a directory you will overwrite the one that has been stored if you save this new file with the same name. The safest way of ensuring that this does not happen is to rename the file when in PipeDream (◇ FC). However, changing the name at the save menu is easy enough – just press ◇ Y to remove the old name and insert the new one.

Now move down the menu to the 'save selection of rows' option and answer Y(es). The cursor will move slightly to the right, ready for you to enter your condition:

```
(A1>9 & A1<21) & (B1="D^#") | (C1>0)
```

Note that you need to reference a column by including the column letter *and* a row number. But you can insert any number here – it makes no difference to the operation. PipeDream simply begins at cell 1 in the column and works downwards, checking at each row whether the condition has been reached.

By providing this facility, PipeDream has certainly supplied an extremely useful way of selecting specific rows of a spreadsheet – perhaps to insert into a word processed document.

Plain text

Sometimes you will want to save a spreadsheet, or part of it, as 'plain text'. That is, with all PipeDream's own layout commands stripped out so that another word processor, say, can accommodate it. The 'plain text' option in the file save page allows you to do this.

You should note, however, that the effect of saving the file like this will be to save cells that contain formulae *as the formulae* – not the results. So, a cell that contains the function SUM(A1A10) will appear in that way – not with the actual summation. This can be a useful feature when trying to debug a more complex spreadsheet model – being able to read the formulae and follow through some often complex logic often shows up where illogical errors have been made.

Recalling the file

As far as recalling (loading) a file is concerned (◇ FL), again the main options available are the same as we used when considering PipeDream's word processing features. A file can be loaded in its entirety and merged into another document. With spreadsheets, however, a third option in the file loading page can be useful. Thus, just as it was possible to save a selected subset of the spreadsheet, so is it possible to specify a range of rows that should be loaded.

Maybe you have a very large spreadsheet and you only want the first 10 rows loaded. In this case answer Y(es) to the option to 'limit to range of rows' and then supply the range, with cell references separated by a space. This option can be particularly useful when you want to merge a spreadsheet into a word processed document – often it is not necessary to merge the complete spreadsheet, just a range of rows will do to make the point. And even these can then be edited as normal once they have been merged into the document.

Finally, the 'plain text' option appears again. In this case, specifying Y(es) will cause TAB characters within the file to be printed onscreen as a series of spaces. To compare the effects of plain and normal text, save a sample spreadsheet as plain text and then load it first as normal text and then as plain text. When the plain text option is *not* set, the spreadsheet appears in a confused state, with highlighted Is at the end of each line (these are the TAB characters). When it is loaded as plain text, however, the complete picture is there to see.

Summary

PipeDream was designed to be a spreadsheet application, and it performs its task well. It supplies a wide range of mathematical, statistical and logical functions that can be used, both independently and combined, to generate very complex and powerful spreadsheet models. As with the word processing aspects of this application, a full range of display, editing and file management features is also available.

The next chapter will consider ways of expanding the Z88's application in the area of forecasting – this time in terms of data and time management.

5

Managing your life

If you talk to anyone who is vaguely knowledgeable about computers, especially computers for the office, and ask about the main applications of these machines they will probably mention three: word processing, spreadsheets and databases. It is the last of these, databases and data management, that this chapter will consider.

Strictly speaking a database is just as its name suggests – a base of data. So this book is a database, as is a telephone directory or the Encyclopaedia Britannica. But when most people talk about a *computerised* database they mean a program that lets you manipulate data of various kinds. With a database program you should be able to search through the information stored on the computer to extract relevant information, sort it into various kinds of order, and maybe even create new sets of data from the old.

Although the Z88 lacks a formal database program of this kind, you can still use the data management aspects of the machine to do most of the operations that a conventional kind of database does. In this chapter we will consider two ways of developing a database on the Z88: using PipeDream to build up a formal set of information, and using the Diary option to develop a personalised database for time and other kinds of management.

A PipeDream Database

To understand how the Z88's word processing capacities can create a database, consider a formal database such as the telephone directory. We are able to use it efficiently because we know exactly how information is stored in it; it helps us to know where to begin searching for the name we want and thus how to find the telephone number.

The formal nature of this kind of database is generated by the various 'fields' in it. Indeed, it is the arrangement of these fields that defines the database structure, just as the arrangement of formulae in the spreadsheet's cells defined the spreadsheet model.

So, most telephone directory databases probably comprise a field that has the surname, and then the initials. Next comes one that contains the first line of the individual's address, then the exchange, and finally the number. Knowing this structure, it is relatively simple to look up your friend's telephone number.

Now imagine these five fields arranged across a page, with information about different individuals in separate rows – just like the telephone directory. It doesn't take a giant leap in thinking to realise how PipeDream can be used to generate a database structure: the fields are simply consecutive columns in the spreadsheet. These columns can be made as wide or as narrow as you like, to accommodate different field widths, for example. So an address field may need 20-30 character spaces, say, while the initials field may only require four.

Developing the Database

To develop your PipeDream database you first need to determine which fields you require, their order and their widths (the maximum number of characters they are likely to contain). For the telephone directory, for example, we might require:

Column	**Field**	**Width**
A	Surname	15
B	Initials	6
C	Address line	30
D	Exchange	15
E	Number	7

Set PipeDream into its word processing mode (□P) and enter these various field names into row 1, with one name per column. Remember to TAB to each column in succession and to alter the width of each column as appropriate (◇ W). Of course, you can also use ◇ W *after* you have entered information into the database. So don't worry too much about selecting accurate field widths at this stage.

As well as expanding the field widths to fit everything in, it might also be sensible to fix this row, so that when the display scrolls the headings remain visible. So, with the cursor still on the first row, issue the command ◇ LFR.

Now you simply enter the appropriate information for each individual, taking one individual per row. Do not worry about putting everything in alphabetical order; you can get PipeDream to do that for you later.

```
PIPEDREAM                                                                              OZ
BLOCKS        ..............A . . . B . . . . . . . . . . . . . . . C . . . . . . . D . . . E . . . . . F
CURSOR     __1 Surname      Initl  Address line               Exchange      Tel no
EDIT         2
FILES        3 Jones        J K    1 The High Street          Westend       209456
LAYOUT       4 Jenkins      F W    27 The Rise                Northend      372980
OPTIONS      5 Williams     H      32 Westend Street          Southend      123455
PRINT        6 Johnson      H G J  7 Willow Grove             Eastend       210321
```

Fields in a PipeDream database

Having entered all your information you can begin to manipulate it in much the same way as a conventional database would let you do. But before doing so it is always good practice to save the file (◇ FS) – just in case you issue the wrong command and end up with a scrambled database.

Sorting

To start with you could sort the entries into ascending or descending order using PipeDream's sort command (◇ BSO).

First mark the block of entries you wish to sort by issuing the ◇ Z command. Take the cursor to row 2 of column A (the first entry) and press ◇ Z. Then take it either to the end of your entries (◇ ↓) or to the end of the entries you want to sort. Thence to the *last* column of the final entry to be sorted (◇ CLC), and press ◇ Z again.

It is important to ensure that the *whole* of each entry is highlighted as a block – not just the column (field) you want to sort on. If you do not highlight the complete entry like this you will end up with a rather jumbled database.

Now simply issue the sort command (◇ BSO) and tell PipeDream on which field (column) you wish to sort. For example, if you want a telephone directory in which all surnames are arranged alphabetically, sort on column A. If you want all the telephone exchanges to appear together, then sort on column C.

The second question in the menu asks whether you want to sort in reverse order (Z-A or 9-0). This is fairly obvious.

The final question, concerning updating references, refers to sorting a spreadsheet. If you were to change the default answer to Y(es), then PipeDream would go through all the active cells and check to see whether any of the cells that are being rearranged are also referred to by formulae in other cells. If so, then these references are changed accordingly. Naturally, this can be a time-consuming process so do not do it unless you have some spreadsheet functions within your database – as we will discuss later.

Having sorted your database on one field, of course, there is nothing to stop you from performing the same process again using another column as the sorting key. For example, you may first sort according to surname. Then, by blocking all individuals with the same surname, you could next sort according to the exchange, and so on.

Searching

Databases are excellent for searching through seemingly endless lists of information to find the one entry you need. Before they were invented this was usually done, inefficiently, using small index cards or some such system. Naturally, with PipeDream's efficient search – and replace – facilities you will soon be able to find the entry you require.

Simply issue the ◊ BSE command and enter the string (name, part of an address, and so on) that you require. To make the search more efficient it is useful to specify the column (field) you want to search through, though this is not entirely necessary.

When a match has been found, you can continue the search for others using the ◊ BNM (Block Next Match) command.

Remember, too, that you can use any of PipeDream's wildcards while searching. For example, the pair of characters ^# represents 'any set of characters, while ^? represents 'any single character'. So, if you cannot remember your friend's house number, "^# The High Street" should find it for you.

Conditional Searches

Although you cannot do conditional searches onscreen, as it were, you can certainly use PipeDream's selection criteria to choose which entries to print. For example, you may want to print all individuals whose telephone exchange is in Birmingham, or all those whose exchange is in Birmingham but whose surname is *not* Jones.

To print the database, as with a word processed document issue the command ◊ PO (Print Out). Leaving the 'print only range of columns' option at its default 'No' will mean that all columns in each row will be printed.

The second question in the list 'select rows to print' is the one that will enable you to choose your output. Change the default to Y(es) and then enter the selection

```
PIPEDREAM
BLOCKS        ....   Print only range of columns     No                      D . . . E . . . . . F      OZ
CURSOR       _1 Sur  Select rows to print            Yes C1="Westend"         Tel no
EDIT          2      Wait between pages              No
FILES         3 Jon                                                           209456
LAYOUT        4 Jen                                                           372980
OPTIONS       5 Wil                                                           123455
PRINT         6 Joh                                                           210321
```

Doing a conditional search

criterion as you wish, using the conditional operators & (AND), | (OR) and ! (NOT).

So `C1 = "Birmingham"` will print all entries whose exchange is Birmingham.

`C1= "Birmingham" ! A1 = "Jones"` will print all the Birmingham exchanges other than for the Jones's.

As with both word processed documents and spreadsheet formulations, the final option in the print menu lets you wait between pages to enable you to insert single sheets into the printer.

Combining Database, Spreadsheet and Word Processor

So far we have found a use for PipeDream that emulates the functions of many of the database programs that are available on the market today. With some more thought, however, we should realise that a spreadsheet is little more than a numerical database, and that the two functions could be combined to considerable effect.

For example, say you have a database of members in your club. Taking financial information such as the subscription rate or the cost of posting continual reminders to attend, you could generate a pretty sophisticated data management system. Just combine the ideas of database fields and spreadsheet cells within the same 'document'.

Say we generated the standard club membership database of:

Column (cell)	Field	Width
A1	Surname	15
B1	Initials	7
C1	1st address line	25
D1	2nd address line	15
E1	3rd address line	10
F1	Membership category	3
G1	Subscription	5

You could use the spreadsheet conditional expressions to make life a little easier. For example, say you have two membership categories, family and single, and each has a different subscription rate of 20 and 10 respectively. By inserting the following formula into cell G2 (the first subscription cell) and replicating it down the page, you will not have to enter the subscription information at all. PipeDream will do it for you:

```
IF(F2="F",20,IF(F2="S",10,"ERR"))
```

This reads as: 'if the value in cell F2 is "F" then enter 20; otherwise if the value in F2 is "S" then enter 10; otherwise enter "ERR".' The final 'ERR' is useful to 'flag' the fact that a membership category other than F or S has been entered.

And you could go one step further. Adding the function SUM(G2G30) at the bottom of the database list (assuming your list extends to row 30), say, will automatically add up your subscription income for you.

Finally, of course, there is nothing to stop you from adding words around the database/spreadsheet combination. Simply take the cursor back to column A, set the margin to an appropriate length and type away merrily. You could, for example, send a standard letter to all club members, informing them of the current membership list and asking for their new subscription. And, by using the @ref@ function, you could even incorporate into the letter the member's name, address and subscription rate.

The possibilities are endless.

Dates and Diaries

As well as this standard kind of database, we often carry around with us another, more free-text, database called a diary. This is a base of data that is constantly updated and which is organised mainly in terms of dates and times, rather than specialised fields.

The Z88's Diary function is a powerful system that lets you jump to specific dates almost instantaneously, select particular kinds of diary entries – say all those that relate to meetings with your boss – and print out various diary selections. You can even have a number of different diaries filed away at the same time. For example, at different times you could load your social diary or your work diary or even your colleague's diary.

Accessing the Diary

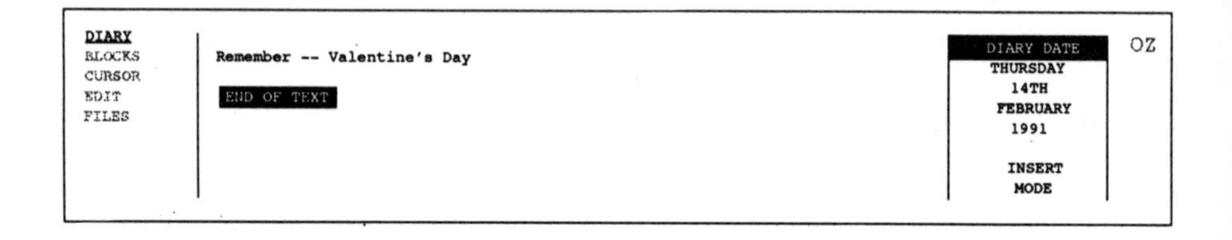

The Diary page (□D)

Like PipeDream, you can enter the Diary function from any activity – this time by issuing the □D command. An empty diary page greets you, opened at the current date. The panel to the right provides details of the day, and also indicates when the batteries are getting low. In addition, as you will notice, the full eight screen lines are available for your diary details.

You can now simply enter information as you would a normal diary, using almost all of the PipeDream commands to edit it if necessary.

Since there is no limit to the number of lines you can enter into a diary page (other than memory limitations, of course) you might as well use one entry per line. The command ◇EMF (Edit Memory free) indicates the amount of free memory that is available to you within the Z88.

Within the Diary option the TAB key operates as a normal 'tab' key, every eight steps across the page. This is useful for helping with the page layout – you could enter the meeting time in one column, for example, the person with whom you are meeting in another, and so on.

Moving around

One of the most useful features of your own pocket diary is that it allows you to flick quickly to a particular date and to see what entries have been made for that date. To be equally effective a computer-based diary must have such speedy movements incorporated into it – and the Z88 has.

By always 'opening' at today's date, the Z88 Diary makes life much easier from the beginning. However, a few simple page turning commands let you move even more quickly through the diary. Thus, pressing the □ key at the bottom of the keyboard along with the up and down arrow keys turns the diary pages over one day at a time – the up-arrow going backwards in time and the down arrow looking into the future.

Flicking through a series of empty pages, however, can be both a time consuming and a time wasting exercise. So the Z88 has another set of options that allow you to move backwards or forwards by *active* days – these are days that have some information contained in them. Again, you use the □ key, but this time you use it with the left (previous active days) and right (next active days) arrows.

Wherever you end up in the diary, you can instantaneously get back to today's date by issuing the command ◇ CT (Cursor Today). And, as with PipeDream, you can mark a specific diary entry and return to it using the ◇ CSP (Cursor Save Position) and ◇ CRP (Cursor Return to Position) commands.

Finally, you can leap to the beginning of your diary (at least to the first active day) by issuing the command ◇ CFAD (Cursor First Active Day); go to the end (the start of the last active day) by issuing the command ◇ CLAD (Cursor Last Active day).

Using the Calendar

As well as providing these cursor speed movements, the Z88's Diary is also intimately related to its calendar, more about which in the next chapter. However, it

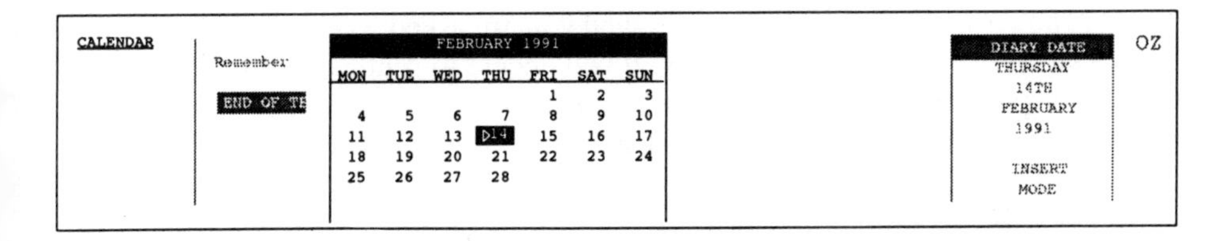

Active days on the calendar

is important to point out here that you can move quickly between diary dates – and even years – simply by entering the calendar application (□C) *from within the diary* and switching to the relevant date on the calendar.

The next chapter will show how to do this in detail. As soon as you have found the date you want, press ESC and the Z88 will return to its Diary mode – with the page open at the right date. (As the next chapter will show, if you press the ENTER key at this point you will be prompted for a date for the calendar prompt to move to.)

While in the calendar, notice that some dates may have a triangular marker next to them. These are the active days; days which contain diary entries.

Blocking off the Diary

Most of the block operations we encountered in PipeDream work in similar ways within the Diary. Thus, by marking a relevant block you can copy or move it to another part of the diary – on the same day or another day – using the ◇BC or ◇BM commands. You can also delete it using ◇BD.

However, there is an interesting difference between the precise ways in which these operations work in the Diary and in PipeDream. Thus, if you issue one of the block commands *while the cursor is in the highlighted area*, the Z88 refuses to carry out the instructions and issues an annoying bleep with the error message 'overtypes' displayed in the side panel.

Only when you take the cursor outside the highlighted area will the operations work as they should do – which was not the case with PipeDream, of course.

Listing the Diary

The Diary has an additional command over PipeDream, which lists the diary either to the screen or to a printer.

When you issue the ◇BL (Block List) command, you are given the option to list the diary to the screen and/or to the printer, and you are asked whether you want to list the whole diary or just a marked block. If you decide to send your list to the screen the Z88 displays the diary eight lines at a time and stops; press the Space bar to see the next eight lines. When it is listed to the printer, however, the print out is continuous.

```
Thursday 14th February 1991
Remember Valentine's Day

09.00    Meet with Jim in his office
12.00    Lunch with Fred


Friday 15th February
08.30    Breakfast meeting with the gang
10.25    Taxi for airport
14.00    Take off - flight BA 1563
15.30    Arrive Frankfurt
18.00    Meet with Herr Steiner
```

Listing the Diary to a printer

Searching and Replacing

The Z88's Diary search feature is similar to PipeDream's, except that it also provides a chance to print a list of the entries to the screen and/or to the printer. The list that is created is organised in terms of diary entry days.

As with PipeDream, the Diary's search facility is activated by the ◇ BSE command. You simply enter the string of characters that you want to search for, indicating if necessary whether you want upper or lower case to be equated (remember, the default is 'yes', so that searching for 'the' will find 'The' and 'THE', for example). By

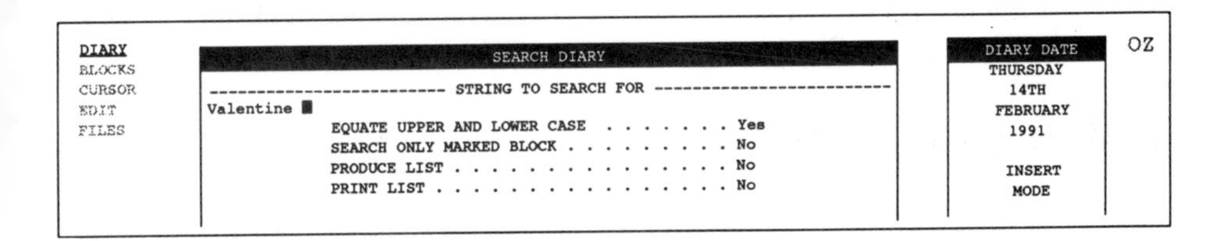

A Diary list after searching

changing the second option in the menu, you can also search only through a marked block, rather than through the diary as a whole.

Unfortunately the Diary does not allow wildcards when stipulating the string to be searched for.

Diary lists

The final two options in this list refer to 'lists'. If either of these are left at their default 'No' value, then the Diary's search routine works in much the same way as PipeDream's – it moves the cursor to the first occurrence of the string that you have specified. This means that you will see the surrounding lines of text on the diary page.

Again, as with PipeDream subsequent occurrences of the string can then be found using the ◇BNM command. The Diary, however, has an additional command (◇BPM – Block Previous Match) which allows you to search backwards through the diary.

Producing a 'list' on the other hand, displays all the lines of text in which the target string is found. The advantages of this are two-fold: firstly, you do not have to keep issuing the ◇BNM command to find subsequent occurrences of the string in your diary. As the function's name suggest, the Diary produces a list for you.

Secondly, all the occurrences of the string are grouped together under each day's heading. So you could quickly produce a list of all meetings with the MD, for example. At a glance you will be able to see when you are to meet her and at what time.

To take full advantage of this feature, of course, you will need to ensure that each diary entry only takes up one line, and that the information is laid out neatly in columns.

Replacing characters with others, using the ◇BRP command, works in exactly the same way as it does with PipeDream.

Deleting the Diary

Since your diary can start on Tuesday 1st December 4713 BC and run until 31st December 18253 AD, it is clear that a considerable amount of information may be stored within the Diary's memory. For this reason it is often useful to do some 'housekeeping' and clear out diary entries for all dates up to the current one, having first printed out the relevant days before deleting them, of course (◇BL).

To do this, the easiest technique is to move to the first active day (◇ CFAD) and mark the block beginning (◇ Z). Then move to the current day (◇ CT). Move back by a day (□ ↑), go to the end of that day's entry (◇ ↓) and mark the end of the block (◇ Z). Now return to the current day (◇ CT) and delete the marked block (◇ BD).

Deleting the *whole* diary is a similar process. Go to the first active day (◇ CFAD) and mark the block beginning. Leap to the last active day (◇ CLAD), take the cursor to the end of that page in the diary (◇ ↓), and mark the end of the block. Press the ENTER key to take the cursor off the end of the block and issue the ◇ BD command.

Diary Filing

Saving diaries

If you ever issue the ◇ PURGE command from the Index page, you will remove any suspended diary you may have in memory. So it is always a good idea to save diaries on a regular basis. This is easily done using the ◇ FS command, and you can save the whole diary, or just a marked block. When you carry out this operation the Z88 simply asks you for a filename under which the diary should be stored.

Loading files and diaries

The complementary operation, to load files into the diary (◇ FL), has two modes of operation. First, you can load an ordinary text or spreadsheet file into the currently displayed date. To do so, however, you should remember to save the PipeDream file as plain text – otherwise you will also load all manner of spurious control characters into your diary.

Second, you can use this command to load a different diary into the diary module – perhaps your social diary or the meetings diary.

If you leave the option 'start loading at diary date' at its default 'No' state, the diary entries will be made according to the days under which they were saved – on whatever date your diary is currently opened. So, even if your diary is open at the page for 1st January 1990, for example, information about meetings on 31st December 1989 will still be loaded back into that day.

By changing the option to Y(es), however, you can force the new diary to be loaded at the date at which your diary is currently opened. Say the first entry in the diary that was saved was 1st January 1989, and the second entry was for 2nd January 1989. By changing the 'start loading data at diary date' option to 'Yes', and by making 10th

February 1990 the current diary date, say, then the new diary will have what was 1st January 1989's information loaded into 10th February 1990 and what was 2nd January 1989's information loaded into 11th February 1990:

	Old diary	**New diary**
Base date:	1st January 1989	10th February 1990
Base + 0:	1st January 1989	10th February 1990
Base + 1:	2nd January 1989	11th February 1990

Although this facility may seem rather useless at first sight, it can be extremely useful for transferring repeating information from one month to another, say, or from one year to the next. A social diary full of birthdays, for example, could easily be generated by saving one year's diary of birthdays as a file and loading it into subsequent years.

One feature to note when loading diaries is that the new diary does *not* overlay the old one – information is appended to the end of each page in turn. To begin with a completely clean diary you will need to ◇KILL the suspended diary file from the Index page. But do remember to save it first.

Diary to PipeDream and Back Again

By saving and loading files it is relatively easy to integrate the Diary and PipeDream, and thus help to save time. For example, you can create a diary file within PipeDream simply by beginning each day's entry with the date, preceded by a percent (%) sign. When this file is then loaded into the diary the information will be put into the relevant days.

So, when it is loaded into the Diary, a file that contains the following information will create the relevant diary for you:

```
%1/1/1989
10.30        Meet with Mr Jones
11.30        Visit the dentist
%3/1/1989
10.30        Coffee with Fred
%4/1/1989
09.00        Management team meeting
10.00        See the MD
```

Note that the way in which you specify the date should conform to the date type setting in the screen options page (◇S). You can choose between a European (day/month/year) format and an American one (month/day/year).

Remember that you *must* save this PipeDream file as 'plain text'. Now, when you load the file into the Diary module, assuming the 'start loading data at diary date' option is set to its default 'No' the information will be added to the relevant day's pages: 1st January 1989, 3rd January 1989 and 4th January 1989.

If you set the 'start loading data at diary date' option to 'Yes', with the current page open at 10th December 1990 say, then the three day's information will be added to 10th December 1989 (the current diary date), 12th December 1989 (two days on), and 13th December 1989 (three days on from the diary date).

Loading a diary into PipeDream is simply the opposite of this process. In this case save the diary using the ◇ FS command and load it into PipeDream in the normal way. You will find that the right margin will have to be extended and the percent signs also appear before each date. These can be easily removed, of course, using the search and replace function (◇ BRP) (search for % and replace with nothing) and changing the 'Ask for confirmation' option to N(o).

Summary

This chapter has considered data management on the Z88. Simply by using some of the standard word processing and spreadsheet features available within PipeDream it is possible to generate a valuable database system that rivals commercial ones. with this system you can sort, search, replace and select database items at will.

The Z88's Diary application takes this idea a little further. It provides an efficient organiser-based diary that allows you to select entries and sort them for easy time management.

The next chapter will discuss the additional 'popdown' facilities available on the Z88 that will help organise and analyse information that's common to all the applications so far.

6

Popdowns

As well as the standard office-user applications based around the computerised word processor, spreadsheet and database, the Z88 also offers three 'popdown' facilities that can be activated at any time, and whatever you happen to be doing at the time. They are called popdowns because that is how they operate – when you call them they pop down over your main operation and let you do some ancillary task. Then, when you press the ESC key, they pop back again into obscurity.

These three popdown applications are the clock and alarm, the calendar (which, as we have already seen, interacts with the Diary), and the calculator. As you activate any of these applications, each one overlays the other on the screen.

The Clock and Alarm

Although these are two separate operations, their functions are obviously interrelated.

Clock

The simplest of the popdowns, the clock, is called up either from the Index or by pressing □T (Time) at any point in your Z88 work. A panel appears just right of centre of the screen, giving details of the current date and time.

To change either the date or the time, highlight the 'set' option by pressing the right arrow once. When you press the ENTER key the panel changes to let you edit the current settings. Remember, the date can either be displayed in European format (day, month, year) or American format (month, day, year). You can switch between

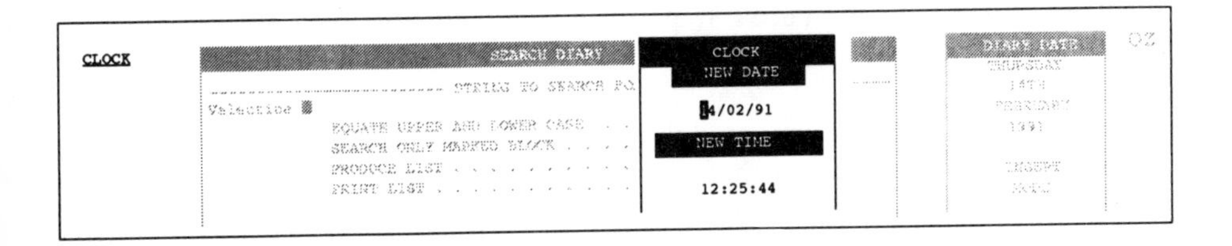

Setting the clock

the two formats from the screen options menu (□S). Take the cursor to the bottom option in the second column and simply press E(uropean) or A(merican) as you wish.

Having altered the date and/or the time, press the ENTER key to return to the clock panel; the new date and time will be displayed. It is important to note, however, that the new settings do not come into operation until you press the ENTER key. So, if you do want to set your Z88's clock to coincide with the strikes of Big Ben you make the change at any time up till the right moment. Then press ENTER on the first strike.

Pressing ESC returns you to your original application.

Alarm

Whereas the clock is just a simple version of the digital watch that you are probably wearing on your wrist, the same analogy cannot be made as far as the alarm is concerned. This feature is far more flexible than the conventional alarm clock next to your bedside. You can get the Z88's alarm to display a message reminding you

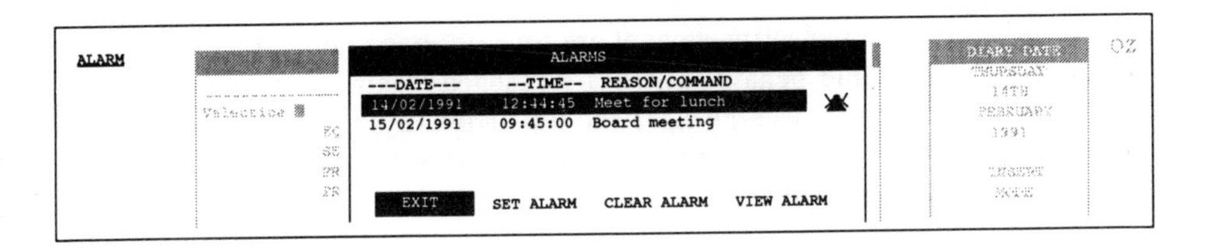

The Alarm clock (□A)

why the alarm has been set, you can make it repeat its alarm at predetermined intervals, and you can even use it to perform some automatic operations like calling a friend at 2.00 a.m., or whatever.

When you call up the alarm module using the command □A (Alarm), you are presented with a wide panel that spans almost half the Z88's screen. Across the bottom are four options, while the main part of the panel is left blank but will display the various alarms you have set. The number of alarms you set, and the length of time for which they can be set, is under your control. Remember, the Z88's calendar extends to 31st December 18253!

To set an alarm simply use the right arrow key to move the cursor over to the second option ('set alarm'); notice that if no alarms are displayed in the panel the Z88 sensibly does not allow you to go beyond this option. Then press ENTER to display the alarm editing panel.

The screen that greets you here looks very similar to the editing panel for the clock, with just a few extra features. The date and time shown are the settings which were current when the 'alarm set' action was called. It is a simple matter to change them to the relevant settings for your alarm. Use the left and right arrow keys to move to different parts of each setting; press the up and down arrow keys to switch from one setting to another.

It may be that all you want is for the bleeper to sound at a particular date and time, in which case after setting the alarm simply press ENTER and the new alarm will show itself in the panel.

Alarm functions

If you want to use some of the alarm's other features, however, *do not* press ENTER. Instead, press the down arrow key to move into an area just right of the time setting. Here you can enter your message to remind you why you set the alarm. For example, messages like 'Time to see the MD', or 'Get up in the morning' can be rather more helpful than simply the sound of an alarm ringing.

Along the bottom of the settings panel are four options that deal with the way in which the alarm should behave. These are reached, again, by pressing the down arrow key – but then you use the right and left arrow keys to switch between them. And, just to confuse you, the alternative settings within each of the four options are varied by using the up and down arrow keys.

Options

The first option lets you decide whether you want the message to be displayed along with the bell, or just the message on its own. You can switch between having the bell on or off by using the up or down arrow keys.

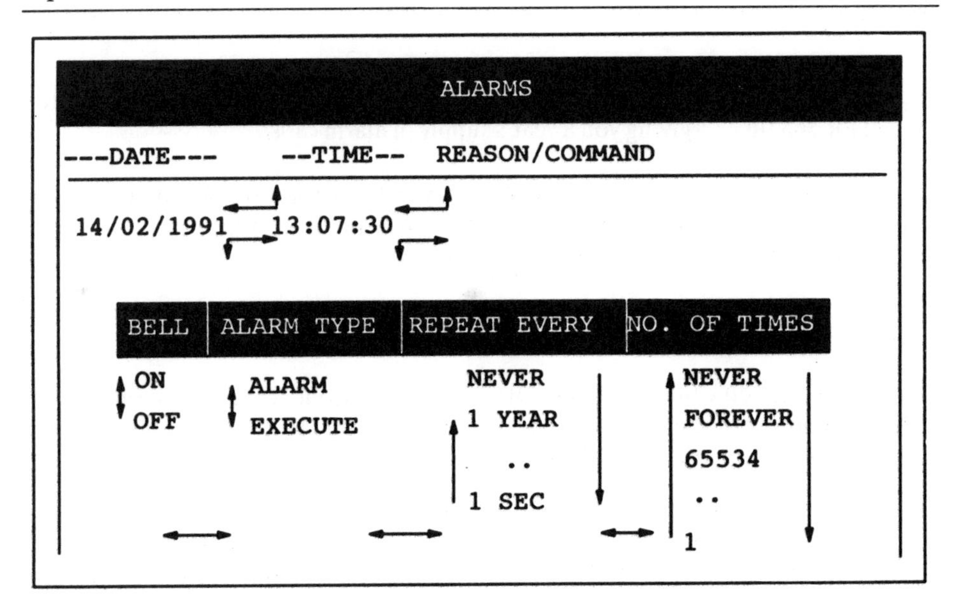

Moving around the alarm functions

Next is an option that enquires how you want the Z88 to react when the alarm date and time are reached. You can either have it behave as an alarm, with or without the bell as you have just set it, or you can ask the machine to execute a previously written program that has been filed in a particular format called a CLI file. More will be said about CLI files in Chapter 9 but, again, you can switch between the two alternatives using the up and down arrow keys.

If you are using the alarm to execute a CLI file, the name of the CLI file should be inserted into the 'reason/command' area to the right of the time on the top row.

Thirdly, you can ask to have the alarm repeated at specific intervals. Use the *down* arrow to switch between never (no repeats, which is the default value) and every second, minute, hour, day, week, month or year.

Having chosen your unit of repetition (hours, days, or whatever), the *up* arrow alters the value of that unit. So, you could repeat every two days, for example, or five years. Having switched into this part of the repetition setting you will find that both the up and the down arrow keys will change this aspect of the setting.

Finally, the 'number of times' setting lets you choose how often this alarm repetition should occur, ranging from never (the default value) to forever. Between these two extremes you can use the up and down arrows to vary the number of times the action will occur in single steps between 1 and 655434 times.

So, you might set the wake-up alarm to repeat itself daily (that is, a repetition rate of 1 day) for 365 times – giving you a year's supply of alarm calls.

Finally, just to confuse you again, although you had to use the down arrow to get from the 'reason/command' setting to the 'alarm on/off' setting, to return in the other direction you need to use the left arrow key.

Having made all of the settings as appropriate, press ENTER and the alarm will appear in the display panel.

Unfortunately you cannot edit an alarm once it has been set. You can only clear it (the third option at the bottom of the display panel) and then reset it. If you want to clear a repeating alarm, press 'Clear' twice.

As its name suggests, the fourth option (View Alarm) lets you see the full range of settings that you have made for a specific alarm. If one or more of the repetitions have been used, the 'number of times' setting will be updated to show the number of repetitions remaining.

For both the Clear and View alarm options, you first need to use the up and down arrow keys to take the highlighting cursor to the alarm setting that you want to take action on. Then you use the left and right arrow keys either to clear it or view it.

Setting the alarm

Having set one or more alarms you can continue to use the Z88 in whatever way you wish. But it is important to realise that the alarm is not properly set until you leave the Alarm module by pressing the ESC key. If you simply turn the Z88 'off' using the two shift keys, nothing will happen until you turn it on again. Then the alarm will ring.

When the alarm time is reached the Z88 utters seven short piercing bleeps and flashes a small alarm bell icon in the top right hand corner of the screen. Remember, though, that the whole sound circuit can be turned off from the screen display options (□S) – so do not turn off this setting and expect the alarm to sound!

After the alarm has sounded, if you press □A the flashing bell icon will also be displayed next to the relevant alarm – just to remind you which one is ringing.

All this still happens if the Z88 is turned 'off' when the alarm rings. In this case, however, the flashing word 'LOCKOUT' appears above the flashing bell icon at the top right hand corner of the screen. Although the screen will also appear to be turned on, showing your activities as they were when you switched the machine off, the keyboard will be totally 'locked out', so that no key works.

This is done to ensure that the machine will not be accidentally operated. You can restore the keyboard to its rightful situation by switching the machine off and on again (press the two SHIFT keys together, twice).

The Calendar

We have already come across the Z88's calendar function when dealing with its Diary. Pressing □C (Calendar) produces a neat display of the days in the current month, with the current day highlighted. If you enter the calendar via □C, rather than from the Diary option (□D), however, you will *not* find the diary's active days highlighted with a small triangle to the left of them.

FEBRUARY 1991

MON	TUE	WED	THU	FRI	SAT	SUN
				1	2	3
4	5	6	7	8	9	10
11	12	13	14	15	16	17
18	19	20	21	22	23	24
25	26	27	28			

The Calendar (□C)

Moving through the calendar

You move through the calendar either by using the up and down arrow keys – on their own or with the SHIFT or ◇ keys – or by going directly to a specific date.

Day-to-day movement through the calendar is performed using the left and right arrow keys. To go from week to week press the up and down arrow keys; for month to month press the SHIFT key with either the up arrow (backwards by a month at a time) or down arrow (forwards in time) keys. The same arrow keys when used with the ◇ key speed backwards and forwards a year at a time.

To leap directly to a specific date, simply press ENTER. The Z88 will ask you to enter the date that you want to go to (remember the European or American format),

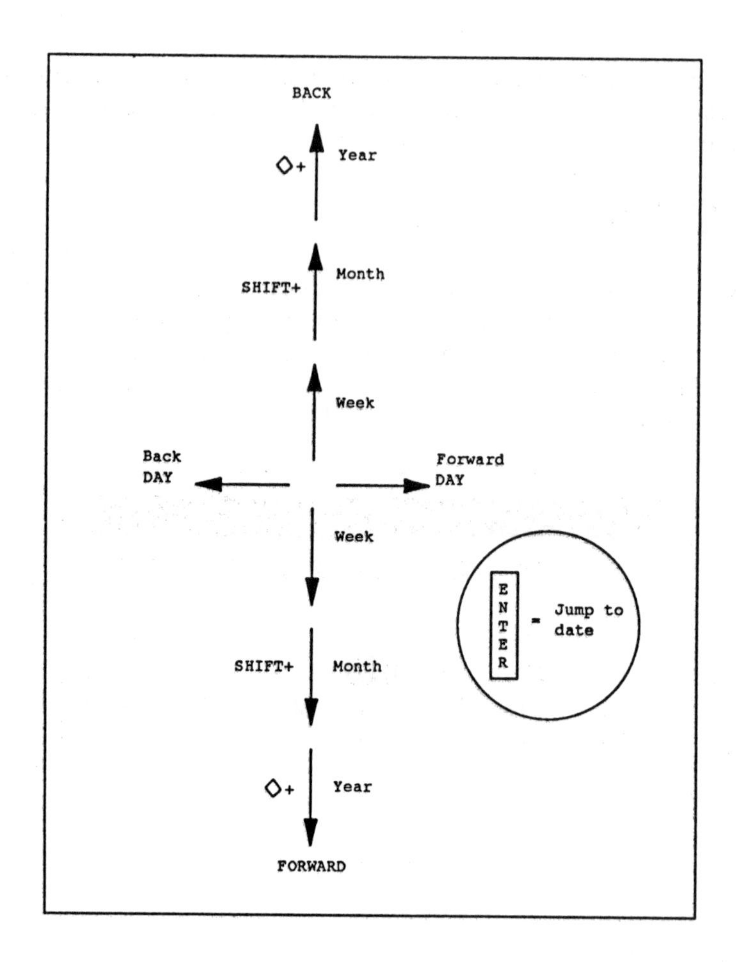

Moving around the calendar

and ENTER again will take you here. If it is easier, you can enter the date in numbers and words if you wish. For example, 15 Dec 1947 or Dec 15 1947 (in this case it does not matter whether you have set the date format to be European or American). If you add the letters 'bc' after the year part of the date, the Z88's calendar goes back beyond the first Christmas.

One word of warning about interpreting some of the earlier dates: the days and dates shown are consistent with the New style (Gregorian) calendar. So, they will not tally with historical dates before 14th September 1752 (for Britain) or 14th October 1582 (for continental Europe). Nevertheless, the standard rules for leap years is included in the calendar generating program:

Every year is a normal year (365 days), except
every 4th year which is a leap year, except
every 100th year which is a normal year, except
every 400th year which is a leap year, except
every 3200th year which is a normal year, except
every 80000th year which is a normal year.

The Calculator

The Z88's calculator (which is activated by pressing □R) comes equipped with the four standard arithmetical functions (+,-,*, and /), a percent key, 10 memories, and a very handy imperial to metric converter. Each of these operations, as well as entering the numbers themselves, can be performed either by using the arrow keys to take the cursor to the appropriate square on the calculator display, or by pressing one of the letters of the function or the number itself.

For example, pressing 'S' will activate the memory storage routine (and highlight the 'StoM' square); pressing '5' will enter the number 5 in the calculation box. If you use this shortcut option the calculator always helpfully moves the cursor to the appropriate part of the display and highlights the relevant box.

Using the calculator for the normal arithmetic functions should be fairly straightforward. Values and operations should be entered as they are seen in a formula. For example, 5+4+9/3. To get the answer press the equals key (=), *not* the ENTER key.

The ENTER key provides a shortcut for repeating numbers. So, if you wish to enter 666, for example, just press 6 and the ENTER key twice.

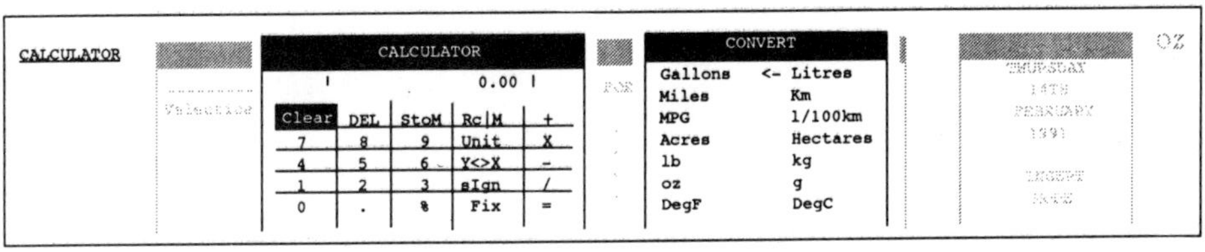

The Calculator (□R)

The DEL key cancels the operation that you have just done. So, if you enter 456 but intended to enter 466, press DEL and the display will show 45. Press it again and it shows 4 – now enter the correct 66.

To clear a calculation completely, press C(lear).

Memories

The Z88 has room for up to 10 memories, numbered 0 to 9. To save a calculation or part of one to memory press S(toM) and supply the number of the memory location that you've decided on. If you add one of the operators +, -, * or / *before* giving the memory location, then the value in the location will be added to, subtracted from, multiplied by, or divided by the new value – and the result stored back into the specified location.

So, say you have the value 5 already stored in location 1. If you then perform a calculation that leads to the answer 10 and S(toM) / (divide into) location 1, you will find the value 0.5 (5/10) has been stored.

Constants and Percents

Constants are very useful if you have to do frequent arithmetical calculations using the same values. For example, say you have a series of goods whose prices are shown net of VAT. You will need to multiply each price by the constant value of 1.15 to find the gross price.

To set the calculator into constant mode, press the operation that you want to perform twice and a 'K' will appear in the top right hand corner of the calculator panel. So, to obtain your gross prices enter 1.15 X X; then your series of net values followed by = each time:

`1.15 X X`
`4.5=` shows 5.17
`8.9=` shows 10.23

and so on.

The percentage operation works in the same way as it does on all other pocket calculators. You can obtain a specific percentage of a value, and you can determine what percentage of a number a specific value represents.

To find out what 45% of 99 is, for example, simply enter '45*99%' (you will find that the answer is 44.55). To find out what 36/78ths is as a percentage, however, enter '36/78%' (the answer is 46.15).

You can extend these simple percentage operations to consider discounts and surcharges.

For example, say you are due a 12.5% discount as a result of buying a case of wine that comes to £75.90. Enter:

```
75.9X12.5% -
```

and you'll find out how much you have to pay (£66.41).

On the other hand, you may have a 12.5% surcharge on your goods. In this case enter:

```
75.9X12.5% +
```

and you'll find out that you will have to pay a total of £85.39.

Y X

The Y X box, which is reached simply by pressing 'Y', lets you toggle between the last two values displayed on the calculator's answer panel. For example, if you had just entered the calculation 4+5+6, without having pressed =, the display will still show the final 6. Press Y, however, and you will see 9, the result of adding 4+5; press Y again and 6 will reappear.

The numbers swap between 9 and 6 because the Z88 computes each calculation as it goes along. This means that it only has to store two numbers at a time.

Sign and Fix

The Sign box (I) simply changes the sign of the value displayed from minus to plus and back again with repeated pressings. To enter a negative number, enter the value and press I; pressing I again removes the negative sign, and so on.

Fix fixes the number of decimal places shown on the screen. Press F and then a number (between 0 and 8) to show this number of decimal places. If you need to work with very large numbers (larger than the screen can accommodate, that is) the Z88 will automatically switch into scientific notation. In this case, the number that follows the E shows how many times the value before it should be multiplied by 10. So,

1.567E3	=	1537
1234.5E5	=	123450000

You can also enter very large numbers into the calculator using this scientific notation.

Imperial/metric conversions

The final function on the Z88's calculator is possibly one of the most useful for the travelling Z88 user. It performs automatic imperial/metric conversions.

To operate this function, first enter the value you that want to convert into the calculator display panel as usual. Next press U to take the cursor to the conversion panel to the right of the calculator. You then use the up and down arrows to highlight the kind of conversion you want to do: volume, distance, speed and so on. The left and right arrows change the *direction* of the conversion: imperial to metric or vice versa. When you press either the left or the right arrow the *destination* of the conversion direction becomes highlighted.

So, to convert 50 degrees Fahrenheit to degrees centigrade, first enter 50 into the calculator. Press U to take the cursor to the conversion panel and use the down arrow key to go to the bottom of the panel where the temperature conversions reside. Now ensure that the direction of the conversion is correct (press the right arrow). Finally press the ENTER key, and you will find that 50 degrees F = 10 degrees C.

Summary

The Z88's popdown facilities provide additional facilities for organising, managing, and interpreting your information. The clock and its associated alarm supply an ever-ready time function which you can use either for information (the time and date, for example, can be used in the word processor, spreadsheet and Diary applications) or for automatically activating the Z88 at predetermined times.

The calendar supplies a wide range of date functions which, when used with the Diary, allows you to go immediately to any date. Finally, the calculator provides facilities for both simple and complex computations, as well as a valuable imperial/ metric converter.

The next chapter will consider ways of printing out all the information currently inside the machine.

7

Printing it all out

The considerable power and value of the Z88, with all of its independent yet integrated features, would be worthless if you could not translate the information that appears onscreen into material that other people can read. For all the prophesies made about the complete electronic office, hard copy – generally on paper – is still the most commonly used medium for passing information from one person to another.

At this point the Z88's self-contained and almost infinite flexibility leaves us, since to produce some hard copy we need another machine to do the printing. Luckily, of course, printers abound in the current world, arriving in all shapes and sizes, and with a variety of qualities and costs.

If you have access to a printer then as long as you also possess a cable to connect your Z88 to it you can print out all of the material currently stored inside the Z88 – and more.

Printer Varieties

Before considering the Z88's printing facilities in more detail, it is appropriate to discuss the range of printers available these days. Essentially there are four kinds, and each type can have either a parallel or a serial interface (connector). The four kinds are daisy wheel, dot matrix, ink jet and laser printers.

Serial and Parallel Interfaces

Information from the computer enters the printer via its interface – a connector that is usually at the back or the side of the machine. The *kind* of interface determines how the printer treats this information as it arrives.

If your printer has a serial interface, which is usually a D-shaped connector that is composed of 25 pins in two rows, the information from the computer is expected to arrive as a sequential string of data. Although very fast data transfers can take place via serial interfaces, without specific information about how fast the string is arriving and how the characters being transmitted are arranged, the printer would not be in a position to know when one character ends and another begins. For this reason, considerable care must be taken to ensure that the transmission speed and other aspects are carefully defined before the information is sent to the printer. We shall consider how to do this later.

Parallel interfaces, on the other hand, send and receive the information in blocks – usually of eight 'bits' at a time. Since all the relevant information about each character is received by the printer at the same time, in parallel, there is no need to stipulate the transmission speed, or any of the other features so beloved of the serial interface. Although the parallel connector is also D-shaped, it is generally a tongued and grooved affair with a row of contacts above and below a horizontal groove.

Appendix 5 shows the a wiring diagram for connecting the Z88 to a serial printer.

Printer Types

Daisy wheel printers

These printers produce the characters on a page by using a wheel of spokes, at the end of each is the imprint of a separate character. To print a character the printer mechanism very quickly spins the wheel so that the relevant character is at the top, and then strikes it against the paper – with the printer ribbon in between. In this way each character is perfectly formed, exactly as with a conventional typewriter.

Although this may seem a rather cumbersome way of going about things, daisy wheel printers can be quite fast. They can print up to about 60 characters a second – although in general, the faster they print the more they cost.

The main drawback of the daisy wheel printer is that the character shapes are fixed. Although you may be able to change a daisy wheel in mid-printing, it is often a time-consuming and fiddly business. So it is unlikely that you will be able to have italic characters in the middle of a piece of text, for example, or be able to change fonts entirely. The major advantage of the three other kinds of printers is that they each supply this flexibility.

Dot matrix printers

These printers operate under the control of both some intelligent circuitry inside the printer and the computer itself. As their name suggests each character is composed of a matrix of dots, and the more dense the matrix the better the final character looks. The dots are created by the printer head which is generally made up of a vertical row of pins, each of which is 'fired' against the ribbon as the head moves over the page.

Since the firing pattern is under software control, theoretically *any* character shape can be produced – as well as pictures. Also, since there are no moving parts to worry about, other than the head moving horizontally and the pins in and out, the printing speed is considerably faster than a daisy wheel printer. Speeds of up to 200 characters per second are easily obtainable, even with very cheap dot matrix printers.

Many modern dot matrix printers offer users a trade-off between speed and quality. You can generally choose between having fast 'draft' print outs, in which you can see that the document has obviously been produced from a computer because individual dots are visible, and 'near letter quality' (NLQ). When producing documents in NLQ the printing speed is considerably reduced because each section of the character is printed twice – and sometimes more – with very small position shifts. This has the effect of joining up the dots and so masks them much more effectively.

Obviously, these printers have to receive certain commands to perform many of their printing operations (for example, to print in italic font, go to the beginning of the next page, and so on). Most of these 'print codes' now conform to a standard known as the Epson standard, named after the Japanese printer manufacturer. More will be said about this standard, and how to accommodate non-standard printers, later.

Ink jet printers

Both daisy wheel and dot matrix printers can be noisy; they work by a piece of plastic or metal constantly hitting the printer's platen. Ink jet printers, on the other hand, do not operate by impact; they work by firing a very thin jet of ink at the paper – the direction of firing is usually controlled by electrostatic charges.

Like dot matrix printers they can create all manner of different fonts (the electrostatic charge is under software control) and they are very fast. Their main drawback is the relationship between the ink and the paper (most ink jet printers need paper which can absorb the ink very quickly) and their relative scarcity.

Their silence and relative light weight, however, make ink jet printers ideal companions for the Z88.

Laser printers

At the top end of all the printer scales (cost, quality, size, and so on) are laser printers. These operate as a cross between dot matrix printers and ordinary desktop photocopiers. So, characters are formed as matrices of dots (albeit very high density ones), and the printing is done by electrostatically bonding carbon granules to the paper – like a photocopier.

Over the past year of so laser printer technology has improved considerably. As far as the Z88 user is concerned, however, their main disadvantage lies in the fact that they do not generally respond to the same, simple, commands as dot matrix or other printers; because of their almost infinite flexibility in printing facilities they require information in the form of a computer language, and special 'drivers' are needed to accommodate this. Nevertheless, some laser printers do accept information in the form of standard Epson codes, and Z88 printer drivers are available for others (particularly the HP LaserJet series of laser printers).

Parallel and Serial Connections on the Z88

The Z88's connector, on the right hand side of the machine, only works in the serial mode. This means that you can connect the Z88 directly to a *serial* printer, but not to a parallel one. To operate a parallel printer from the Z88 you will need to purchase a special serial/parallel conversion unit that translates the information being received in serial format into the parallel format that the printer understands.

To accommodate both kinds of printers Cambridge Computers have produced two different cables. The serial cable simply has a 9-pin D connector at one end that plugs into the Z88 and a 25-pin D connector at the printer end.

The parallel connector, on the other hand, has a smallish black box attached to the printer connector end of the cable. This is the serial/parallel conversion unit and in operation is totally 'transparent' to the user – you will not know it is there. For it to work properly, however, both the transmit and receive baud rates shown in the screen panel (□S) *must* be set to 9600 baud.

Serial settings

Whereas parallel printer owners may now begin to print to their heart's content, those with access to serial printers must first set the speed and other attributes of the Z88's serial port to the values that the printer expects to receive.

To do this, enter the screen based options (□S); the serial port settings are shown in the final column. Without going into too much detail about the parameters at this stage (more detail can be found in Chapter 10) you must first determine the receiving baud rate (speed) of your printer from the printer manual (you may have to switch some small switches inside the printer to set the baud rate). Then make sure that the Z88's transmitting baud rate is exactly the same. If you take the cursor to this option in the screen panel you can flick through the various baud rates available on the Z88 by pressing ◇ J.

As far as the parity and Xon/Xoff settings are concerned, you can probably leave them as they are for the moment. However, if you find that your serial printer does not receive the information properly (maybe it misses characters periodically) then you should experiment with these settings. Again, ◇ J helps you flip through the possibilities.

Echoing to the Printer

Although it is possible to print information directly to the printer using some of the application's commands like ◇ PO in PipeDream or ◇ BL in the Diary, sometimes you may want to have a direct copy of everything that appears on the screen – as and when it appears. For example, you may be connected to another computer via the Z88's terminal utility (see Chapter 10) and wish to have a 'hard copy' of all the information that arrives down the telephone line.

The process by which you send information both to the computer's screen and to the printer is known as 'echoing' to the printer. It is very easy to accomplish – simply press the three keys □, + and P in succession. For the plus key you do not have to press SHIFT and the +/= key to get '+'; just press the +/= key – that will be enough.

When you invoke this sequence of commands the letters CLI appear at the far right hand side of the screen. This shows that a small, 'internal', program is being activated called a Command Line Interpreter (more about which in Chapter 9). Now, whatever is sent to the screen, say from a file or incoming from another program, will be printed at the printer.

To conclude the echoing process, press the 3-key sequence:

□-P

A word of warning about using the □+P operation, however. If you do so without having a printer attached to your Z88 you may find that the computer 'hangs' on you. It expects to be able to send information to the non-existent printer. If this happens, press the SHIFT and ESC keys together to abort the CLI process.

Interestingly, the sequences □+P and □-P are not the only ways of 'redirecting' information to the printer – as we shall see later.

Directory listing

One very useful function of this procedure is to obtain a listing of all the files in your current directory.

To do so, first switch into the Filer panel (□F) and ask to 'catalogue files' (◇ CF). Next turn on the echoing process (□+P) and simply press the ENTER key when the request for a 'name' appears. Information about all of the files in your directory will be printed to both the screen and your printer. Finally, round off the process with □-P to remove the CLI message on the screen.

The Printer Editor

Whenever you are in an application like PipeDream and send information to the printer, before letting it out of the serial socket on the right hand edge of the machine the Z88 actually passes the data through a kind of translator.

As its name suggests, this piece of software translates some of the PipeDream commands in your document into codes that your printer can understand. For example, it has to translate the Highlight 1 (underline) instruction into the codes which your printer uses to turn on its underlining activities. Then, the next time it encounters the highlight code as your document passes through the translator, the appropriate instructions to turn *off* the printer's underlining function will be substituted.

As with most aspects of the Z88 the full translation facility can operate from default instructions. In this case the default translation codes are those necessary to operate an Epson or Epson-compatible printer (the most common form of dot matrix printer these days). If you have access to this kind of printer, therefore, it is unlikely that you will need to worry about the printer translator.

However, as with most of the Z88's features, you can also alter the translation system to suit your own printer and maybe even application.

To do this you enter the Printer Editor option from the Index page, or press □E from any current activity. This takes you into a 2-page group of options that lets you change almost any aspect of the printer code translations that you want. You can even translate specific characters to print others – say to print an 'x' wherever the document contains a 'y'.

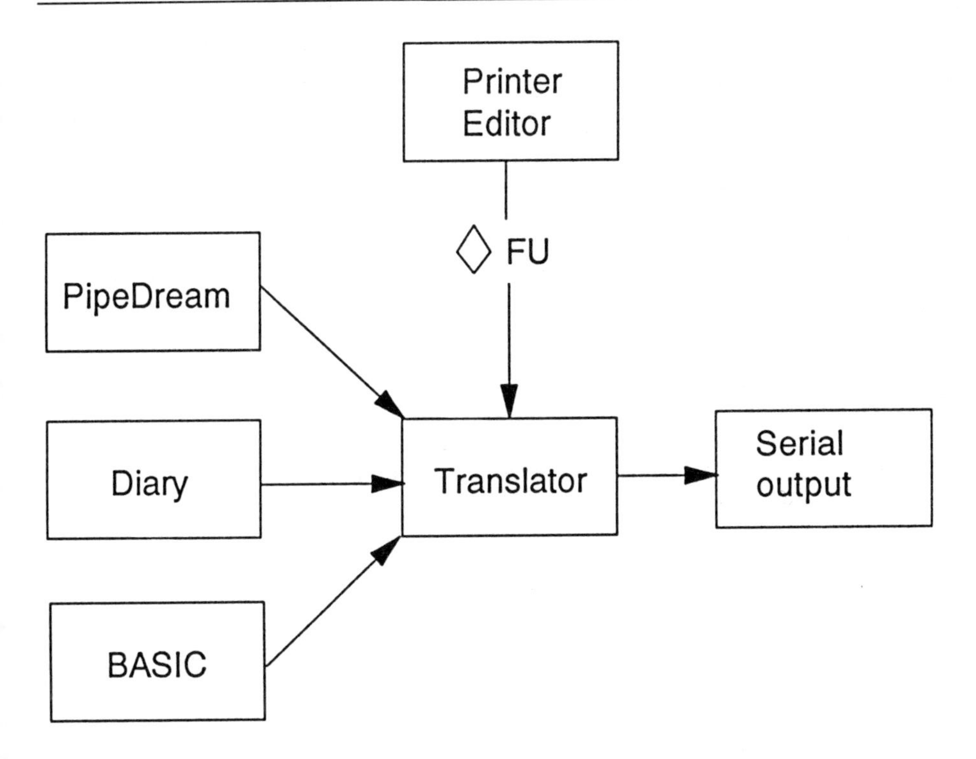

Using the Printer Editor (□E)

More usefully, this facility can be used to print some of your printer's special characters. For example, say you have produced a document that contains passages in French. As long as you use unique characters in your document for each accented French character – say % for á, $ for ç, and so on – you could get the printer translator to print your document correctly each time it encounters one of these special characters.

Printer Control Codes

To be able to use this Printer Editor properly, you need to have access to your printer's manual and some rudimentary understanding of the meanings of its control codes.

If you have a dot matrix or ink jet type of printer, a quick flick through the printer manual will demonstrate the wide variety of printing effects available. As well as the standard bolding and underlining, it probably also has the facility to print characters of different heights, densities, and so on. And it is likely that you will be able to alter layout aspects such of your document such as varying the left hand margin, text justification and line spacing.

Each of these printing enhancements will be accompanied by a set of numbers in your manual. It is these numbers that have to be entered into the Printer Editor for the translator to work properly. Most have a sequence that begins with the number 27. This known as the 'escape' code.

So, for an Epson-compatible printer to switch into Elite pitch (12 characters to the inch) you will need to send the two codes 27 and 58 to the printer; to select the French international character set from the many resident in the printer you will have to send the three codes 27, 82 and 3 to the printer. And so on.

ASCII

In addition to understanding something about printer control codes, you should also know about ASCII codes.

Obviously, each character in any of your documents is not stored in the Z88's memory in terms of the character's shape such as 'b' or 'z'; the Z88 deals with numbers. The decision as to which number represents which character has now been standardised across all kinds of computers and is known as the ASCII (American Standard Code for Information Interchange) code. These codes are shown in Appendix 1.

So, the word 'test', for example, will be stored in the computer as 116, 101, 115, 116. The Z88 'translates' these values into the more familiar characters for you when it displays information on the screen.

Modern printers also understand the meaning of these ASCII codes. When they receive a particular code their own software translates it back into a character shape – or at least into the actions needed to print the shape.

So, when sending characters to the printer we send the ASCII codes down the cable rather than the characters themselves. It is these numbers that the printer translator intercepts and changes. And it is the instructions for making the change that we can alter using the Z88's Printer Editor.

Changing the Editor

When you first switch into the Printer Editor the default printer 'driver' (translator) for an Epson-compatible printer appears. You can confirm this by looking at the left hand panel of the screen. If ever you want to return to this default editor, simply issue the command ◇ FNEW.

```
PRINTERED   PRINTER CODE     1      ON   Underline 27,45,1         OFF 27,45,0        Off Yes   OZ
CURSOR         EDITOR        2  String        Bold 27,69        String 27,70           at Yes
FILES                        3       Ext. sequence                                     CR Yes
                             4             Italics 27,52               27,53              Yes
              PRINTER        5           Subscript 27,83,1             27,84              Yes
               Epson         6         Superscript 27,83 0             27,84              Yes
               Page 1        7           Alt. font 15                  18                 No
           Page 2: SHIFT ↓   8        User defined 27,120,1            27,120,0           No
```

The printer editor's first page

On the first page of this editor appear the codes that will be sent to the printer when you use any of the eight highlight commands within a PipeDream document. Associated with each highlight command are the codes needed to turn it on and off.

On the second page (which you reach by pressing SHIFT and ↓) are a set of options that will send a sequence of codes to the printer at the beginning and end of each document, tell the Z88 how to treat page breaks and line feeds, and consider how 'microspacing' should be handled on the printer.

Finally, the page provides you with nine opportunities to instruct the editor to translate your special characters for you (international versions of the Z88 supply 28 translation chances). Within the default Epson printer driver the first character translation is done for you: to translate the pound sign into a sequence of characters that the printer can understand.

To alter a specific set of printer codes, simply take the cursor to the first code in the relevant sequence and change it to the new setting. For example, to change the sequence of printer codes for turning on Highlight 1's underlining function, put the cursor on the '2' of 27 at the top left hand corner of the 'underline' setting. Now simply enter the new string of codes, each separated by a comma. In the same way you will need to change the sequence of printer codes to turn off underlining on your printer.

The final set of options in the third column of the first page lets you control how the printer should behave when it meets a carriage return in your document (which takes the printer head back to the beginning of the line, and turns the platen up by a line). You can set each of the eight highlight codes to switch off the highlight when a carriage return code is reached, or not as you wish.

If you decide that a highlight code should be automatically switched off at the end of each line you will need to insert the highlight code in your PipeDream document at the beginning of each line you want highlighted. So, to highlight a quotation block, for example, you would have to add Highlight 2 at the beginning of each new line in the block.

If the option in the last column is set to N(o), however, the highlight will remain active until you specifically turn it off with a second highlight code. Although this can save you considerable time when producing your document you must be very careful not to turn on a highlight and forget to turn it off!

Most of the eight highlight settings are fairly self-explanatory, and each conforms to the eight highlight codes we noted when discussing the layout of PipeDream documents in Chapter 3. Remember that the first four (underline, bold, extended sequence and italic) display different characters on the PipeDream screen, so there should be little chance of forgetting to turn off these highlight codes. The remaining four, however, do not produce unique screen displays.

Of course, by being able to tamper with the printer codes for each highlight command you do not have to keep to the 'official' description of them. By adding the appropriate codes to the bold highlight, for example, you could make Highlight 2 (bold) produce both bold *and* italic print.

Standard strings

As well as entering printer codes in terms of the numbers that your printer manual supplies, often you can also enter them into the Editor as letter strings. For example, on a standard Epson-compatible printer the codes to print in double width characters are 27, 87, 49 *or* 27, "W", "1" (87 is the ASCII code for "W" and 49 is the ASCII code for "1"). You can enter code sequences like this, although you should enclose the characters in double quotation marks.

You can also use this feature of the Editor to help produce some standard phrases for your printer. So, instead of having to enter 'Yours Sincerely' into the end of each PipeDream-produced letter you could put this phrase into a highlight code – say Highlight 8: "Yours Sincerely" (the quotation marks are important). Now, when you want to include this phrase in your letter simply issue Highlight 8 in place of the phrase; when the time comes to print it the two words will appear on paper for you.

Finally, of course, you can 'mix-and-match' numbers and characters within the codes. For example, if you enter the following codes into Highlight 8 for an Epson-compatible printer:

```
27,14,"Yours Sincerely"
```

they will print 'Yours Sincerely' in double width characters.

Symbolic entry

Not only can you enter printer codes as numbers and character strings, but you can also use the standard ASCII symbols to represent the values 0 to 31. You simply enter the relevant two- or three-character set *in upper case*:

0	NUL		Null – does nothing
1	SOH	)	
2	STX	)	
3	ETX	)	Special codes for data transmission
4	EOT	)	
5	ENQ	)	
6	ACK	)	
7	BEL		Sounds printer bell
8	BS		Back space
9	HT		Horizontal tab
10	LF		Line feed
11	VT		Vertical tab
12	FF		Form feed
13	CR		Carriage return
14	SO		Shift out (usually sets double width text)
15	SI		Shift in (usually sets compressed text)
16	DLE		
17	DC1		Device control 1 – for receiving data
18	DC2		Device control 2 – usually turns off SI
19	DC3		Device control 3 – usually deselects printer
20	DC4		Device control 4 – usually turns off SO
21	NAK	)	
22	SYN	)	
23	ETB	)	Special codes for data transmission
24	CAN	)	
25	EM	)	
26	SUB	)	
27	ESC		Escape
28	FS	)	
29	GS	)	
30	RS	)	Special codes for file structures
31	US	)	

So, to turn Highlight 8 into a code for printing double width characters, for example, you might simply add the letters 'SO' to the print translation string, instead of having to remember that the ASCII value for this code is 14.

To add an extra line at the end of this string you will need to add CR (to take the printer head back to the beginning of the line) *and* LF (line feed). The command LF on its own will simply roll the platen up by one line, starting the next line's printing at the column where the previous line ended.

Page two

Page two of the Printer Editor provides some more useful translation facilities.

The first two options let you enter strings of codes that will be sent to the printer at the beginning of a document before it is actually printed. You might wish, for

```
PRINTERED   PRINTER CODE     Printer on 27,64         Translations   A   B   C    OZ
CURSOR        EDITOR        Printer off                Character 163
FILES                       End of page 12            Changes to 27,82,3,
                          Allow line feed Yes          Character
              PRINTER        HMI: Prefix              Changes to
               Epson              Suffix               Character
               Page 2             Offset              Changes to
            Page 1: SHIFT ↕
```

The printer editor's second page

example, to have all your document printed in Elite (12 pitch) typeface, in which case you would enter the codes 27, 58 here for an Epson-compatible printer. You might also wish to set the printer so that it can print the French character set. In this case the codes in the 'printer on' string should read:

27, 58, (to turn on Elite print) 27, "R", "1" (to produce the French character set).

The 'printer off' string performs the same kind of action at the end of the printing session. Here you may wish to reset the printer to its default values.

Once again, these printer codes can contain strings of characters as well as numbers. The message "Good morning" for example, entered into the 'printer on' string might make an interesting greeting for anyone using this particular printer driver.

The next two translation options ('end of page' and 'allow line feed') deal with the way the Z88 treats line feeds.

When most printers are sent a form feed character (ASCII code 12) they will advance the paper to the beginning of the next page (the appropriate number of lines can often be varied by using special printer codes that could be sent as part of the 'printer on' string). If you enter this value into the 'end of page' option, then the printer will quickly go to the beginning of the next page, rather than having to issue line feeds. This is both quicker and quieter.

If you have not set the number of lines between the top and bottom of your page correctly, however, using this code can create some unfortunate effects; different pages will begin at different positions. It is sometimes 'safer', therefore, to remove this code (replace it with 0) and let PipeDream do the form feeding by issuing the appropriate number of carriage returns at the end of each page.

Allow line feed

Sometimes printers will insert their own line feed when the print head gets to the end of a line; sometimes they expect a line feed command to be issued from the computer. Obviously, if the computer adds a line feed to the end of each line of text as well as the printer, or both the printer and the computer fail to add a line feed, unfortunate printing effects will occur.

For this reason, the fourth option in the printer editor lets you add, or not add, a line feed code to the end of each printing line. Unfortunately, however, the function does not work in the earlier produced Z88s which have either the 2.2 or 3.0 operating system. To check which operating system resides in your machine, go to the Index page, press the HELP key and then the left arrow key.

Microspacing

Certain printers can print text using microspacing, in which the space between characters is variable (often in multiples of 1/120ths of an inch). This produces a more evenly spaced effect and is particularly useful when you are printing text which is right justified.

To do this, however, you must tell the printer how many 120ths of an inch steps should be allocated to printing subsequent characters. This value is known as the Horizontal Motion Index (HMI). Your printer manual will tell you the precise codes to send. Some require only a set of codes before each character (prefix), others require them after each character (suffix), while others require both prefix and suffix codes.

To print a file in microspacing, before you issue the ◊ PO command to print your document you must have informed PipeDream that you will wish to use microspacing by issuing the ◊ PM command. This adds the message that you will be 'microspacing' to the options page (◊ O).

Character translation

Finally, you can translate up to nine different characters when they are sent to the printer. It is here that you can change '%' into ç, for example, or '|' into ü.

The nine possible translations are supplied as a 3x3 table on the right hand side of the second Printer Editor page. In the first line of each 'cell' you enter the ASCII value of the character that you want translated, while in the second line you put the character or sequence of characters to be printed instead.

The default Epson printer driver contains the sequence of codes needed to translate the keyboard pound sign into an appropriate symbol at the printer. Thus, the ASCII code for the pound sign on the keyboard is 163 (see Appendix 1). To print this symbol the default driver first switches into the British international character set (27, 82, "3"), prints the pound sign (35), and then switches back to the American character set (27, 82, 0). So, the full translation sequence that you will see is:

```
27, 82, 3, 35, 27, 82, 0
```

As with the other translation facilities provided by the Printer Editor, the possibilities for interesting and useful printing effects are limitless if you use this translation table with imagination.

For example, you can still enter characters as strings enclosed in quotation marks. So you could translate "%", say, to print the faithful "Yours Sincerely".

Updating and Saving

Any changes that you may have made to the printer editor do not come into operation until you issue the 'update file' command ◇FU. This *must* be issued while the printer editor is onscreen.

It is important to note that this printer editor will not affect the way the printer operates if you are echoing the screen to the printer using the □+P and □-P command sequences. It only comes into play when you are sending characters to the printer through one of the Z88's own applications.

Because you may wish to have a number of printer editor files available for different printers, or for different interpretations by the same printer, the Z88 allows you to save your newly created printer editor as a file, and load another one ready to become operative.

For this you use the standard ◇FS and ◇FL commands. But again note that the new printer editor does not become operative until you issue the ◇FU command.

The only way to exit from the printer editor is to return to the Index.

```
PIPEDREAM  A1                                                              OZ
BLOCKS         ............A . . . . . .B . . . . . .C . . . . . .D . . . . . .E . . . . . .F
CURSOR      1   27,45,1
EDIT        2 ! 27,69
FILES       3 # 27,52
LAYOUT      4 $ 27,83,1
OPTIONS     5 % 27,83,0
PRINT       6 & 15
```

A printer editor page in PipeDream

Printer Editor Files

Once you have saved it, you can easily read the Printer Editor file using PipeDream. Simply load it into PipeDream (◇ FL) as plain text. There you will see each of the control code sequences following a special character: a space on line 1, a ! on line 2, a # on line 3, and so on. These characters represent the ASCII character for the line number plus 31. So, line 1 in the Printer Editor is the ASCII code 32 (space), line 2 is the ASCII code 33 (31+2 = !), and so on.

Since it is possible to create and edit printer editor files in this way, you can use this facility to give specially designed printer editor files to a friend, say – even via a modem and telephone line as we will see in Chapter 10.

Summary

The Z88's printing facilities are as flexible as its other applications. By being able to interrupt the information flow before it leaves the computer on its way to the printer, you can perform a number of translations to create various printer drivers for different purposes.

The next chapter will discuss some of the interesting opportunities provided by the Z88 via its BASIC programming language.

8

Basic programming

The Z88 does not only provide powerful facilities for integrated word processing, spreadsheet, diary, database and other work; it is also a very sophisticated computer. Indeed, it is precisely this application which makes the machine so flexible. By being able to program it in a variety of different ways we can make the various parts of the electronic applications inside the computer do a variety of new and different things.

As well as the applications we have discussed so far, then, the Z88 arrives equipped with what has become one of the most popular programming languages: BASIC – an acronym for Beginners All Symbolic Instruction Code.

The Z88's Basic implementation is a special form of the computer language that was developed for the BBC Microcomputer and used in the early TV programs that looked at the wonders of computing. For the most part, therefore, programs that have been written to run on the BBC Micro will also work inside the Z88 – although some modifications may sometimes have to be made to take account of the Z88's 8-line screen.

For readers who have experience of BBC Basic, the major difference between the Z88's version and the full implementation on the BBC Micro is the absence on the Z88 of statements that concern sound, graphics and colour – for obvious reasons. Also there are no 'FX' commands. Otherwise all the Basic statements operate in much the same way as they do on the BBC Micro.

The purpose of this chapter is *not* to teach the reader how to write Basic programs; that subject is far larger than the space available. Instead, we will consider some of the features of the Z88's implementation of Basic that make this particular variation so useful.

Indeed, the interested reader who wishes to delve into the insides of Basic is urged to obtain more detailed reference manuals for BBC Basic on the Z88. Two in particular are: *The BBCBASIC(Z80) Reference Manual* by D J Mounter (M-TEC Computer Services), and *The Z88 Developer's Notes* by J Harrison and M Elton (Cambridge Computers). The second book will be of value to both BBC and Assembler programmers.

BBC Basic in Summary

As well as the standard features supplied by Basic, BBC Basic provides control over a number of other computing activities.

For example, like the BBC Micro's Basic you are given full control over the screen and its appearance. Using the 'VDU' statement, you can define windows within the screen area, create your own graphic symbols, and take control over the cursor movement and other operating functions.

BBC Basic also supplies a built-in assembler, which enables you to write programs in assembly language if you so desire. Indeed, you can 'mix-and-match' Basic and assembly language statements within the same program, perhaps using assembly language when speed is needed and Basic when displaying instructions to the user.

And BBC Basic provides facilities for fully interacting with the Z88's operating system. With this you can develop programs that will interact with other Z88 operations – and even control them from within Basic. Chapter 9 will illustrate this aspect in more detail.

Basic Basic

Like other Z88 applications, Basic can be accessed at any time and from within any application. In this case the significant key presses are □B. This produces a simple Basic editing screen with the familiar chevron prompt. There are no Help functions available in this application.

When entering Basic statements it is important to remember that BBC Basic insists that all keywords like 'PRINT' or 'RUN' are entered in upper case; otherwise you will be presented with the annoying and unhelpful 'Mistake' error message when you try to RUN the program. To make life slightly easier, therefore, when you enter the Basic editor the CAPS LOCK key is automatically activated, and 'CAPS' is shown in upper case letters in the bottom right hand corner of the screen.

To enter lower case characters you will have to turn off the caps lock action by pressing the CAPS LOCK key again. However, you can 'invert' the action of the key instead so that, whereas normal entry of alphabetic text will be in upper case, if you want to enter lower case letters you should press the SHIFT key together with the letter you want to enter.

To invert the caps lock operation press the □ and CAPS LOCK keys *together* – this time it is important that they are both pressed together. The display at the bottom right hand corner of the screen changes to the lower case 'caps', to show you that the CAPS LOCK key function has been inverted. Now, no matter how many times you press the CAPS LOCK key to turn the feature on and off, the inverted nature of this key will remain (this works even when you are using other Z88 features such as PipeDream).

To return the caps lock key to its normal, upper case, operation press the ◇ and CAPS LOCK keys *together*.

Basic and PipeDream

When a BBC Basic program is saved to a file, to save space it is first 'tokenised'. That is, all of the Basic keywords are reduced to unique one-character tokens that the Basic interpreter can understand – but no-one else. Although the Basic statements appear on the screen as recognisable English, therefore, they are not stored as such.

Although this feature can be annoying if you wish to create a 'word processed' Basic program, it is still possible to compose a Basic program using the PipeDream word processor and then to 'read' it into the Basic interpreter. The benefits of doing this, of course, are that the full range of PipeDream's facilities become available to you, including search and replace, and forward and backward scrolling. Such facilities are often very useful when developing a long program.

PipeDream to Basic

To develop a Basic program in PipeDream, ready for running in Basic, the first line of your PipeDream file *must* contain only a dot and a J (.J) (in upper case). Then, having written the document (in this case a program), save it in the normal way using the ◇ FS command and stipulating that it is 'plain text'.

When you are in Basic, the standard LOAD statement will only load a program which has been saved in the normal, tokenised, form. So we have to resort to another trick to read the recently PipeDream-created program into Basic.

Say you have saved your program document with the file name 'test'. From within Basic issue the command:

`*CLI .*test` (note the dot)

This will read the file into Basic, ready for you to edit, Run, Save, or whatever.

Although you will probably use this function when there is no other program resident in the Basic interpreter, if another program *is* resident the function will *append* the new program to the end (which provides a useful way of joining two programs together). To ensure that the PipeDream-generated program is the *only* program within Basic, insert the keyword NEW into the program at line 2 (that is, after '.J').

Basic to PipeDream

Because of the tokenising effects of Basic, it should be equally obvious that it is not possible to 'read' a Basic program directly into PipeDream. If you try to load such a program (◇ FL) you will see some recognisable words, but also a considerable amount of incomprehensible material.

To translate the Basic program back into a more readable form for PipeDream you first need to 'spool' it to a file. Then load that file into PipeDream – again as plain text.

Although this operation may sound complicated it is actually quite simple. Make sure that the program you want to spool has been loaded into Basic and issue the command:

```
□+S
```

Like the printer echoing operation described in the last chapter (□+P), this key sequence also echoes what appears on the screen. In this case, however, the information is sent to a special file called S.SGN which resides in the device called ':RAM.-' (see Chapter 2).

Having turned on the file-spooling function you should LIST the program. Then simply end the spooling with □-S. So the full sequence should be:

```
□+S
LIST
□-S
```

If you now enter PipeDream (□P) and load the file (◇ FL) called ':RAM.-/S.SGN' as plain text you will see your Basic program appear in pristine condition. You can then edit it at will, ready to save again and '*CLI' it back into Basic – but remember to add '.J' at the beginning.

Basic editing

The developers of the Z88's BBC Basic have included a simple line editor into the application. In immediate mode (that is, when entering a statement but before having pressed ENTER), the majority of PipeDream's editing functions are available:

DEL	Backspace and delete
←	Cursor right
→	Cursor left
◇ DEL	Delete line
◇ D	Delete to end of line
◇ G	Delete character
◇ S	Swap case
◇ T	Delete word
◇ U	Insert character
◇ V	Insert/overtype
◇ ←	Start of line
◇ →	End of line
SHIFT←	Previous word
SHIFT→	Next word

(Interestingly, these editing functions are also all available to users when they are entering information that has been requested by a Basic INPUT statement.)

Once you have pressed ENTER, however, the statement leaves the immediate mode and is entered into the program. Unlike with the BBC Micro you cannot edit it later. Unfortunately the whole line will have to be re-entered.

You can overcome this disadvantage, however, by including a line-editing procedure at the end of your Basic program. The following procedure, developed by Cambridge Computers, could be written in PipeDream and appended to the end of each program as you develop it (using *CLI). Remember to add the instruction '.J' as the first line, though not NEW.

```
65500 END
65501 DEF PROCE(B)
65502 REM (C) Cambridge Computer Ltd.
65503 IF B = 0 THEN ENDPROC
65504 A=OPENOUT ":RAM.0/EE.CLI"
65505 B$=":RAM.0/E.CLI"
65506 PRINT#A,"."+B$
```

```
65507 PRINT#A,".J","LIST"+STR$(B),"PROCF"
65508 CLOSE#A
65509 *CLI .*:RAM.0/EE.CLI
65510 ENDPROC
65511 DEF PROCF
65512 A=INKEY(0)
65513 A=OPENIN B$
65514 INPUT#A,A$,A$
65515 CLOSE#A
65516 A=OPENOUT B$
65517 PRINT#A,".J",A$
65518 PTR#A=PTR#A-1
65519 BPUT#A,0
65520 CLOSE#A
65521 *ERASE :RAM.0/EE.CLI
65522 VDU 8
65523 OSCLI "*CLI ."+B$
65524 ENDPROC
```

Having appended this procedure to your program, you edit a particular line simply by issuing the command PROCE(line number to edit). For example, PROCE(20). The original line will be sent back into 'immediate' mode, ready to be edited as you wish.

You can also use this procedure to duplicate lines. For example, say you have the statement:

```
25 PRINT A
```

and you wish to make this line 35 also. Simply issue the instruction PROCE(25) and then change the line number from 25 to 35 when the statement appears. You will find that you have *both* lines 25 and 35 in your program.

Some Basic Commands

Although the version of Basic employed in the Z88 is much the same as BBC Basic, it is useful to consider a few of the operations that are available to you when developing a program.

Run, Chain and Stop

As usual, you start executing a program using the Basic command RUN. Before it begins execution this routine will clear all variables within the Basic area – *except* the variables A% to Z% and @%. You can use these variables, therefore, to transfer information from one program to another – at least on a limited basis (@% is a special print formatting variable).

If you want to start a new program without clearing all the variables, however, you can use the statement:

```
GOTO line number
```

CHAIN is a variant of RUN, which both loads and runs the program whose name follows the CHAIN statement. So:

`CHAIN "example"`	will load the program 'example' and run it;
`CHAIN a$`	will load and run whatever program name resides in the variable a$.

As with Run, CHAIN clears all variables except for A% to Z% and @%.

To stop a program simply press the ESC key, although the command STOP within a program has the same effect. When you have concluded a program's operation in this way all variables remain uncleared, so it is possible to interrogate the value of a particular variable:

```
10 DIM A(20)
20 FOR I = 1 TO 5
30   A(I) = RND
40 NEXT
50 STOP

RUN

STOP at line 50
FOR I = 1 TO 5:PRINT A(I):NEXT
-1.26667692E9
1.525973E9
1.7025572E9
 500718324
-1.9585173E9
```

RUN and CHAIN can be shortened to RU. and CH.

New and Old

From the beginning BBC Basic was developed with user's mistakes in mind, and the NEW and OLD statements are good examples of this forethought. As with most implementations of Basic the statement NEW clears out the Basic area in memory and prepares the Basic interpreter to accept a new set of instructions. A program that is 'newed' is effectively wiped from the machine.

Because errors can be made and you might issue a NEW instruction by mistake, however, the designers of BBC Basic introduced the complementary instruction OLD. This reverses the effect of NEW and restores the program to life in its original form.

However, this revitalising instruction will only work if no new lines have been added or deleted and no new variables have been created since the NEW instruction.

Auto and Renumber

Like many Basic implementations BBC Basic provides the facility for automatically entering statement line numbers, saving you the bother of having to type them into the program yourself.

If you issue the command AUTO on its own, line numbers will begin at 10 and increase by 10 for each new line. However, you can stipulate the starting number and/or increment by adding the appropriate values after the AUTO command:

```
AUTO start number, increment
```

For example,

`AUTO 100, 5`	will start at line 100 and increase by 5 each time
`AUTO 100,`	starts at 100 and increases by 10; and
`AUTO ,5`	starts at 10 and increases by 5.

It is *not* possible to use the AUTO command from within a program.

Having entered your line numbers and developed your program, RENUMBER renumbers them for you and automatically changes any line number references as appropriate. The command uses the same parameters as AUTO, but increments of greater than 255 are not allowed. For example, say you have the program:

```
 10 INPUT A
 20 IF A  THEN GOTO 100
 30 PRINT "Your account is in surplus":GOTO 110
100 PRINT "Your account is in deficit"
110 END
```

Now renumber it, starting at line 1000, and increasing in steps of 20:

```
RENUMBER 1000, 20
```

This would produce:

```
1000 INPUT A
1020 IF A  THEN GOTO 1060
1040 PRINT "Your account is in surplus":GOTO 1080
1060 PRINT "Your account is in deficit"
1080 END
```

You *can* use the RENUMBER statement from within a program, but when the job has been done the program will end and return you to the Basic command mode.

If you try to RENUMBER a program (or enter AUTO) with an incremental size of zero, the Z88 will return an interesting error message: 'Silly'.

AUTO and RENUMBER can be shortened to AU. and REN.

List

All versions of Basic provide the command LIST to list a program to the screen. BBC Basic's LIST command, however, can be tailored to your own requirements.

The standard command is 'LIST start line, end line'. So,

`LIST`	lists the whole program;
`LIST ,100`	lists up to line 100;
`LIST 200,`	lists from line 200; and
`LIST 150,500`	lists from line 150 to line 500.

When the program is listed a screenful is displayed at a time; you must press the Space bar to move on to the next page. Pressing ESC aborts the listing.

When listing a program the standard format is for a space to be printed between each line number and the beginning of each statement. Two additional spaces are also printed between the end of each line number and statements within a FOR..NEXT loop and within a REPEAT..UNTIL loop.

However, you can change this format by issuing the LISTO command before LIST. LISTO must be followed by a number which ranges from 0 to 7. This is calculated by adding the following values as appropriate:

Format	**Value**
Space between line and statement	1
Two spaces for FOR.. NEXT loops	2
Two spaces for REPEAT.. UNTIL loops	4

So, for all three options to be 'on' LISTO should be followed by 7 (1+2+4), which is the default LIST setting. To have two spaces for FOR..NEXT and REPEAT..UNTIL loops, but not otherwise, use LISTO 6 (4+2). And so on.

Remember, to print a list of your program you should issue the CLI command □+P before LIST, and conclude the echoing to the printer with □-P. When you do this, the listing scrolls continuously without stopping at the end of each page. Abort the command by pressing the SHIFT and ESC keys together.

Trace

The command TRACE ON helps you determine how your program is progressing, and is very useful for 'debugging' it – that is, finding out where things are going wrong. When TRACE is ON the line numbers are printed to the screen as they are being executed.

You can limit the line numbers that will be printed to the screen. If you issue the command 'TRACE X', only line numbers smaller than X will be displayed. So:

TRACE 100 will only display line numbers below 100.

This is an extremely useful facility since you can incorporate TRACE within a program. Since you can also set 'X' to be a variable, judicious use of the controlling line value and placement of TRACE within the program should soon make your Z88 help you determine why the program is going wrong – and how to put it right.

You can turn TRACE off either by issuing the command TRACE OFF or if Basic encounters an error in your program.

On Error and Report

Error trapping can be made even more effective using BBC Basic's ON ERROR command. Whenever the interpreter notes an error, rather than the program simply stopping its control will be passed to the ON ERROR statement. So, if you have the statement 'ON ERROR GOTO 100' at the beginning of your program, for example, if ever Basic encounters an error the program control will be passed to the statement in line 100. This could be some routine that reports the error and does something about it.

The ON ERROR facility must be used with a certain degree of caution, however. If your error handling routine (at line 100, say) itself contains an error the program will enter an endless loop and the only way out will be to reset the Z88. You can avoid having to do this by including the statement:

```
dummy = INKEY(0)
```

at the beginning of your error handling routine. This will allow you to exit from Basic by pressing the INDEX key.

The statement ON ERROR OFF returns the error handling ability to BBC Basic.

In conjunction with ON ERROR, BBC Basic provides three other statements which should help to identify the nature and location of the error:

ERL supplies the line number on which the error was detected.

ERR supplies the Basic's own code number of the error reported. The complete list of these codes and their associated meaning are available in Mounter's *BBC BASIC(Z80) Reference manual*. However, it is not necessary to have access to the complete list because the Basic command REPORT supplies the error in reasonable English.

Take the following example:

```
 10 ON ERROR GOTO 100
 20 INPUT A
 30 PRINT B
 40 END
100 dummy = INKEY(0)
110 PRINT "Error found in line ";ERL;" code number ";ERR
120 REPORT
```

This will produce:

```
RUN
? 3
Error found in line 30 code number 26
No such variable
```

Of course, you can use the variables ERR and ERL to take even better control over your program. For example, if line 110 in the above program is changed to:

```
110 IF ERR = 26 then B=100:GOTO ERL
```

the error will be trapped and the program can continue:

```
RUN
? 3
           100
```

Basic Memory

The Z88's memory is a very complex affair but, to some extent, can be under your control. By understanding a little about how programs are organised in memory it is possible to operate with more than one program resident at the same time. Indeed, with some knowledge of assembly language you could have more than one program *working* at the same time. That aspect of the machine goes beyond the confines of this book, however.

Here is a very simple block diagram of the Z88's memory:

```
--------------------
BBC Basic
--------------------
Stack
-------------------- HIMEM (16384 on basic machine;
                     49152 on expanded machine)

                     LOMEM
-------------------- TOP

Program

-------------------- PAGE (8960)
Basic's workspace
--------------------

Z88 operating system
--------------------
```

As was explained in Chapter 1, a Z88 is said to be 'expanded' if you have inserted at least a 128k Ram pack into slot 1 at the front of the machine. If slot 1 is empty (even if a Ram pack is in slot 2), then the machine is said to be a 'basic' machine).

The important aspects to note about this 'map' are the four memory variables: HIMEM, LOMEM, TOP and PAGE.

PAGE represents the location in memory where your program starts; TOP is the highest location of the program itself. So, if you issue the instruction:

```
PRINT TOP - PAGE
```

you will see how large your program is.

As a program works away Basic requires some temporary storage areas to hold various pieces of information – generally intermediate calculations. This it carries out in the 'stack' which gradually 'moves' down the memory area as it is filled up, the bottom of which is indicated by the memory location called HIMEM. As more room is used up HIMEM is pushed 'down' the memory area until it reaches LOMEM, the next location above TOP. When this happens the Z88 will report that there is 'No room'.

More than one program in memory

Essentially, you have the area between PAGE and HIMEM in which to place your programs, with LOMEM acting as a buffer to stop the stack encroaching on your programs. Because BBC Basic lets you alter the values of PAGE, LOMEM and HIMEM you can have multiple programs in your machine at the same time.

You should know, however, that PAGE can only be altered by 256 locations at a time. So in memory the PAGE boundaries are at locations 8960, 9216, 9472, 9728 and so on. Because it is always handy to have these page boundaries available, if you enter the following sequence of keystrokes from the Basic screen (though not within a Basic program) they will be printed out for you:

```
□+P
FOR I = &2300 TO &4000 STEP 256:PRINT I;:NEXT
□-P
```

Injudicious changing of these variables can lead the machine to 'crash', so you should be careful of casual use. However, the following provides an example of how you can have two programs operating at the same time.

Let us enter a simple program:

```
10 PRINT "This is the first program"
```

You can LIST it to check that the one-line program has been entered correctly, and PRINT TOP to see where the program ends in memory (8996). If you RUN the program, of course, the Z88 will display the statement "This is the first program".

Now change the PAGE to the first boundary:

```
PAGE = 9216
```

and LIST the program that you know is inside the Z88. Nothing appears. Now enter your second program:

```
10 PRINT "This is the second program"
```

If you PRINT TOP you will see that the top of the Basic program area has increased from 8996 to 9253.

RUNning this program will display the message "This is the second program". Switch PAGE back to 8960 (PAGE=8960) and RUN again – you will see the message "This is the first program".

The second program will stay in memory, and will be perfectly operable, even if the NEW statement is issued when PAGE is set at the base of the first (8960).

With sensible programming, of course, it is possible to transfer control between programs:

Return to the first program (PAGE=8960) and add the following two statements:

```
20 PAGE = 9216
30 RUN
```

Switch to the second program (PAGE=9216) and add the following statement:

```
20 PAGE = 8960
```

Now return to the first program (PAGE=8960) and RUN it. You will see the two messages appear, and control will be returned to the first program.

This facility could make a rudimentary security system: when listing the first program a would-be hacker would be unable to see the second statement in the higher page area – which might contain password information.

If you do 'play' with the memory locations like this the only way of removing all programs will be to set PAGE individually and NEW each program in turn, or issue the ◇ PURGE command from Index.

Printing Basic

Layout

Printing information from within Basic is performed using the PRINT statement. As in most implementations of the language you can use the comma (,) to 'tab' to the next screen position (for most purposes, the screen is divided into zones that are 10 characters wide). Numeric values are printed right justified. Using the semi-colon (;) will print the value at the next available position, and the apostrophe (') forces a new line.

So:

```
PRINT "Test",A
```

will print the letters 'Test' at the left hand edge of the screen and the value of A starting at position 11. If A is only a single digit, therefore, it will actually be printed at position 20. If it is two digits long it will be printed at positions 19 and 20, and so on.

```
PRINT "Test";A
```

will print the letters 'Test' at the left hand edge of the screen, immediately followed by the value of A.

```
PRINT '"Test";A
```

will skip a line before printing 'Test' and the value of A.

Print format

The PRINT format can be changed using the variable @%, which gives control over the width of the print zones and the number of decimal places to print. It has the general form:

```
&ABCD
```

where A, B, C and D are hexadecimal values.

A determines whether or not the PRINT statement should take note of this @% formatting instruction. So if A = 01 then the printing format will be affected by @%, otherwise @% will be ignored and the default printing format will be used (which is G9 – General format nine characters wide – see below).

B determines the format:

00 General format (G)
01 Exponential format (E)
02 Fixed format (F)

In the general format (G), values above 0.1 to 1 and integers are printed as they stand. Numbers less than 0.1 and greater than the range set will be printed as exponential values.

In the E format values are printed according to the scientific (engineering) notation; and fixed format values (F) are printed with a defined number of decimal places.

C determines the number of digits to print.

D sets the width of the print zones.

So:

&01020205 tells the PRINT statement to use this function (01), sets a fixed format (02) with two decimal places (02) and a print zone of 5 (05) characters wide.

&01000A0D tells the PRINT statement to use this function (01), sets a general format (02) with a maximum of ten characters before entering the exponential format (0A) and a print zone of 13 (0D) characters wide.

Decimal and hexadecimal

You should notice from this last example that the values within the @% statement must be in hexadecimal notation. You can get Basic to print the hexadecimal value of any number by adding the tilde (~) sign before it. For example:

```
PRINT ~13        0D
PRINT ~12        0C
PRINT ~10        0A
PRINT ~9         09
```

Printing values in Basic

Whereas it is easy to print statements and values from the Basic's command mode (you just echo to the printer using □+P) you cannot do this from within a Basic program, or at least not as easily.

The problem arises because the □+P sequence begins a set of instructions within the Z88 using an operation known as the Command Line Interpreter or CLI. This will be discussed in more depth in the next chapter. However, as its name suggests, the CLI will only interpret command lines – not program statements.

The Basic statement OSCLI (Operating System Command Line Interpreter) can pass information to the CLI, however, and this can be used to turn the printer on and off again. To use it, the commands to turn on the printer must be put into a normal PipeDream file and called from there. So create the following two line file and save it, say in :RAM.0, *as plain text* using a file name such as 'printon':

```
#+P
.S
```

To turn on the printer from within a Basic program issue the statement:

```
OSCLI("CLI .*:RAM.0/printon"):dummy=INKEY(0)
```

All PRINT statements will now be sent both to the screen and to the printer. To turn it off at the appropriate place within the program issue the command:

```
OSCLI("CLI #-P"):dummy=INKEY(0)
```

The 'dummy=INKEY(0)' part of both statements ensures that the program 'looks' to the keyboard – a CLI command does not become active until the next attempt to read a character from the keyboard.

Unfortunately, there are two drawbacks to using this method. First, you can only do it once in a program; you cannot turn the printer on and off at will. Second, although the 'printer off' statement turns the printer off it does not end the CLI operation. That is simply 'suspended' and has to be cleared by pressing the ◇ and ESC keys together. Until you do this, subsequent LISTings of the program to the screen will not stop at the end of each page.

Print#

Another way of turning the printer on and off, and thus sending material to it from within a Basic program, is to make the Z88 believe that the printer is simply a device like another computer. Once you have 'opened' this device and initialised the printer you can use the PRINT# statement to send information to it.

You open the printer as a device by issuing the statement OPENOUT. It has the format:

```
handle = OPENOUT ":PRT"
```

where the 'handle' is a variable that the Basic interpreter will recognise as being the printer.

To select and deselect the printer, we have to send a sequence of control codes to this handle:

To turn the printer on:

```
PRINT#handle,CHR$(5)+"["
```

To turn the printer off:

```
PRINT#handle,CHR$(5)+"]"
```

Now we can use the PRINT# statement to send information to the printer – though the information *must* be in the form of a string. And at the end of each line of information we must also send the instruction to feed a line:

```
BPUT#handle,CHR$(10)
```

Finally, the printer must be shut down (the file closed) with the statement:

```
CLOSE#handle
```

So, the following small program will print even numbers to the screen and odd numbers to the printer:

```
10 handle=OPENOUT":PRT"
20 PRINT#handle,CHR$(5)+"["
30 FOR i = 1 TO 20
40    A=RND(10)
50    IF A MOD 2 = 0 THEN PRINT A
60    IF A MOD 2 = 1 THEN PRINT#handle,STR$(A):BPUT#
                          handle,10
70 NEXT i
80 CLOSE#handle
```

Line 10 opens the printer file, and the printer is turned on in line 20. Line 40 is a simple way of generating random whole numbers, in this case between 1 and 10. Lines 50 and 60 test to see whether the random number is odd or even. If it is odd then print it to the screen. But if it is even the program is told to print the number at the printer as a string (STR$(A)) and send a line feed.

Printer enhancements

If you use this method of printing information from within a Basic program there are a number of printer enhancements you can also use:

Sequence	Meaning
`PRINT#handle,CHR$(5)+"U"`	Underline
`PRINT#handle,CHR$(5)+"B"`	Bold
`PRINT#handle,CHR$(5)+"X"`	Printer's extended characters
`PRINT#handle,CHR$(5)+"I"`	Italics
`PRINT#handle,CHR$(5)+"L"`	Subscript
`PRINT#handle,CHR$(5)+"R"`	Superscript
`PRINT#handle,CHR$(5)+"A"`	Alternative font
`PRINT#handle,CHR$(5)+"E"`	User defined attributes

These attributes will automatically be reset at the next carriage return, as long as you have given that instruction in the Printer Editor. Luckily, you do not have to issue a carriage return instruction each time you want to turn off a printer attributes. The statement

```
PRINT#handle,CHR$(5)+"S"
```

makes the Z88 think it should enter a carriage return, without actually doing so. For example:

```
10 a=OPENOUT":PRT.0"
20 PRINT#a,CHR$(5)+"["
30 PRINT#a,CHR$(5)+"U"+"Test"+CHR$(5)+"S"+"ing":BPUT#a,10
```

will underline just the 'Test' part of 'Testing'.

Finally, you should remember that all of these PRINT# instructions pass through the Printer Editor. So any alterations you have made to the translations within your Printer Editor will appear when printing from Basic.

Controlling the Screen

As well as giving you full control over your printed output, BBC Basic also lets you fine-tune your screen display to such an extent that you can control the cursor movement, create windows and define your own characters. This is all done using a very powerful statement: VDU.

The VDU statement comes in two forms. It is either followed by a single value or a sequence of values.

When the VDU statement (which can be shortened to V.) is followed by a single value between 0 and 127 it 'prints' the ASCII character associated with that value to the screen – although sometimes the action may be to move the cursor or ring a bell rather than printing a visible character.

So, VDU 97, for example will print 'a'; VDU 36 prints '$'. As well as these obvious features the Z88 can print a number of other attributes:

VDU 7	Makes the Z88 beep
VDU 8	Moves the cursor back one character
VDU 9	Moves the cursor forwards one character
VDU 10	Moves the cursor down one line
VDU 11	Moves the cursor up one line
VDU 12	Clears the text area

`VDU 13`	Moves the cursor to the start of the current line
`VDU 127`	Prints a black square
`VDU 160`	Prints three dots
`VDU 163`	Prints £

Try the following:

```
10 VDU 9,9,9,163,163,163
20 VDU 10,8,163,10,8,163
30 VDU 8,8,163,8,8,163,8
40 VDU 11,163,10,10,163
```

Each of these VDU codes could be defined within a program as variables. For example, the same effect would be produced by the following program:

```
10 right=9:left=8:down=10:up=11
20 char$="£"
30 VDU right,right,right,ASC(char$),ASC(char$),ASC(char$)
40 VDU down,left,ASC(char$),down,left,ASC(char$)
50 VDU left,left,ASC(char$),left,left,ASC(char$),left
60 VDU up,ASC(char$),down,down,ASC(char$)
```

Extended sequences

If you intend to use the extended form of the VDU statement then the first number of the special sequence must always be 1. This facility opens a range of possibilities for controlling the screen display. With it you can generate special characters, set text attributes, define text justification, and create windows.

Cursor movement

First, you can send the cursor directly to a particular position on the screen using the VDU command:

```
VDU 1, 51, 64, 32+x, 32+y
```

where x and y are the column and row numbers respectively. For example, to send the cursor to the middle of the screen you would issue the command:

```
VDU 1, 51, 64, 80, 36
```

The special sequence VDU 1, 50, 88, 32+x moves the cursor to position 'x' along the same row, while the equivalent sequence VDU 1, 50, 89, 32+y moves the cursor to row 'y' in the same column.

Special characters

The following VDU sequences produce a range of special characters, many of which we have already experienced in various Z88 activities:

`VDU 1,32`	Three dots
`VDU 1,33`	The Z88 bell symbol
`VDU 1,39`	The grave accent
`VDU 1,42`	Square
`VDU 1,43`	Diamond
`VDU 1,45`	The Z88 Shift symbol
`VDU 1,124`	An unbroken vertical bar
`VDU 1,224`	The Z88 Space symbol
`VDU 1,225`	The Z88 Enter symbol
`VDU 1,226`	The Z88 Tab symbol
`VDU 1,227`	The Z88 Del symbol
`VDU 1,228`	The Z88 Esc symbol
`VDU 1,229`	The Z88 Menu symbol
`VDU 1,230`	The Z88 Index symbol
`VDU 1,231`	The Z88 Help symbol
`VDU 1,240`	An outline arrow pointing left
`VDU 1,241`	An outline arrow pointing right
`VDU 1,242`	An outline arrow pointing down
`VDU 1,243`	An outline arrow pointing up
`VDU 1,244`	A bullet arrow pointing left
`VDU 1,245`	A bullet arrow pointing right
`VDU 1,246`	A bullet arrow pointing down
`VDU 1,247`	A bullet arrow pointing up
`VDU 1,248`	A left pointer
`VDU 1,249`	A right pointer
`VDU 1,250`	A down pointer
`VDU 1,251`	An up pointer

Text attributes

In addition to these characters, you can set other attributes. The first time the attribute command is encountered it is set 'on', the next time it is set 'off':

`VDU 1,66`	Bold
`VDU 1,67`	Cursor
`VDU 1,70`	Flash
`VDU 1,71`	Grey print
`VDU 1,76`	Caps lock
`VDU 1,82`	Inverse video

`VDU 1,83`	Vertical scrolling
`VDU 1,84`	Tiny font
`VDU 1,85`	Underline
`VDU 1,87`	Horizontal scrolling
`VDU 1,127`	Reset *all* toggles

You do not have to send multiple VDU codes to the screen each time you want to change one or more attributes, and you do not have to remember which state each toggle is currently in. Using another extended VDU sequence it is possible to force a complete set of attributes to be switched on or off at the same time.

You perform this trick with the VDU statements:

to turn attributes on:	`1, 49+n, 43, sequence of codes`
to turn attributes off:	`1, 49+n, 45, sequence of codes`

In these statements 'n' represents the number of attribute codes that are to be turned on or off. So, to turn on a reverse video and tiny font effect, you would send the VDU sequence:

VDU 1, 51, 43, 82, 84 (two attributes are to be turned on; 49+2=51)

To turn off the cursor you would send the VDU sequence:

VDU 1, 50, 45, 67 (only one attribute is to be turned off; 49+1=50)

Finally, it is possible to set certain attributes for a specific number of characters already onscreen. Although this only applies to flashing, grey, reverse and underlining, it can save considerable time.

VDU 1, 50, 65, 32+n applies the current toggle to the next 'n' characters.
VDU 1, 50, 69, 32+n inverts the current toggles for the next 'n' characters.

For example:

```
10 CLS
20 PRINT TAB(0,0)
30 PRINT "TEST"
40 PRINT TAB(0,0)
50 VDU 1,71,1,50,65,34,1,71
60 PRINT
```

This short program prints the word 'TEST' at the top left corner of the screen (lines 20 and 30), returns the cursor to the starting point (line 40), sets the grey attribute, turns the first two characters grey (32+2=34), resets the grey attribute (line 50), and takes the cursor down to the next line so that you can see the effect.

Notice that you can combine a number of VDU commands on the same line – as long as each command begins with the ubiquitous 1.

Margins and text justification

Within a window (see below) you can set both the margins and the text justification.

Sequence	Effect
VDU 1, 76, 32+n	Set left margin to 'n'
VDU 1, 82, 32+n	Set right margin to 'n'
VDU 1, 50, 74, 76	Left align the text
VDU 1, 50, 74, 67	Centre text between margins
VDU 1, 50, 74, 82	Right align the text
VDU 1, 50, 74, 78	Set normal justification (the default)

Whereas some of these command sequences might produce peculiar effects on the screen if you enter them in immediate mode, when they are included as part of a program the effects work well. For example:

```
10 left=76:centre=67:right=82:default=78
20 VDU 1, 50, 74, left
30 PRINT "Left"
40 VDU 1, 50, 74, centre
50 PRINT "Centre"
60 VDU 1, 50, 74, right
70 PRINT "Right"
80 VDU 1, 50, 74, default
```

Windows

The Z88 makes considerable use of windows within its various applications. For example, the text you enter when you are word processing goes into one window, the right margin of which you can define. In another window on the left hand side of the screen you may see the help information, while a narrow window on the right contains information about the current state of the operating system, perhaps warning you when the battery is low.

Within Basic, you can define up to six such windows, referred to simply by a number from 1 to 6.

The following VDU sequence defines a window:

```
VDU 1, 55, 35, 48+n, 32+x, 32+y, 32+w, 32+d, type
```

where:

n	is the window number
x	is the start column (left hand) of the window
y	is the start row (top) of the window
w	is the width of the window
d	is the depth of the window
type	is the type of window, defined as:
	54 no margins drawn
	129 draw left and right margin lines
	130 draw shelf brackets (blocks at the top of left and right lines)
	131 draw margin lines and shelf brackets

Once you have defined a window you can send information to it using one of the following VDU sequences:

`VDU 1, 50, 72, 48+n`	Direct output to window 'n' maintaining the display attributes previously set for this window.
`VDU 1, 50, 73, 48+n`	Direct output to window 'n' resetting attributes to default values.
`VDU 1, 50, 73, 48+n`	Direct output to window 'n', resetting display attributes to default and clearing window.

When text and other information is sent to a window, the normal scrolling functions of the display are turned off. Remember, though, that both horizontal and vertical scrolling can be turned on using the attribute sequences described already. So, to turn vertical scrolling on and off use VDU 1, 83. Horizontal scrolling is toggled with the sequence VDU 1,87.

To force a scrolling movement upwards or downwards, use the following sequence:

`VDU 1, 255`	Scroll current window upwards
`VDU 1, 254`	Scroll current window downwards

Finally, a couple of sequences to 'grey' the current window, which produces the effect that you see when using a pop-down such as the calculator. For example:

`VDU 1, 50, 71, 43`	Grey the current window
`VDU 1, 50, 71, 45`	Ungrey the current window

Multiple beeps

The following sequence of codes rings the Z88's bell a number of times:

```
VDU 1, 52, 33, 32+n, 32+w, 32+l
```

where:

n	is the number of beeps
w	is the wait time between beeps in 10 msec units
l	is the length of each beep in 10 msec units

For example, the sequence:

```
VDU 1, 52, 33, 36, 132, 232
```

will produce four beeps, each 2 seconds long (200+32) with a wait time of 1 second (100+32) between them. A word of warning: if you set the number of beeps to be less than 0 the Z88 will continue the sequence forever. Only a soft reset (◇ PURGE at the Index page) will stop the noise.

Box characters

The VDU sequence:

```
VDU 1, 50, 42, 64+c
```

prints a variety of characters that will let you build up grids of various shapes and sizes, depending on the value of 'c' in the VDU expression.

The variable 'c' can range between 1 and 15, and the shape that will be produced is created by adding the appropriate values from the following cross hair shape:

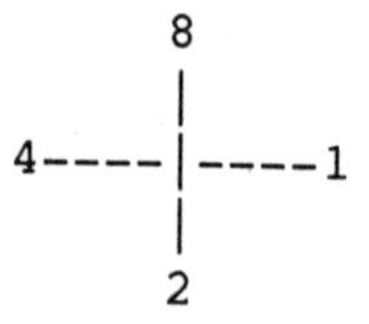

So, to produce a T-shaped character with the bar pointing right you would use the VDU sequence:

```
VDU 1, 50, 42, 75
```

In this case the value of c is 8+1+2=11 (64+11=75).

If c is given the values of just 1, 2, 4, or 8, then an arrow will be produced that points in the appropriate direction. For example,

```
VDU 1, 50, 42, 65
```

will draw the shape →.

The following Basic program draws a series of boxes across the screen, using some of these characters:

```
 10 VDU 1,50,42,67
 20 FOR I = 1 TO 5
 30   VDU 1,50,42,71
 40 NEXT I
 50 VDU 1,50,42,70
 60 PRINT
 70 VDU 1,50,42,73
 80 FOR I = 1 TO 5
 90   VDU 1,50,42,77
100 NEXT I
110 VDU 1,50,42,76
```

User Defined Characters

With all the facilities available with judicious use of VDU statements, it is not surprising to find that BBC Basic has one more surprise up its sleeve. With a little thought you can define your own characters, and with even more you can create some startling effects.

User-defined characters overwrite the current characters between '@' and DEL in the ASCII table – that is between ASCII codes of 64 and 127 inclusive. The characters themselves conform to a 6x8 matrix.

At first, defining a character may seem a little daunting but it is quite easy really. You simply take the 6x8 matrix and shade in the squares you wish to appear 'black' in your character. Then add up the total shaded squares for each row, starting from the top. Shaded squares in the first column have a value of 32, those in the second column have a value of 16, column three's squares have a value of 8, then 4, 2, and 1. To this total, add 128 for the final row value.

For example:

value	32	16	8	4	2	1	
column	1	2	3	4	5	6	Total
row1			0	0			12+128=140
2	0	0	0	0	0	0	63+128=191
3	0	0			0	0	51+128=179
4	0	0			0	0	51+128=179
5	0	0			0	0	51+128=179
6	0	0			0	0	51+128=179
7			0	0			12+128=140
8			0	0			12+128=140

To define the character, use the sequence:

```
VDU 1, 138,61,char_code,r1,r2,r3,r4,r5,r6,r7,r8
```

where char_code is the ASCII code of the character you wish to create (64 to 127) and r1 .. r8 are the the final row totals.

For example, to turn the '@' character (ASCII code=64) into the character we designed above we would enter the VDU sequence:

```
VDU 1,138,61,64,140,191,179,179,179,179,140,140
```

If you now print character 64 to the screen (VDU 64) you will find that the '@' character remains. To print the user-defined character number 64 you need to issue the sequence of codes:

```
VDU 1, 50, 63, char_code
```

In this case:

```
VDU 1, 50, 63, 64.
```

Big characters

We can use this facility to produce large characters which are composites of smaller ones, of course. For example:

```
VDU 1,138,61,64,0,0,0,191,191,0,0,0
```

will define character 64 as the left part of a large arrow.

```
VDU 1,138,61,65,0,140,142,191,191,142,140,0
```

defines character 65 as the right hand portion.

Now, VDU 1,50,63,64,1,50,63,65 will print the complete design.

With judicious use of cursor control movements, all via appropriate VDU sequences, some pretty startling effects can be obtained.

Star Commands

As well as the commands necessary to develop and run a program, the Z88's Basic also provides a few facilities to control the filing system from within Basic. These routines are accessed by commands that begin with an asterisk – hence the name 'star' commands.

*CLI

This accesses the Command Line Interpreter. It has already been considered when discussing how to load a PipeDream file into Basic. The next chapter discusses use of the CLI in more detail.

*DELETE and *ERASE

These commands are synonymous and delete the specified file from the directory. For example:

```
*DELETE test
*ERASE test
```

Only one file can be deleted at a time. To delete multiple files you should use the erase facility in the Filer (□F; ◇ ER).

*NAME

This command is used to 'name' the current Basic program you are working on. The name you supply, which can be up to 15 characters long, appears in the 'YOUR REF' column on the Index page. For example:

```
*NAME First program
```

*RENAME

This renames a file in the directory. Its format is:

```
*RENAME oldname newname
```

OSCLI

Whereas each of the above commands can be activated from the immediate mode in Basic, they cannot be included within a Basic statement without change. To do so you need to invoke the OSCLI command which has the format:

```
OSCLI (string)
```

where 'string' represents the star command without the star.

For example, to give the current Basic program a name automatically you would use the statement:

```
OSCLI("NAME First program")
```

To delete the file called 'test' from within Basic the statement would be:

```
OSCLI("DELETE test").
```

The advantage of using star commands within OSCLI is that the file names and other parameters can be entered as a string. For example:

```
10 PRINT"What is your name "
20 INPUT NM$
30 OSCLI("NAME "+NM$)
```

This will give the current Basic program the name which has been supplied via the INPUT statement.

Summary

The BBC Basic supplied with the Z88 is very similar to its parent implementation designed for the BBC Microcomputer. With it users can create a wide range of effects and can begin to take the Z88 into realms that are not covered by its conventional applications. This will become more apparent in the next chapter when we consider how to program the Z88's fundamental operating system.

9

Inside the Z88

Apart from communicating with the outside world, we have now looked at all of the specialised facilities that the Z88 offers: word processing, spreadsheets, database facilities, BASIC programming, and so on. We have also considered how Cambridge Computers incorporated various Z88 programs to help with the management of these facilities. And we have discussed how the memory is maintained, how files are stored and recalled, and how the information contained within files can be displayed on the screen and/or on the printer.

The only application that remains is the very specialised one of communicating with other computers, either directly or via the telephone line – and this will be discussed in detail in the next chapter. But before we can communicate properly we need to understand a little about how the Z88 organises its own operations, and this is the purpose of the present chapter.

This chapter, then, will look in more detail at *how* the Z88 manages to perform all of these tricks at the same time. Remember, you can switch from one application to another at the press of a key, and return to the original application just as easily. And when you return you get back to exactly the same place as you left.

To organise all this power and flexibility the Z88 needs some fairly sophisticated management routines inside it, and these are embodied in what is called the 'operating system'. The Z88's operating system is called OZ (*O*perating system for the *Z*88), and its presence is always indicated to you by the two letters you can see in the top right hand corner of the Index page.

By understanding a little about how OZ operates it is possible to carry out some simple yet sophisticated operations. But despite their simplicity they can take the

Z88 out of the bounds of an impressive office-based laptop computer and into the sphere of a sophisticated control system which you can use to tailor many of your office applications.

Device Control

The basis of all computer operations is the control of information between one 'device' and another. When you process words on the Z88, for example, you are expecting the machine to take the information from the keyboard, manipulate it according to some programmed instructions, and to send the results of these manipulations to the screen. In this case, then, the Z88 is required to deal with the two devices: keyboard and screen.

Sometimes, however, you will want the information to be sent to a printer instead. Or the information may be extracted from an internally stored file and sent to the screen. Each of these beginning and endpoints to the flow of information (keyboard and printer; file and screen) are called devices.

The Z88 recognises a variety of such devices and supplies the facilities to control how information flows between them. These are:

```
:RAM.0    Ram in slot 0 – the internal memory
:RAM.1    Ram in slot 1 – external memory
:RAM.2    Ram in slot 2 – external memory
:RAM.3    Ram in slot 3 – external memory
:RAM.-    A temporary area of Ram used by the Z88
:SCR.0    The screen
:ROM.0    )
:ROM.1    ) A ROM (Read Only Memory)
:ROM.2    )
:ROM.3    )
:PRT.0    The serial port – via the printer driver
:COM.0    The serial port – not via the printer driver
:INP.0    Standard input
:OUT.0    Standard output
:NUL.0    Null (used to 'waste' certain kinds of
           information)
```

Binding devices

Later in this chapter we shall see how information can be directed between pairs of these devices. For the present, however, it is useful to reconsider some of the discoveries we made in previous chapters in the light of this idea about redirecting the flow of information.

We have already considered four of the devices listed above. These are the keyboard, screen, printer, and memory (files). Of these, two can be used to 'input' information into the Z88 (the keyboard and a file) and three can be used as output devices (the screen, printer and a file).

Input:-	Keyboard	File	
Output:-	Screen	Printer	File

When it is operating normally, the Z88's input and output initially concern the keyboard and screen respectively. In computer jargon they are *bound* together. However, we have already seen how it is possible to change the bindings. So:

to bind the keyboard to a file use	□+K and □–K	(Key)
to bind the screen to a file use	□+S and □–S	(Spool)
to bind the screen to a printer use	□+P and □–P	(Printer)

For example, you could bind the screen and filing system to create a file which lists all the files in your directory. Enter the Filer □F and request a catalogue of files. Then press the three keys □+S and you will see the letters 'CLI' appear in the right hand panel. Press the ENTER key to obtain the directory information and, when it has finished scrolling to the screen, press the three keys □–S. The CLI indicator will disappear.

If you now switch into PipeDream (□P) and load the file (◇FL) called :RAM.-/S.SGN as plain text, you will see the full directory information.

In this way, then, we have rebound the screen to a file to produce the file S.SGN. Then we bound the file to the screen to display it.

:Ram.- and versions 2.2 and 3.0

The first two of the three binding operations (□+K and □+S) create special files within the Z88's :RAM.- area called K.SGN and S.SGN respectively. We have already discussed how these temporary files (they are lost if your perform a soft or hard reset) can be copied across to more permanent file storage.

However, it is important to remember that versions 2.2 and 3.0 of the Z88's operating system contains a serious 'bug'. This has the effect of confusing OZ if you issue a soft reset (either by issuing the ◇PURGE command from the Index or by pressing the small reset button on the left side of the machine) while :RAM.- contains files. For this reason, having copied files from the :RAM.- area, it is very important that you immediately erase them. Otherwise problems may arise later if you perform a soft reset without remembering the files in RAM.-. Later in this chapter we will see how to automate some of this chore.

To check which version of the operating system you have in your machine, go to the Index page (□I), press the Help key, and then the left arrow key. Full commercial details of your Z88 will be revealed to you.

The Command Line Interpreter

The main controlling feature of the Z88's operating system is carried out by a powerful function that 'sits' between the keyboard and the system itself and 'interprets' the keys that are pressed. This is known as the command line interpreter (CLI); it accepts information either from the keyboard or from a file.

As far as keyboard input is concerned, in most cases the CLI simply passes on the keys you press directly onto the system and thence to the application you are performing. But for some keys, for example, □ and ◇ or the Menu or Index keys, the CLI interrupts the information flow and transfers the operating control to another part of the Z88's system. This may instruct the machine to wait for other information, on the basis of which it demands a specific action.

For example, wherever you happen to be within the Z88's cornucopia of applications if you press □ and then P the system will be directed to take you into PipeDream. Pressing the □ key followed by B will take you into Basic, and so on.

CLI Files

When you press □ and P or □ and B, all that the CLI does is to interpret information that arrives from the keyboard; the CLI intercepts the □ key and waits for the next letter to tell it where to send the operating system. Since it can also do the same for information that arrives via a file it should be easy to see that we could instruct the operating system to switch into PipeDream from a previously prepared file.

Try the following:

Switch into Pipedream (□P) and ensure that you have a 'clean' document in front of you (◇ BNEW). Now enter the following two lines:

```
#P
This is an example of a CLI file.
```

Save this as a plain text file, using the filename 'test'.

Now return to the Index and ◇ KILL your suspended PipeDream application to prove that what we are about to do is genuine. Then call up the Filer (□F) and 'execute' (◇ EX) the command file that you have just created. So, press ◇ EX and supply the filename: test. As soon as you press the ENTER key the CLI indicator appears in the right hand panel and the Z88 slips into its PipeDream application with the words 'This is an example of a CLI file.' printed ready for you.

With this simple example you have created and executed a CLI file.

Most of the Z88's key presses, and many of its applications, can be 'programmed' into a file in this way. All you have to do is to 'translate' the key presses you normally perform at the keyboard into the a file, using the following special characters if necessary:

File characters	Keyboard presses
#	Holding down the □ key while pressing another key
|	Holding down the ◇ key while pressing another key
~A	Pressing □ and releasing it before pressing another key
~C	Pressing ◇ and releasing it before pressing another key
|[	ESCape key
~S	Shift key
~I	Index key
~M	Menu key
~H	Help key
~X	Delete key
~E	Enter key
~U	Up cursor
~D	Down cursor
~L	Left cursor
~R	Right cursor
##	A single hash (#)
||	A single bar (|)
~~	A single tilde (~)
~.	A single dot at the beginning of a line

Unfortunately, not all keyboard sequences can be represented with these codes. For example, there is no way of representing the CAPS LOCK key or ◇ ESC.

CLI Examples

To illustrate the value of a CLI file, here are two very useful examples. The first returns all your favourite Z88 parameters following a soft reset after issuing the command ◇PURGE from the Index page or having pressed the reset button. The second erases all files in the :RAM.- area before they have a chance of doing any damage should you have to perform a soft reset.

When developing a CLI file it is always a useful exercise to have a piece of paper and a pencil handy, ready to record the key strokes as you perform them on the Z88.

Resetting the parameters

If you perform a soft reset all of the screen and file parameters are reset to their default values. For example, irrespective of whether or not you have an expanded Z88 the default device (◇ SV) will return to :RAM.0.

To reset the parameters you will probably perform the following keystrokes:

Keyboard	CLI file	Meaning
□S	#S	Enter the screen menu
down	~D	Down a line)
down	~D	Down a line) to reach the default directory
down	~D	Down a line)
◇→	|~R	Move cursor to the end of :RAM.0
DEL	~X	Delete the 0
1	1	1 (to set the default directory to :RAM.1)
down	~D	Down a line
down	~D	Down a line
2	2	Reduce the time-out time to 2 seconds
Enter	~E	Press ENTER to update
□F	#F	Enter the Filer
◇SV	|SV	Select device
◇→	|~R	Move cursor to the end of :RAM.0
DEL	~X	Delete the 0
1	1	1 (to select :RAM.1 as the directory device)
Enter	~E	Press ENTER to update
Index	~I	Return to the Index

Enter the CLI sequence shown above into a 'clean' PipeDream file and save it (◇FS) as a plain text file in :RAM.0 (since this is the Z88's default device, the machine returns to this device after a soft reset). For example, save the file as:

```
:RAM.0/RESET
```

Now, after a soft reset (◇PURGE at the Index) you simply have to enter the Filer (□F) execute the reset CLI file (◇EX reset), and your favourite parameters will return.

Erase all RAM.- files

To ensure that you don't have any files resident in your :RAM.- area, the following CLI file will automatically perform any necessary erasures:

Keyboard	**CLI file**	**Meaning**
◇`ER`	`|ER`	Ready to erase
`:RAM.-/*.*`	`:RAM.-/*.*`	All files in Ram.-
`N`	`N`	Do not confirm erasure
Enter	`~E`	Enter
Index	`~I`	Return to Index

Save this CLI file as a plain text file in :Ram.1, for example, :RAM.1/ERASE.

Now the command:

'◇EX erase' issued from the Filer will put your mind at rest.

Stopping the CLI

The only way of cancelling a CLI file while it is running or is 'suspended' is to press the Shift and Esc keys together. To cancel all CLI commands press ◇ESC.

Keyboard CLI Files

Although it is instructive to go through the laborious process of recording individual keystrokes and entering them into a PipeDream file this process is not always necessary because of the Z88's ability to record keystrokes into a file automatically. It does this by redirecting the keyboard to a file – so the keyboard and a file are bound together.

Simply press □+K before going through the complete keyboard procedure that you want recorded as a CLI file. For example, in the resetting the parameters CLI operation above, press □+K before the first □S instruction to enter the screen menu.

Then press □-K at the end of the process. That is, after pressing the Index key at the end.

If you now look at the :RAM.- directory you will find the new file K.SGN which contains all your key presses in CLI format. You can verify this by loading :RAM.-/K.SGN into PipeDream as a plain text file. Note that all the key press codes are on the same line. This does not matter to the CLI; it just makes the file more difficult to read.

If you copy :RAM.-/K.SGN to some more permanent file in :RAM.1, say, and then issue the 'erasing' CLI to remove the file from :RAM.-, you will have produced your new CLI file with much less effort.

Some More CLI Commands

As well as those in the list above, the Command Line Interpreter will accept some other commands in a file to provide even more flexibility. These are preceded by a full stop and *must* be placed at the beginning of a new line in any CLI file you create.

Command	**Meaning**
.S	Suspend the CLI file but retain its current bindings. This means that the CLI sign will remain in the right hand panel and any redirection will remain in force. The Z88 will now accept information from the keyboard. However, the only way to remove the suspension is for the user to press the Shift and Esc keys together.
.Dn	Delay for n hundredths of a second. So .D100 will provide a 1 second delay in the file's execution.
.J	This is the 'jammer'. It instructs the operating system to ignore all special characters like # and | and so not to act on them as CLI commands. This will be especially useful in the next chapter when we consider transferring files between computers.
.*file	Runs the CLI command file called 'file'.

Input and Output Redirection

The last group of CLI commands began the sequence with a full stop. The Z88 provides another set of similar 'full stop' commands that let you control the input and output processes within the machine – which returns us to where we entered this chapter. In other words, these I/O dot commands affect the Z88's binding. As above, these commands *must* be put at the beginning of a new line within a CLI file.

.<infile	takes input from the file 'infile' rather than from the keyboard.
.>outfile	sends output to the file 'outfile' rather than to the screen.
.T<infile	takes input from the keyboard but also sends it to the file called 'infile'. (This is like □+K.)
.T>outfile	sends output to the screen, but also sends it to the file called 'outfile'.
.=printfile	sends the printer output to the file called 'printfile' *before* it is sent to the printer filter (□E).
.T=printfile	sends the printer output to the file called 'printfile' *via* the printer filter (□E).

Each of these commands can refer to devices as well as to named files. For example, to re-direct the screen output to the printer as well as to the screen you could use the command:

```
.T>:PRT.0
```

It is this aspect of the command files that makes use of the :NUL.0 device – in order to turn off the redirection of an output in the middle of a CLI file operation. The NUL device is very much a theoretical entity, insofar is it is not actually present in the computer. So it 'absorbs' output because the machine believes that it is present when it is not.

Some aspects of using these dot commands was illustrated in the Basic line editing program that we considered in the last chapter. To recap, the program created a file called 'EE.CLI' which contained the following CLI sequences:

.RAM.0/E.CLI	All further information is sent to the file called E.CLI, rather than to the screen.
.J	To 'jam' the CLI so that the next listing would not be taken as a CLI command.
LIST	To LIST the line that we wish to edit.
PROCF	To call the editing procedure.

Then, this CLI file was activated with the CLI command:

```
*CLI .*RAM.0/EE.CLI
```

We could have changed line 65504 in the line editing program, for example, to have read:

```
.=PRT.0
```

which would have sent the line information to the printer rather than to the file E.CLI.

Booting CLI Files

As we have seen, all CLI files are executed either from the Filer (□F) using the execute command ◇ EX, or from the alarm (□A). When using the Alarm we set it to execute at a certain time by supplying the CLI file name within the 'reasons' area of the Alarm menu.

However, there is one special CLI file which, if filed in an Eprom sitting in slot 3, will automatically be executed following a soft or a hard reset. This file *must* be called:

```
BOOT.CLI
```

When you do a soft or hard reset the operating system looks to see whether an Eprom is resident in slot 3 and, if so, whether the file BOOT.CLI is present.

If this file is present it is automatically copied across to the :RAM.- area and executed from there. It would be very useful, for example, to make the parameter-resetting CLI that we developed above your BOOT.CLI.

However, you must remember the problems about leaving files in RAM.- if a subsequent soft reset is needed. So, if you do use the Z88's self-booting facilities, do ensure that you also use the erasing CLI immediately afterwards – just in case you need to soft reset your machine at some time in the future. To ensure that you do this you could execute the ERASE.CLI file at the end of RESET.CLI, although you will have to stop short of the final press of the ENTER key or you will be trying to erase a file that is in use.

CLI and Basic Files

Having developed the idea of being able to command the Z88 through its own Command Line Interpreter, now comes the really fancy work: combining Basic and

CLI commands to produce your own applications as combinations of bits and pieces from different existing applications.

We started to see the beginnings of such a set of procedures when we used Cambridge Computer's Basic line editor in the last chapter. In this respect, the important lines are those between 65504 and 65508:

```
65504 A=OPENOUT ":RAM.0/EE.CLI"
65505 B$=":RAM.0/E.CLI"
65506 PRINT#A,"."+B$
65507 PRINT#A,".J","LIST"+STR$(B),"PROCF"
65508 CLOSE#A
65509 *CLI .*:RAM.0/EE.CLI
```

The system creates a temporary file, called EE.CLI, into which the appropriate CLI commands were written. It uses variable names (B and B$) to introduce the variable line number. This CLI file is then executed from Basic in line 65509.

So this idea develops a CLI file which is then executed. But we have also seen already how CLI command strings can be incorporated directly into a Basic statement using the OSCLI command. For example, within a different kind of program, line 65506 could have been written as:

```
65506 OSCLI("CLI ."+B$):x=INKEY(0)
```

(Remember the need for the statement 'x=INKEY(0)' to 'force' the CLI to take action.)

By combining Basic and CLI in this way, therefore, it is possible to develop powerful and interactive programs. As an example, we will develop a simple interactive program that deletes a file from the directory. In this case, however, it asks the user which file to delete, rather than the individual having to remember a sequence of Filer commands.

```
10 CLS
20 INPUT "Which file do you want to delete ",f$
30 OSCLI("CLI #F~Cer"+f$+"~E~E~I"):X=INKEY(0)
```

In this simple, three line program, the first two lines are obvious. Reading from left to right in line 30, the OSCLI command line, we see the instructions:

`CLI`	Call the CLI
`#F`	Call the Filer
`~Cer`	◇ ER
`+f$`	Basic adds the name of the file to be deleted
`+`	Continue with the CLI string
`~E`	Enter – the file name
`~E`	Enter – 'yes' to the question to delete the file
`~I`	Return to the Index page

We could, of course, have written line 30 as:

```
30 OSCLI("DELETE "+f$):X=INKEY(0)
```

but it is more interesting to play with CLI commands.

Returning to Basic

When you use a Basic program to run a sequence of CLI commands, at the end of each OSCLI string you *must* return to Basic (#B). If you do not, the program controller obviously will not be in a position to move on to the next statement in the program.

So, say you wish to produce a program that erases a series of files, then you will need to include a series of OSCLI commands:

```
10 INPUT"How many files do you want to delete ",N
12 DIM f$(N)
20 FOR I = 1 TO N
30   INPUT"What are the file names ",f$(I)
40 NEXT
50 FOR I = 1 TO N
60   OSCLI("CLI #F~CER"+f$(I)+"~E~E#B"):X=INKEY(0)
70 NEXT
80 OSCLI("CLI ~I"):X=INKEY(0)
```

Notice the CLI command #B at the end of the OSCLI string in line 60; it returns the operating system to Basic. It is also important explicitly to command the CLI to enter the Filer (#F) at the beginning of each entry into the OSCLI statement. Otherwise, the reverse problem would occur and the Z88 would remain in Basic following line 60.

Two Applications

To use the skills we have just developed to better effect than simply deleting a set of files from the directory, here are two applications. The first creates a useful 'front end' menu for naive users. It makes it unnecessary for users ever to have to know the commands necessary to enter an application, and can also be extended to set up parameters if necessary.

The second application produces a powerful mail-merge facility for PipeDream that is presently lacking in the application. One standard letter, for example, could be sent to any number of people in a personalised fashion.

The menu

```
20 CLS
40 PRINT"                   MENU"
60 PRINT"A PipeDream                 E Terminal"
70 PRINT"B Spreadsheet               F File exchange"
80 PRINT"C Diary                     G Calculator"
90 PRINT"D BASIC                     H Alarm"
100 PRINT'"Which application do you want to see ";:INPUT
           app$
110 APP=ASC(app$)-64:IF APP<1 OR APP>8 THEN VDU7:GOTO 20
120 ON APP GOSUB 200,210,220,230,240,250,260,270:GOTO 20
200 OSCLI("CLI #P"):X=INKEY(0):RETURN
210 OSCLI("CLI #P"):X=INKEY(0):RETURN
220 OSCLI("CLI #D"):X=INKEY(0):RETURN230 OSCLI("CLI
            #B"):X=INKEY(0):RETURN
240 OSCLI("CLI #V"):X=INKEY(0):RETURN
250 OSCLI("CLI #X"):X=INKEY(0):RETURN
260 OSCLI("CLI #R"):X=INKEY(0):RETURN
270 OSCLI("CLI #A"):X=INKEY(0):RETURN
```

Whereas this application is quite straightforward, it can be made more comprehensive by adding further OSCLI command lines or executing CLI files *from within* a particular subroutine.

For example, say you wish to set up the PipeDream parameters for your naive user, the subroutine at line 200 could become:

```
200 OSCLI("CLI #P"):X=INKEY(0)
201 *CLI .*SET
202 RETURN
```

Where the CLI file called 'set' could have the following option changes:

```
~C0~DnD~~D~D~D70~D~D~D~D~D~D~D~D~D~D~D~D~D~D~D//My
company//~E~Cw100~E~Ch70~E
```

Reading from left to right, this CLI sequence enters the options menu (~ C0), moves down a line to turn off the borders (~ Dn), moves down to set the page length to 70 lines (70), changes the header information to print 'My company' at the top of each page, and alters the column width and right margin positions.

The same line, of course, could have been included within the OSCLI command in line 200. The value of using the *CLI.*filename route, however, is that you can develop the appropriate parameter setting CLI file by using the □+K and □-K route.

Mail merging

The following scheme uses the fact that, although you can compose documents on PipeDream, it is really a spreadsheet so your document can incorporate many of the spreadsheet functions. In this case we will use PipeDream's ability to:

- include a reference to a cell (@ref@)
- Index a cell
- print just a single column

The system expects you to develop your standard letter in column A, as is usual when using PipeDream as a word processor. It is important that the width of column A is set to be the same as the right hand margin. Where variable information is to be printed, the document should make reference to an appropriate cell in column C, which itself will refer to information in column B. This is where the PipeDream 'Index()' command will come in handy.

For example, say you wanted to send the following letter to three people:

```
Dear <person's name>,
This is just to remind you that you your account is
currently overdrawn to the amount of £<amount owed>. We
would be grateful if you would remit the outstanding
balance soon.

Yours Sincerely
```

In column B you should list the names and then the amount owed in each case. This is the variable information. For example:

Cell	**Information**
B1	Jim
B2	49.50
B3	Fred
B4	67.89
B5	John
B6	45.34

This information, of course, could arise from a previously prepared file – simply load the file (◇ FL) and 'Insert' it into slot B1.

The system will operate by inserting into column C the appropriate Index() statements that will tell PipeDream from where to take the information. So, when the first letter is printed, the Index command in C1 will point to the cell that Contains 'Jim' and the command in C2 will index '49.50'. On the next print run, the index pointers will move to 'Fred' and '67.89' respectively.

For this reason, the actual letter should be couched in the following terms:

```
Dear @C1@,

This is just to remind you that you your account is
currently overdrawn to the amount of £@C2@. We would be
grateful if you would remit the outstanding balance soon.

Yours Sincerely
```

Remember, the function '@ref@' takes the information from the referenced cell and inserts it into the document.

Finally, when printing out the letter, we need to be able to tell PipeDream how many lines are to be printed. You will remember that you can do this by using the option supplied in the print menu (◇ PO) that asks you to 'select rows and columns'. Thus, we must design some selection mechanism, the easiest of which will be to enter a special value, such as 1, into column C for the length of the letter.

So, TAB to column D and enter 1 in cell D1. This must be entered as a spreadsheet expression: ◇ X and then 1. Now, say your letter extends from rows 1 to 10, enter ◇ BRE..d1..d1d10 to replicate the value of 1 down the next 10 rows of column D.

Save this document (◇ FS) with the filename "MM".

To recap:

- Type the standard letter into column A, having set the column width to at least the right margin. Where variable information is to be inserted, enter @Cx@ where 'x' represents its position in the information list (1 for the first, 2 for the second, and so on).
- Add the variable information to column B.
- Enter the value 1 into cell D1 and replicate this cell for the number of rows taken up by your letter.
- Save the document with the filename "MM".

Now for the Basic program that will merge together the two sets of information and print out separate letters:

```
10 INPUT"How many letters ",N
20 INPUT "How many variables ",V
30 ch$="%"
40 OSCLI("CLI #P~CFLMM~E#B"):X=INKEY(0)
50 LOC=0
60 FOR I = 1 TO N
70    FOR J = 1 TO V
80       LOC=LOC+1
90       OSCLI("CLI #P~CcgsC"+STR$(J)+"~E~Cx~Cdindex
                (2,"+STR$(LOC)+")~E#B"):X=INKEY(0)
100    NEXT J
110    VDU7
120    OSCLI("CLI #P~Cpoyal~Dy~CdD1=1~E#B"):X=INKEY(0)
130    OSCLI("CLI .D500"):INKEY=(0)
140 NEXT I
```

Before you run this program, ensure that you do not have any PipeDream documents are suspended in your Z88. 'Kill' any that you see shown on the Index page.

When you run this program, it will:

- Ask you how many different copies you intend to print and how many variables there are in each copy (lines 10 and 20)

- Load the document into PipeDream (line 40).

- For each variable of the first copy, insert the appropriate Index() reference into the relevant cells in column C (line 90 – looped between lines 70 and 100). Notice that each time this is done, the Z88 switches into PipeDream at the beginning, and back into Basic at the end.

- Print the document (line 120), but only the information in column A (~ Cpoya1) using D1=1 as the criterion for selecting which rows to print (~ Dy ~ CdD1=1). Notice the need to delete the criterion each time before inserting D1=1. This arises because PipeDream remembers the selection criterion each time. So simply entering 'D1=1' would add this character string each time, producing an ever-increasing (and meaningless) criterion.

- Wait for five seconds, just in case the printer is too slow to keep up with the Z88 (line 130).

- Having printed the document, the procedure is repeated (line 140) with new Index() references inserted into the relevant cells in column C.

Summary

This chapter introduced the idea of controlling the Z88 directly from within its own operating system. In this way extremely powerful developments can take place that use parts of the Z88's individual applications in novel ways – particularly when they are combined with standard Basic programs.

The final chapter will show how such skills can be put to good effect by making the Z88 communicate with other computers – even if they are on the other side of the world.

10

Tomorrow the world

For all their power and sophistication, computers would be limited if all this information that they generate remained locked inside them. For example, it would be no use using the word processor to create the perfect manuscript if everyone who wanted to read it had to sit at the computer terminal and watch the words scroll past. Even the Z88's sophistication, compactness and portability would not save it from extinction if it had to be passed from one individual to another before the spreadsheet data it so expertly creates could be appreciated.

Happily, of course, this state of affairs does not exist. With just a few simple commands and a cable connected to some other device, the information that is stored inside the machine can easily be extracted. We saw an example of this in Chapter 7 when discussing the variety of ways in which we can get the Z88 to 'talk' to a printer and control its actions. All that is required is the right kind of cable connecting the two devices; the Z88 and the printer does the rest.

Modern printers, of course, are not just the electronic equivalents of their mechanical precursors, the typewriter; they are very sophisticated computing devices in their own right. If you lift the lid on one you will see a similar maze of electronic circuitry to that which is inside your computer.

This being so, it does not take too great a leap in thinking to realise that the printer could be replaced relatively easily by another computer. After all, the Z88 does not mind what kind of device is receiving the information which it is transmitting – as long as something is.

Then, with an active computer at the other end, rather than the device being just a passive printer, we have the bases for some very sophisticated information transmission systems. Indeed, as this chapter will demonstrate, you could set up the situation in which two or more computers are connected by cables that circumnavigate the world; and they will still 'talk' to each other and act on the information that each sends.

So the Z88, via its 9-pin serial port on the right hand edge of the machine, can take part in this developing communications system that will see us into the next millennium. And it can do so as easily as the most powerful mainframe computer.

Kinds of Communications

When discussing communication between two computers a distinction is often made between the simple situation in which two computers are connected together with a cable attached to their serial connectors, and that in which they are connected to each other via the telephone line. In the first case the computers correspond with each other directly, usually to transfer files between one and the other. In the second, however, the information from one first has to be translated into a form that the telephone line can accommodate; then it is retranslated by the receiving computer at the other end. This is normally done by a special device called a 'modem' that is interposed between the computer's serial connector and the telephone line.

The Z88 can accommodate both kinds of communication systems. For the first it uses a simple file transfer application called Imp-Export. This is activated either

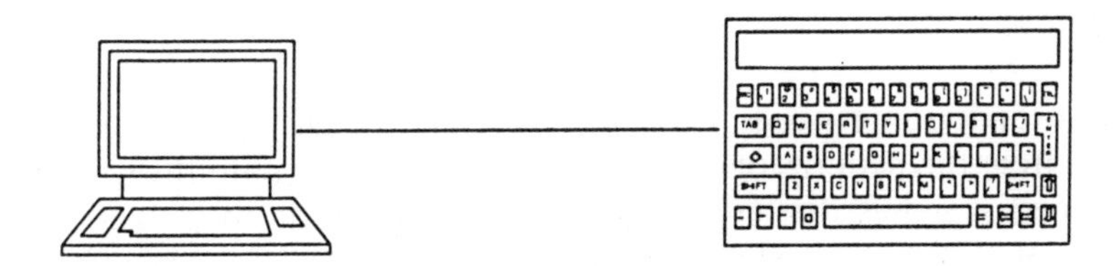

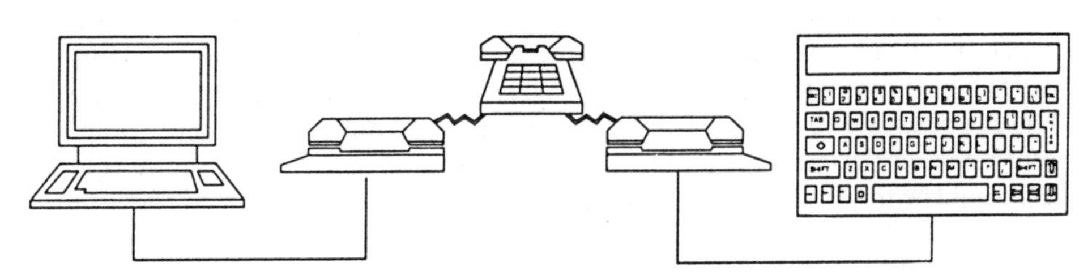

Computer-computer and computer-modem communications

from the Index page or by pressing □X. Interactive communication between remote computers (and, indeed, also between closely connected ones), however, is carried out using the Terminal application. Like Imp-Export this can be activated from the Index page – or by pressing □V.

Bits and Baud

When you decide to connect two computers together to make them communicate with each other, you need to understand a little about the nature of computer communications. If the transmitting and receiving computers are not set up correctly, the messages that are passed between the two devices will be lost.

In human terms the problem is a little like when two people talk to each other: if one uses a language that the other does not understand, or speaks too fast, or if the receiver is deaf, then the communication is likely to be unsuccessful. Some information might be passed between the two, but its quality and quantity is unlikely to be high.

As humans we communicate with speech sounds or visually by recognisable character shapes. Computers, on the other hand, deal with electronic pulses; indeed, part of their sophistication lies in being able to translate these pulses for us into display characters that we can understand. As far as computer-computer communication is concerned, of course, the machines do not have to perform this translation; they can communicate with each other in their own language.

ASCII

Just as we understand words from their sound patterns, computers recognise characters from the patterns of electronic pulses that are sent to them. These days, the sequence of pulses that create each character conform to a standard system known as ASCII (American Standard Code for Information Interchange). As long as both the transmitting and the receiving computer can 'understand' ASCII codes, the characters will be sent and received accurately.

Each character in the ASCII system is composed of eight possible pulses, each of which it called a 'bit' (the eight bits are known as a 'byte' – computer memory is defined in terms of the number of such bytes available). Confusingly, each of these bits can be created by the presence the or absence of a pulse. For example, where '1' represents an electrical pulse and '0' indicates no pulse, the capital letter 'A' (but not 'a') would be transmitted as the following sequence:

```
1 0 0 0 0 0 1 0
```

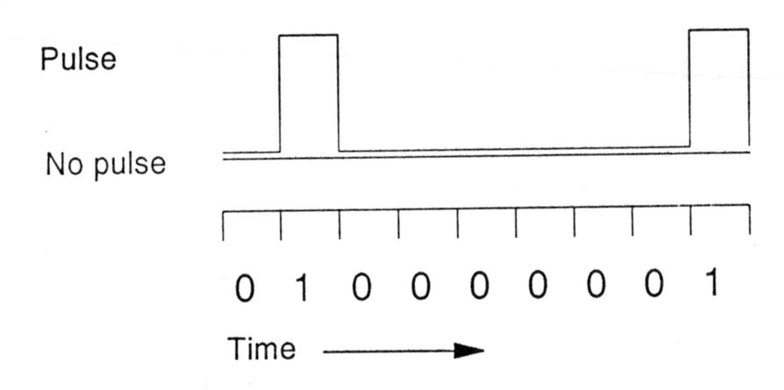

The letter A in bits

With different combinations of eight 1s and 0s it is possible to create 256 different sequences. This is the maximum number of character codes that '8-bit' computers (which comprise most of the 'cheaper' micro computers) can deal with.

If you were to produce a list of all 256 possible sequences, the sequence 00000000 would be first and 11111111 last. Numbering the list from zero to 255, the bit sequence for 'A' (10000010) would have a value of 65. This is the ASCII value for 'A', as you can see in Appendix 1.

You could prove this fact by entering Basic on the Z88 (□B) and then:

```
PRINT ASC("A")
```

Similarly,

PRINT CHR$(65) will respond with 'A'.

How is the value of 65 calculated? It is actually quite simple:

If the first bit has a value of 1, the second a value of 2, the third 4, then 8, 16, 32, 64 and finally 128, you simply count the values where the bit equals 1. So:

value	1	2	4	6	8	16	32	64	128	
A	1	0	0	0	0	0	0	1	0	
Count	1							64		Total=65

Since all the alphabetic characters have ASCII values that are lower than 128, for most purposes it is not necessary to use the highest bit (128). For this reason, many communication systems operate on just seven bits; the eighth is assumed to be zero. Obviously, this increases the number of characters that you can send from one machine to another within a given time.

Baud rates

Having seen how characters are generated, ready to be sent from and to the Z88, it is now important to understand how they are transmitted and received.

The first priority is to ensure that the information is transmitted at the same 'speed' as that which the receiving station is expecting. Obviously, since the information transmitted is in terms of pulses or not pulses (1s or 0s), the receiving computer must know how fast to expect the information. Otherwise it will be unable to differentiate between a sequence of pulses or no pulses.

The transmission speed is called the 'baud rate'. This actually refers to the number of signal changes that occur each second – that is a change from a 0 to a 1 or from a 1 to a 0. At lower 'speeds' this corresponds to the number of bits transmitted per second but, because of additional procedures that the computers have to go through, at higher speeds this simple relationship between baud and bits/second does not hold.

Happily, most people do not need to worry about this slight distinction between the two terms. These days there are standard baud rates that most computers can accommodate, all of which – except 4800 baud – are available on the Z88:

75, 300, 600, 1200, 2400, 4800, 9600, 19200, 38400

In addition, the British Viewdata system, which is used by Prestel, uses a baud rate known as 1200/75, in which information is passed in one direction at 1200 baud and returned at 75 baud.

Parity

Obviously, as with human-human communication, the faster the information is transmitted the more likely it is that errors will creep into the process. This is particularly true when information is passed via the public telephone system.

When communicating via the telephone line, the most common transmission speed is 1200 baud – although increasingly modems are becoming available that will accommodate 2400 and even 9600 baud without too much error.

As some check that the code has been sent correctly, most communicating devices use rather inventive techniques to check each letter as it is being passed between them. As each character is made ready to be sent, the transmitter counts the number of 1s in the character and then adds a 0 or a 1 to make the final bit count either odd or even. This extra bit is known as the parity bit, and you can define it as being odd or even. If no parity count is employed, then the system assumes that eight bits are being transmitted.

Xon-Xoff

When computers are communicating with each other, they often need a system whereby one can 'tell' the other to stop transmitting temporarily – perhaps because the receiver needs to assimilate the information it has obtained (perhaps to save it). The same effect often occurs in human terms – you may ask the person speaking to you to wait for 'a second' while you try to assimilate what he has said.

In computer terms, this process is known as 'handshaking' and the system employed is known as 'Xon-Xoff'. Again, both computers in the communication process need to know under which rules they are communicating – with handshaking on or off.

Z88 Communications Parameters

The message so far, then, is simply that the communications parameters of baud rate, parity and handshaking must be set to be the same on both the transmitting and receiving computers – otherwise the communications will go astray and one device

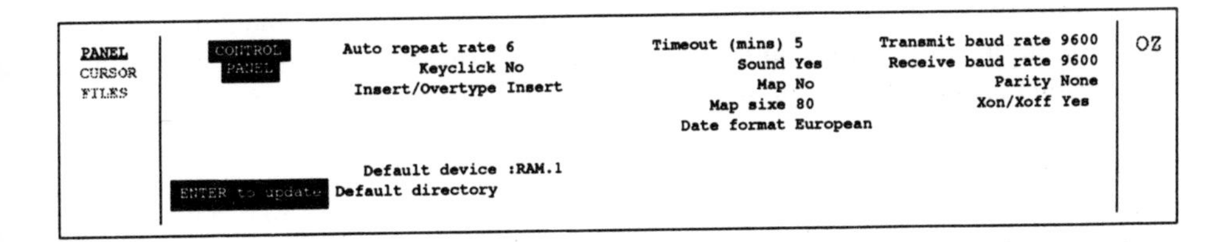

Changing the communications in the screen options page (□S)

will not 'understand' the other. The choice of which settings to use is yours alone – although if you are communicating with a remote computer the choice may be made by the other computer owner.

The Z88's communications parameters are easily set and changed from the screen options panel (□S). They all appear in the final column. As with all Z88 options you can cycle between the various possibilities using the command ◇J. So, to find out which baud rates are available for transmission, for example, take the cursor to the first option in the final column of the screen menu and continue to press ◇J until the baud rate you require appears.

As you will see, the Z88 lets you set the transmission speed for the Z88 in its transmitting and receiving modes separately. Although this provides considerable flexibility, most communications systems will demand that the transmission and reception processes are carried out at the same speed.

Having set the speed, parity and handshaking parameters, you are ready to enter the world of Z88 communications.

Local Computers

The first situation we should consider is when two (or more) computers are connected together directly. They do not actually have to reside next to each other; with appropriate lengths of cable they can be in different rooms, for example. However, the important feature is that the connecting cable extends from one machine directly to the other without any intervening device (other than a switch box, perhaps).

The cable

The cable used in this direct kind of computer-computer communications is known as a 'crossed wire' cable. Pin 2 of one of the connectors is connected to pin 3 of the other, and vice versa. This is necessary because the output of one machine needs to enter the input of the other, and vice versa. Obviously, other connections also have to be made between the two plugs, and these are shown in Appendix 5.

At the Z88 end of the connection you will need the same 9-pin 'male' (pin-based) D-connector that is used to connect the computer to a printer. The kind of connector you should use at the other end, however, will be determined by the kind of computer with which your Z88 is communicating. An IBM PC or a PC-compatible machine, for example, will normally require a 25-way 'female' (socket-based) D-connector. A BBC Micro, on the other hand, will need a 5-pin DIN plug that fits the RS423 connector at the back of the machine.

Communications software

Being unintelligent machines, computers cannot know what to do with information that arrives at their communications sockets nor, indeed, can they know how to send the information. Each end of the link, therefore, needs a program which will perform this service for them.

As far as the Z88 is concerned, it contains a ready-made file-transfer system that can transfer both program and ASCII (text-based) files from and to the Z88. This is the Imp-Export application that is accessed at any time by pressing □X. You can use this to send any file that has been previously saved somewhere within the Z88's directories – though not data that are merely 'suspended'.

There is a variety of different kinds of software that you use at the other end of the link. Some programs are free and can be obtained from many different outlets around the country, while others are commercially available. They all rejoice under the generic name of 'communications software'.

Cambridge Computers have produced a 'Link' range of software for the IBM PC and the BBC Micro, and other programs are available for the Apple Macintosh and the Atari ST. These are very easy to operate and simply require you to indicate whether or not the 'other' machine should send or receive files and, if the process is to send files, the name of the file to be sent.

Instead of using a commercially available *file* transfer program, it is possible to transfer files between the Z88 and another computer using the more sophisticated communications software that you will also use if you want to employ your Z88 as an interactive terminal. This kind of software allows an individual at one machine literally to 'talk' to another at a remote computer – messages appear on the screen in 'real time'.

Because most such software also provides facilities for saving the information that appears on the screen to a file – just like the Z88's □+S function – you can certainly transfer ASCII text files in this way.

Procomm is one of the most famous programs of this genre, which also happens to be extremely cheap because it is shareware (a program for which you pay a small amount of money directly to the author). This program is available for PC-compatible machines and allows text-text transmission as well as other more sophisticated protocols that will be discussed later.

Talking Together

Operating the Z88's Imp-Export application is extremely simple.

To send a file from the Z88 to another computer first load and run the other computer's communications program, setting it to receive files as appropriate. Using PC Link on an IBM PC or a PC-compatible computer, for example, you will simply need to press the appropriate key to 'receive a file' from Z88 and supply the name of the file that you want your transferred data saved as. If you do not supply a name the program will use the name of the file that originated from your Z88.

At the Z88 end, press □X to enter the Imp-Export application and 's' to send. Supply the name of the file that you wish to send, including any directory paths as appropriate, and press ENTER.

As long as your cable is wired correctly and the communications parameters are the same at each end, the file will be sent from the Z88 to your other computer. While the material is being sent the Z88 displays the row number being transferred to give you some idea as to how the transmission is progressing.

To send a file from the other computer to the Z88, in other words for the Z88 to receive a file, the process must be reversed:

First set the Z88 to receive mode (□X and then 'r'). If you supply a file name when requested that name will be used to store the file that is passed to the Z88. This stage is important if your communications program on the other machine has not been designed specifically to interact with the Z88. If it does not transmit a file name then the Z88 will simply remain passive while the data are being transferred because it does not have a file name into which it can store the incoming information.

If you are using a specially designed communications package like PC Link, however, pressing ENTER at this filename prompt will tell the Z88 to use the name of the file supplied by the transmitting machine.

Having set the Z88, turn your attention to the other computer and go through the necessary processes to send a file. Once again, the row numbers will be displayed on the Z88 as it receives the data.

Receiving batches of files

As well as sending and receiving single files, the Z88's Imp-Export utility can also receive a group (batch) of files from the other computer. The procedure works in much the same way as it does for receiving single files – that is, you set the Z88 to receive a batch of files by pressing 'B' and then ENTER twice so that the machine will accept the file names from the other computer.

The only stipulation made is that the sending computer *must* send special codes to tell the Z88 when a file begins and ends and when the group of files has been transmitted. Unfortunately, not all communications programs can do this. For computer programmers who are capable of instructing their computers to send and receive information, however, the following codes will be useful:

Code	Function
`ESC N`	Start of filename
`ESC F`	End of filename and start of file
`ESC E`	End of a file .. more files to follow
`ESC Z`	End of a file .. and end of batch

So, a group of three files sent as a batch would have the following codes:

```
ESC N filename1 ESC F data ESC E ESC N filename2 ESC F
data ESC E ESC N filename3 ESC F data ESC Z
```

When transmitting the information in files, it is important to know that data in the standard character range of &20 to &FF (that is, everything above a 'space' in Appendix 1) is transmitted without modification. Each piece of data in the range &00 to &1F, however, must be prefixed with the sequence 'ESC B'. For example, &32 (space) is transmitted by the computer as &32. The code &18 (◇ X), however, should be transmitted as 'ESC B 18'.

Upload and Download

Communications program designers seem to have a jargon all of their own, as we already have seen with terms such as 'bits', 'bytes', 'baud' and 'parity'. Another piece of jargonised terminology that often catches the unwary is up- and down-loading. These terms are often used in commercial communications software and refer to the *direction* in which the information is transmitted between machines. If you get the direction wrong you *could* lose your file.

If you are dealing with the Z88's keyboard, up-loading means sending information *from* the Z88 to another one; downloading means the opposite: from the other computer to the Z88. This can be very confusing, since each process implies that both computers should be considered to be the central one, at different times. For example, if you are sending information from a PC to the Z88 you are 'uploading' at the PC and 'downloading' at the Z88. Communicating in the other direction means 'downloading' at the PC and 'uploading' at the Z88.

The problem will only arise with a communications program on your other machine that uses this terminology (the Z88's Imp-export application sensibly uses 'send' and 'receive'). When dealing with the other machine, therefore, a simple way of remembering the right directions is to imagine the Z88 sitting on top of your other computer. Then, if you are transferring information *from* the Z88 *to* the other computer, you're *down*loading it at the other computer; *up*loading is the process of going from the other computer *up* to the Z88.

Plain Text or Not

Whenever you send a PipeDream or Diary file to another computer, you should remember that the files contain a considerable amount of information that is additional to the text itself. As previous chapters have explained, this defines how the Z88 formats the file when it appears onscreen and is sent to the printer.

However, it is likely that when you come to deal with the material on the other computer you will wish to have all this formatting information present. For this reason PipeDream offers you the facility to save a file as plain text – the formatting instructions are removed before the file is saved.

If you intend to transfer ASCII files from the Z88 to another computer, therefore, you should take advantage of this facility. However, some specialised communications programs may remove the formatting information for you. For example, using Cambridge Computer's Link suit of programs you can convert the PipeDream file to a format that is more compatible with other word processors *before* sending it.

Of course, you may also decide to incorporate appropriate formatting removal routines into your own communications program. For this reason, Appendix 4 shows the format of both PipeDream and Diary files.

Through the Printer Filter

Whereas the Imp-Export utility provides a very simple and efficient way of sending and receiving files from and to the Z88, it suffers from the simple drawback that ASCII (text) files do not pass through the printer editor on their way out of the machine.

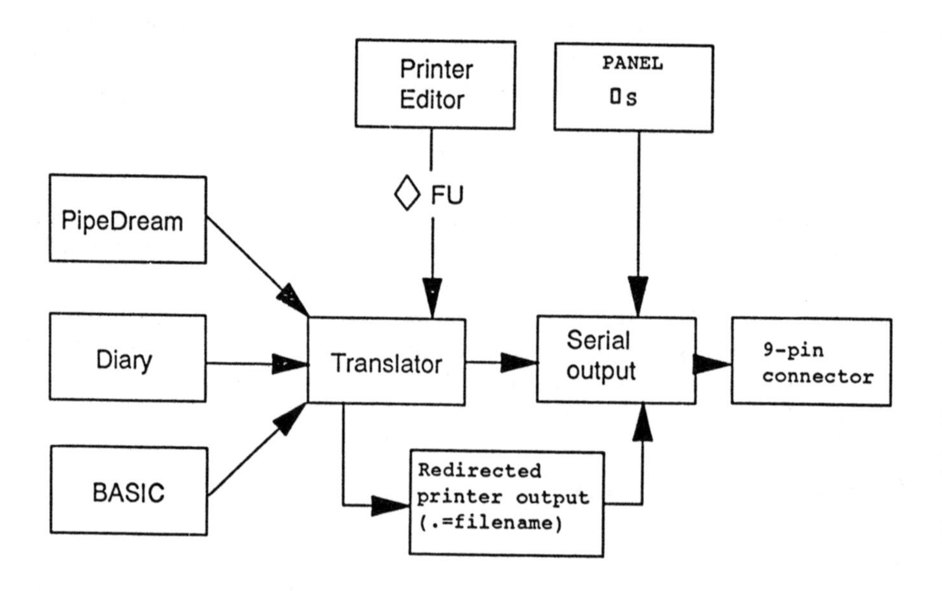

Out through the serial port

The reason for this is obvious: whereas you may wish to have ASCII files translated before they reach the other device, you probably will not wish to have any program files tampered with.

If you *print* files from the application (◇ PO), however, you will send them via the printer editor before it exits the Z88. This means that any translations that you have set up within your printer editor (□E) will be incorporated into your transmitted file – as long as you have updated the printer editor file (◇ FU).

Since the Z88 knows nothing about the nature of the device at the other end of the cable you can easily substitute a computer for a printer and enjoy the benefit of any translations that you have set up in the Printer Editor. Remember to use the computer communications cable, though, rather than the standard printer cable.

Interactive Communications

The kind of communication that has been discussed so far is essentially one way only: a file (or a batch of files) is sent from one machine to the other. Although some return information will have been sent, particularly if you have set the Xon-Xoff handshaking to be on, the communication is not fully interactive.

To effect this kind of communication on the Z88 you should enter the Terminal application (□V), which simply produces a blank screen. Here you enter your messages and receive replies from the person using the computer at the other end of the communication link. Of course, the other end does not actually have to be an individual who is operating the computer – it could just as easily be a computer which is making the responses.

This kind of interactive communication can be accomplished both when two computers are connected directly with each other, as they were when operating the Imp-Export program, or when they are connected to each other via modems and the telephone line.

In whichever way you design the communications set up, the computer at the other end must have running an interactive communications program such as those discussed already. A program such as one of Cambridge Computers' Link suite will not work since it cannot operate interactively.

Procomm and the Z88

To illustrate the ease with which you can communicate interactively we shall use Procomm as the communications program on a PC and connect this computer to the Z88.

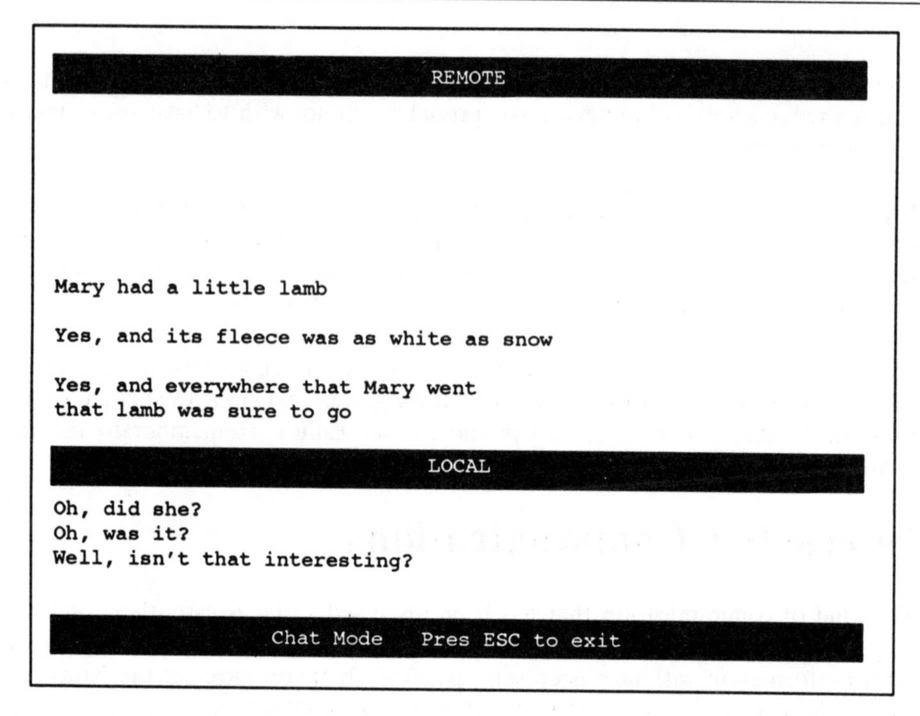

Procomm's chat mode

At the PC end, press Alt and O together to enter Procomm's 'chat' mode. You will see the screen split horizontally, with an area for the PC user's messages and another for messages from the Z88. Now enter the Z88's Terminal application (□V).

As long as you have set the communications parameters to be the same on both machines (using Alt and P in Procomm and □S on the Z88), whatever you type into the Z88 will appear on the 'remote' Procomm screen. And what is entered into the PC will be displayed on the Z88's screen.

You should note, however, that in both cases the information is only transmitted to the other computer when you press ENTER.

Capturing the Text

All good communications programs supply the ability to capture (spool) the text that appears on the screen and save it into a file for future use. With Procomm you do this by pressing the Alt and F1 keys together and supplying a file name for the captured text. Pressing Alt and F1 a second time closes the file. You can then read the information in it using Alt and V, or your own word processor.

At the Z88, end, of course, we have a similar spooling function built into the software: □+S.

If you press the three keys □+S before begin to communicate with the other computer, and then □-S at the end, all the material that appeared on the Z88's screen will be stored in a file called S.SGN in :RAM.-.

To read this information from within PipeDream (□P) load (◇FL) the file :RAM.-/S.SGN as plain text. You will then be able to deal with it as you wish.

Remember, however, the annoying 'bug' that has found its way into the Z88s with operating system versions 2.2 and 3.0. (Press Index, Help and the left arrow to check your operating system version.) It is *very* important that you remove all files from :RAM.- before doing any soft resetting (by pressing the small button inset into the left hand edge of the Z88, for example, or by entering ◇PURGE at the Index).

So, having captured your text to S.SGN, copy this file into a safer area (□F, ◇CO, :RAM.-/S.SGN, :RAM.1/capture) and erase S.SGN from RAM.-.

Remember, too, that information is *only* spooled to S.SGN. So, if you spool another set of text by pressing □+S, then a *new* S.SGN file will be created, overwriting any copy of it that already resides in :RAM.-.

Transmitting Files

When interacting with another computer you may often wish to send a previously prepared file rather than laboriously entering the information at the keyboard. This is particularly important when you use electronic mail, as we shall discuss below.

By judicious operation of the CLI file system, this is very easy with the Z88.

At the beginning of the file you want to send simply add the following two lines at the beginning:

```
#V
.J
Text......
```

Save this file as plain text (for example, with the filename 'tosend') and then 'send' it via the Filer in the following way:

If you are within the Terminal application enter the Filer with □F and ask to execute the file using the command '◇EX tosend'. The #V command at the beginning of the file will return you to the Terminal, '.J' ensures that any characters such as '#' or '.' do not get interpreted as CLI commands, and then the remainder of the file is sent directly to the Z88's serial port and by-passes the screen.

At the end of the operation you are left in the Terminal, ready to continue further interactions with the other computer if you wish.

Since this is a CLI file, of course, you can add a number of other command features to it, including instructions to dial another computer, log on to its services, transmit the file, and then log off, if you so desire.

Telephone Communications

So far we have considered only the situation whereby two computers are connected to each other directly. Now we shall move into more global communications, using the telephone line as our connector.

Most parts of the world are served by the telephone system, which means that somehow you should be able to connect your Z88 to another computer almost anywhere in the world. Remember, a standard telephone line contains many more cables than the few needed to connect two computers together.

The only problem with this Utopian dream, of course, is that the telephone system does not operate with the same kind of pulse system which we use when communicating between two computers. If you were to connect your Z88 directly to the telephone socket in the wall you could do considerable damage both to your computer and to the telephone system.

For this reason, we need to have an intervening box that will translate the computer's output signals into the kind of information that the telephone system can cope with – and at the other end there needs to be an equivalent box that will translate the information back again.

Modems

This service is provided by a piece of hardware called a 'modem' (*mod*ulator *dem*odulator). These come in all shapes and sizes with a wide variety of prices and facilities. Most modern modems will accommodate transmission speeds of 1200 baud, although newer ones can accommodate 2400 and even 9600 baud transmission rates.

The size of modems varies, too, from as small as a box of matches to as large as the Z88 itself. Clearly, being a valuable portable tool the Z88 will be best served by having an equally portable, battery-operated, modem.

As far as cables are concerned, the modem needs *nearly* the same kind of cable to connect with the Z88 as you used when connecting the machine to another computer. The major difference, however, is that pins 2 and 3 are *not* crossed between connectors: pin 2 at one end should be connected to pin 2 at the other, and pin 3 to pin 3.

The output of the modem is then connected directly to the telephone system, using a normal telephone connector.

Auto-dial modems

Some time ago the US firm of D C Hayes developed the idea of a modem that could be instructed by software to dial a number automatically, and also automatically answer a call. These 'auto-dial, auto-answer' modems have become very common and most modern modems conform to the Hayes standard – they are said to be 'Hayes-compatible'.

The Hayes standard contains a number of commands for controlling various operations on the modem using the computer's software. As far as the present discussion is concerned, however, the important command is the one used to dial a number. This is:

`AT Dn` where n is the number you wish to dial.

So, if you issue this instruction directly from your Z88's Terminal the modem will automatically dial the number that you have defined. Once you are connected with the other computer's modem the rest is up to you. Remember though, that all of these operations can be incorporated into a CLI file or, more impressively, into a BASIC program that contains the relevant CLI commands.

Some commercially produced software is available for the Z88 which incorporate these operations.

Electronic Mail and Bulletin Boards

Communicating directly with another computer user via the telephone line, many miles, or even thousands of miles, away, opens up a number of new horizons for the Z88 owner. As interesting, however, is the use of the hundreds of mainly free electronic bulletin boards that are dotted around the world, and the dozens of commercial electronic mail systems that are currently available.

Most bulletin boards are created by hobbyists who dedicate their computer to a telephone line with an auto-answer modem. If you call one of these numbers you will

```
Type 'cix' to login: cix


+-----------------------------------------------------------------------------+
|               Welcome to - The Compulink Information eXchange               |
+-+---------------------------------------------+-------------------------+-+
  |      XXXXX   XXXXXX  XX      XX             |       Provided by:      |
  |    XXXXXXX    XX     XX   XX                |                         |
  |   XX   XX     XX     XX XX   +--------------+           CIX           |
  |  XX          XX      XXX     | Europe's Most | Suite 2,  The Sanctuary |
  | XX   XX     XX      XX XX    |   Advanced    | Oakhill Grove, Surbiton |
  | XXXXXXX     XX     XX   XX   | Conferencing  |      Surrey KT6 6DU     |
  | XXXXX   XXXXXX  XX      XX   |    System     |   Voice: 01 390-8446    |
  +------------------------------+---------------+-------------------------+
  | 01 390-1244  Tricom Modems with V21 V22 V23 V22bis Level 5 MNP 16 lines |
  | 01 399-5252  Tricom Modems with V21 V22 V23 V22bis Level 5 MNP 20 lines |
  | 01 390-1255  Courier HST modems with 9600 HST only Level 5 MNP  4 lines |
+-+-----------------------------------------------------------------------+-+
|    If you type "qix" instead of "cix", this screen will not be displayed    |
+-----------------------------------------------------------------------------+


CIX  Version 1.254  2/5/90

You are on line: tty16

Nickname? (Enter 'new' for new user)
```

The CIX conferencing system

be connected with a computer system that is used by hundreds, if not thousands, of other individuals from around the world. Most of the boards have electronic messaging facilities in which you can leave (electronic) messages and files for named individuals, and also let you download free software. Of particular relevance to Z88 users, of course, are boards which are subscribed by groups of users who have an interest in the Z88 or in the BBC Micro. Appendix 3 provides the current names and telephone numbers of some such bulletin boards – although these numbers may change in the future.

The whole area of bulletin boards is one which extends well beyond the limits of this book. However, *The New Hackers Handbook* by Steve Gold provides a comprehensive exposition of this intriguing area.

As far as electronic mail is concerned, systems such as Telecom Gold supply the facility to send messages and documents from user to user. They operate in much the same way as bulletin boards but their emphasis is primarily directed towards the business user who wishes to transmit text-based messages and memoranda around the world.

Troubleshooting

The novice who enters the world of communications must expect to experience a few teething troubles at the start. Perseverance, however, will reap many rewards.

If you do experience trouble, perhaps you cannot transmit a file from one computer to another, the most likely cause will be first the cable and second the parameters that you have set. If you have built the cable yourself carefully check to see that all soldering joints are firm and that there are no pieces of solder making unexpected connections with another pins. Also, of course, check that that pins are wired correctly.

Assuming that you have purchased the cable, the problem will probably lie in the communications parameters that you have set. First ensure that they're the same on both machines. If they are then you will have to vary them systematically until you obtain success.

When connecting two computers together the most appropriate parameter settings on the Z88 are for no parity and for the Xon-Xoff to be set to 'on'. At the other computer set the parameters to be no parity, 8 bits and 1 stop bit. Your baud rates, of course, are up to you.

Finally, problems sometimes occur with autodial modems when the telephone line takes some time to connect. This is particularly prevalent if you telephone an overseas number, and occurs because most modems 'drop' the line after a preset time if no connection is made. To overcome this you will have to 'instruct' your modem, using the Hayes commands mentioned in its manual, not to drop the line. This instruction, of course, is done via the Z88's Terminal in the same way as you instructed the modem to dial the number.

Summary

The kind of communications discussed in this chapter represent the next important stage for our computerised world. By being able to transfer information between computers over distances ranging from inches to many thousands – and even millions – of miles we are likely to change how we think, work and interact with each other. Indeed, society itself is likely to change.

And the Z88, with its considerable flexibility and portability is likely to be at the forefront of this revolution that will take us into the next millennium.

Appendix 1

ASCII codes

Decimal	Hex	Binary	Keyboard	Meaning	
0	&00	0000 0000	◇ =	NULL	Null
1	&01	0000 0001	◇ A	SOH	Start of file header
2	&02	0000 0010	◇ B	STX	Start of text
3	&03	0000 0011	◇ C	ETX	End of text
4	&04	0000 0100	◇ D	EOT	End of transmission
5	&05	0000 0101	◇ E	ENQ	ESC for printer & screen
6	&06	0000 0110	◇ F	ACK	Acknowledge
7	&07	0000 0111	◇ G	BEL	Beep
8	&08	0000 1000	◇ H	BS	Back space
9	&09	0000 1001	◇ I	HT	Horizontal tab
10	&0A	0000 1010	◇ J	LF	Line feed
11	&0B	0000 1011	◇ K	VT	Vertical tab
12	&0C	0000 1100	◇ L	FF	Form feed
13	&0D	0000 1101	◇ M	CR	Carriage return
14	&0E	0000 1110	◇ N	SO	Shift out
15	&0F	0000 1111	◇ O	SI	Shift in
16	&10	0001 0000	◇ P	DLE	Data link escape
17	&11	0001 0001	◇ Q	DC1	Xon (Device control 1)
18	&12	0001 0010	◇ R	DC2	Device control 2
19	&13	0001 0011	◇ S	DC3	Xoff (Device control 3)
20	&14	0001 0100	◇ T	DC4	Device control 4
21	&15	0001 0101	◇ U	NAK	Negative acknowledge
22	&16	0001 0110	◇ V	SYN	Synchronous idle
23	&17	0001 0111	◇ W	ETB	End of transmitted block
24	&18	0001 1000	◇ X	CAN	Cancel line

25	&19	0001 1001	◇ Y	EM	End of medium
26	&1A	0001 1010	◇ Z	SUB	Substitute
27	&1B	0001 1011	◇ [	ESC	Escape
28	&1C	0001 1100	◇]	FS	File separator
29	&1D	0001 1101		GS	Group separator
30	&1E	0001 1110		RS	Record separator
31	&1F	0001 1111		US	Unit separator
32	&20	0010 0000			Space
33	&21	0010 0001			!
34	&22	0010 0010			"
35	&23	0010 0011			#
36	&24	0010 0100			$
37	&25	0010 0101			%
38	&26	0010 0110			&
39	&27	0010 0111			'
40	&28	0010 1000			(
41	&29	0010 1001			)
42	&2A	0010 1010			*
43	&2B	0010 1011			+
44	&2C	0010 1100			,
45	&2D	0010 1101			-
46	&2E	0010 1110			.
47	&2F	0010 1111			/
48	&30	0011 0000			0
49	&31	0011 0001			1
50	&32	0011 0010			2
51	&33	0011 0011			3
52	&34	0011 0100			4
53	&35	0011 0101			5
54	&36	0011 0110			6
55	&37	0011 0111			7
56	&38	0011 1000			8
57	&39	0011 1001			9
58	&3A	0011 1010			:
59	&3B	0011 1011			;
60	&3C	0011 1100			<
61	&3D	0011 1101			=
62	&3E	0011 1110			>
63	&3F	0011 1111			?
64	&40	0100 0000			@
65	&41	0100 0001			A
66	&42	0100 0010			B
67	&43	0100 0011			C
68	&44	0100 0100			D

69	&45	0100 0101	E
70	&46	0100 0110	F
71	&47	0100 0111	G
72	&48	0100 1000	H
73	&49	0100 1001	I
74	&4A	0100 1010	J
75	&4B	0100 1011	K
76	&4C	0100 1100	L
77	&4D	0100 1101	M
78	&4E	0100 1110	N
79	&4F	0100 1111	O
80	&50	0101 0000	P
81	&51	0101 0001	Q
82	&52	0101 0010	R
83	&53	0101 0011	S
84	&54	0101 0100	T
85	&55	0101 0101	U
86	&56	0101 0110	V
87	&57	0101 0111	W
88	&58	0101 1000	X
89	&59	0101 1001	Y
90	&5A	0101 1010	Z
91	&5B	0101 1011	[
92	&5C	0101 1100	\
93	&5D	0101 1101	]
94	&5E	0101 1110	^
95	&5F	0101 1111	_
96	&60	0110 0000	”
97	&61	0110 0001	a
98	&62	0110 0010	b
99	&63	0110 0011	c
100	&64	0110 0100	d
101	&65	0110 0101	e
102	&66	0110 0110	f
103	&67	0110 0111	g
104	&68	0110 1000	h
105	&69	0110 1001	i
106	&6A	0110 1010	j
107	&6B	0110 1011	k
108	&6C	0110 1100	l
109	&6D	0110 1101	m
110	&6E	0110 1110	n
111	&6F	0110 1111	o
112	&70	0111 0000	p

113	&71	0111 0001	q
114	&72	0111 0010	r
115	&73	0111 0011	s
116	&74	0111 0100	t
117	&75	0111 0101	u
118	&76	0111 0110	v
119	&77	0111 0111	w
120	&78	0111 1000	x
121	&79	0111 1001	y
122	&7A	0111 1010	z
123	&7B	0111 1011	{
124	&7C	0111 1100	|
125	&7D	0111 1101	}
126	&7E	0111 1110	~
127	&7F	0111 1111	
160	&A0	1010 0000	...
163	&A3	1010 0011	£

Appendix 2

Z88 commands

□ Commands

Alarm	□A
BASIC	□B
Calculator	□R
Calendar	□C
Clock	□T
Diary	□D
Filer	□F
Imp-Export	□X
Index page	□I
PipeDream	□P
Printer Editor	□E
Screen	□S
Terminal	□V

Index commands

Card display	◇ CARD
Kill activity	◇ KILL
Soft reset	◇ PURGE

PipeDream ◇ commands

Blocks

Clear mark	◇Q
Copy	◇BC
Delete	◇BD
Mark block	◇Z
Move	◇BM
Next match	◇BNM
New document	◇BNEW
Recalculate	◇A
Replace	◇BRP
Replicate	◇BRE
Search	◇BSE
Sort	◇BSO
Word count	◇BWC

Cursor movement

Bottom of column	◇ ↓
Cursor down	↓
Cursor left	←
Cursor right	→
Cursor up	↑
End of cell	◇ →
First column	◇CFC
Go to slot	◇CGS
Last column	◇CLC
Next column	TAB
Next word	SHIFT →
Previous column	SHIFT TAB
Previous word	SHIFT ←
Restore position	◇CRP
Save position	◇CSP
Screen down	SHIFT ↓
Screen up	SHIFT ↑
Start of cell	←
Top of column	◇ ↑

Edit commands

Add column	◇ EAC
Backspace	DEL
Delete character	◇ G
Delete column	◇ EDC
Delete row	◇ Y
Delete row in column	◇ EDRC
Delete to end of cell	◇ D
Delete word	◇ T
Edit expression	◇ X
Insert/overtype	◇ V
Insert character	◇ U
Insert column	◇ EIC
Insert page	◇ EIP
Insert reference	◇ K
Insert row	◇ N
Insert row in column	◇ EIRC
Join lines	◇ EJL
Next option	◇ J
Number,,text	◇ ENT
Reformat paragraph	◇ R
Split lines	◇ ESL
Swap case	◇ S

File commands

Bottom file in list	◇ FB
Load file	◇ FL
Name file	◇ FC
Next file in list	◇ FN
Previous file in list	◇ FP
Save file	◇ FS
Top file in list	◇ FT

Document layout commands

Centre align	◇ LAC
Decimal places	◇ LDP

Default format	◇ LDF
Fix column	◇ LFC
Fix row	◇ LFR
Free align	◇ LAF
LCR align	◇ LLCR
Leading characters	◇ LCL
Left align	◇ LAL
Margin left	□→
Margin right	□←
Negative brackets	◇ LSB
Negative minus	◇ LSM
Right align	◇ LAR
Right margin	◇ H
Trailing characters	◇ LCT
Width of column	◇ W

Print commands

Alternative font	◇ PA
Bold	◇ PB
Delete highlights	◇ PHR
Extra sequence	◇ PX
Highlight block	◇ PHB
Insert highlights	◇ PHI
Italic	◇ PI
Microspace	◇ PM
Print document	◇ PO
Subscript	◇ PL
Superscript	◇ PR
Underline	◇ PU
User defined characters	◇ PE

Diary Commands

Blocks

Clear mark	◇ Q
Copy	◇ BC
Delete	◇ BD

List diary	◇BL
Mark block	◇Z
Move	◇BM
Next match	◇BNM
Previous match	◇BPM
Replace	◇BRP
Search	◇BSE

Cursor movement

Cursor down	↓
Cursor left	←
Cursor right	→
Cursor up	↑
End of line	◇→
First active day	◇CFAD
First line	◇↑
Last active day	◇CLAD
Last line	◇↓
Next active day	□→
Next day	□↓
Next word	SHIFT →
Previous active day	□←
Previous day	□↑
Previous word	SHIFT ←
Restore position	◇CRP
Save position	◇CSP
Screen down	SHIFT ↓
Screen up	SHIFT ↑
Start of line	◇←
Tab	TAB
Today	◇CT

Edit commands

Backspace	DEL
Delete character	◇G
Delete line	◇Y
Delete to end of cell	◇D

Delete word	◇ T
Insert/overtype	◇ V
Insert character	◇ U
Insert line	◇ N
Join lines	◇ EJL
Memory free	◇ EMF
Next option	◇ J
Split lines	◇ ESL
Swap case	◇ S

File commands

Load file	◇ FL
Save file	◇ FS

Filer Commands

Catalogue Eprom	◇ CE
Catalogue files	◇ CF
Copy a file	◇ CO
Create directory	◇ CD
Cursor down	↓
Cursor left	←
Cursor right	→
Cursor up	↑
Down directory	SHIFT ↓
Erase files	◇ ER
Execute a CLI file	◇ EX
Fetch from Eprom	◇ FE
Name match	◇ NM
Rename file	◇ RE
Save to Eprom	◇ SE
Select device	◇ SD
Select directory	◇ SI
Select first file	ENTER
Select subsequent files	SHIFT ENTER
Tree copy	◇ TC
Up directory	SHIFT ↑

Printer Editor Commands

Cursor movement

Cursor down	↓
Cursor left	←
Cursor right	→
Cursor up	↑
Next option	◇ J

File commands

Load file	◇ FL
Name file	◇ FC
New file	◇ FNEW
Save file	◇ FS
Update driver	◇ FU

Appendix 3

Some useful addresses

Cambridge Computers

Cambridge Computer Ltd.,
Bridge House,
10 Bridge Street,
Cambridge,
CB2 1UE
Tel: 0223 312216
Fax: 0223 358912

M-TEC

M-TEC Computer Services (UK),
Market Place,
Reepham,
Norfolk,
NR10 4JJ

Z88 User's Club

Z88 User's Club,
68 Wellington Street,
Long Eaton,
Nottingham,
NG10 4NG

Z88 protective cover

Cambridge Topper,
49 Olney Road,
Olney,
Bucks,
MK46 5BU

Z88 Bulletin Boards

Compulink Information eXchange

CIX
The Sanctuary,
Oakhill Grove,
Surbiton,
Surrey,
KT6 6DU
Tel: 01-390 8446
Bulletin Board: 01-399 5252

This system operates on most baud rates up to 9600, with no parity, 8 bits and 1 stop bit (N81). It contains 'conferences' (subsections) dedicated to the Z88 and there are a number of Basic and CLI files that you can 'download' to run on your own Z88.

You can try out the system by typing 'NEW' when it asks for your name.

Z88 USA

Bulletin Board: 0101-213-370-2754

This system also operates on N81 with a range of speeds. When you connect through press your space bar a couple of times to 'wake' it up and to enable the American computer to calculate your transmission speed. It contains dozens of programs, hints and tips for you to download to your machine.

Books

The BBC Basic(Z80) Reference Manual for the Z88 by D J Mounter (1989). Published by M-TEC Computer Services (UK). ISBN: 1-871895-00-6.

New Hacker's Handbook by Steve Gold (1989). Published by Century. ISBN: 0-7126-3454-1.

Z88 Developer's Notes by John Harrison and Matthew Elton (1988). Published by Cambridge Computer Ltd.

Appendix 4

Z88 file formats

PipeDream format

Each PipeDream file contains the following information:

- File name
- Option page details (◇ O)
- Column information

The Option Page details, which appear at the beginning of the file, are composed of a list of the option parameter labels and their values *that you have changed from the default values*. Each parameter in the list is preceded with the four characters %OP% and concludes with the carriage return character &0D.

So, the options page details may look like:

%OP%BM8(cr)%OP%FM2(cr)%OP%PL66(cr).....

The various parameters labels are:

AM	Auto/manual
BM	Bottom margin
BO	Borders
DE	Title
DP	Decimal places
FM	Footer margin
FO	Footer
HE	Header

HM	Header margin
IW	Insert on wrap
JU	Justify
LM	Left margin
LP	Leading characters
LS	Line spacing
MB	Minus/brackets
PA	Pages
PL	Page length
PS	Page number at start
RC	Rows/columns
TM	Top margin
TN	Text/numbers
TP	Trailing characters
WR	Wrap

The column information can take two forms. At the beginning of each column of information are details of the column and its size. Then, inserted in the information as appropriate, come details of specific layout and other material.

Each column begins with the following details:

%CO: column letter, width, right margin%

For example, %CO:A,8,72%

Inserted into the text as appropriate are details relating to:

%B%	Bracket format
%C%	Centre align
%Dn%	Decimal places – n is the number
%DF%	Floating format
%Hn%	Highlight character – n is the highlight number
%JL%	Justify left
%JR%	Justify right
%L%	Left align
%LC%	Leading character format
%LCR%	LCR align
%Pn%	Page break – n is the number of lines free; 0 means unconditional
%PC%	Per cent character
%R%	Right align
%TC%	Trailing character format
%V%	Cell is defined as a number cell

Diary format

Each day in the diary uses the following format:

```
%dd/mm/yyy
```
text

For example,

```
%1/1/1989
10.30      Meet with Mr Jones
11.30      Visit the dentist
%3/1/1989
10.30      Coffee with Fred
%4/1/1989
09.00      Management team meeting
10.00      See the MD
```

Appendix 5

Connecting to other computers

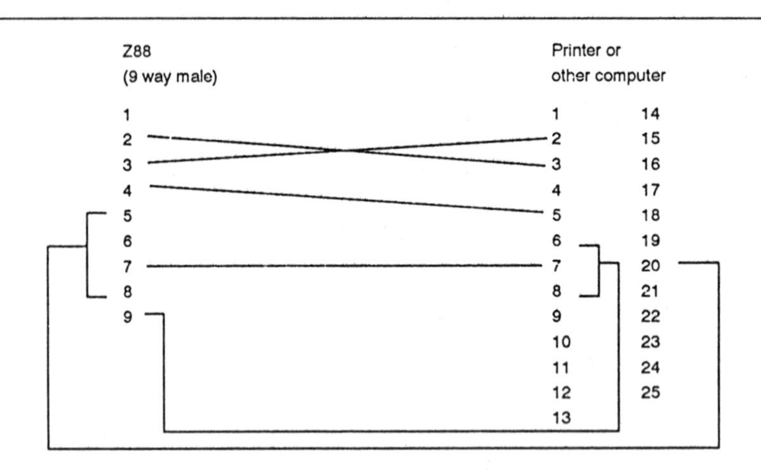

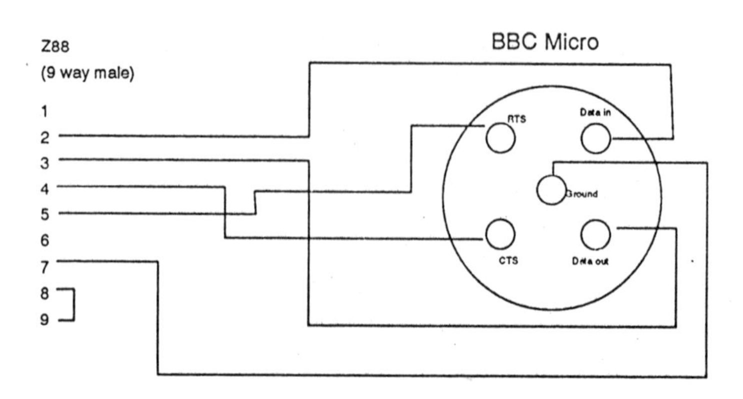

Connecting to other computers

General Index

L

M

N

O

P

Q

R

Diamond Key (◊) Commands

The following commands are all preceded by the 'diamond key' :

Square Key (□) Commands

The following keypresses are all preceded by the 'square key':